'Excellent... great advice, strategies and models. I'd certainly recommend it to our students'
Sarah Speight, Associate Pro-Vice Chancellor for Teaching & Learning, University of Nottingham

'Jonathan has produced a book that will help all students. Using positive, encouraging, age-appropriate language, and easy-to-complete reflective action points, he leads the reader through a journey that makes everything much less daunting. In fact, it comes across as doable – even enjoyable'
Jeremy Dudman-Jones, Assistant Headteacher, Greenford High School, Middlesex

'Supporting students at every step, this book will be a constant source of reference and reassurance throughout their studies and beyond. Importantly, it offers techniques that will help students embrace and overcome the challenges they face – and, ultimately, enjoy the resulting satisfaction and success. I wish I had been able to use this book during my degree studies'
Prof. Derek Bell, visiting lecturer, UCL Institute of Education

'Everything you need to know to succeed in Higher Education'
Gaye Conroy, Study Support Tutor, University of Sussex

THE STUDY BOOK
Essential skills for academic success

Jonathan Hancock

First published in the UK in 2019 by John Murray Learning, an imprint of Hodder & Stoughton.
An Hachette UK company

British Library Cataloguing-in-Publication Data: a catalogue record for this book is available from the British Library.

ISBN 978 1 529 30027 7

eBook ISBN 978 1 529 30026 0

1

The publisher has used its best endeavours to ensure that any website addresses referred to in this book are correct and active at the time of going to press. However, the publisher and the author have no responsibility for the websites and can make no guarantee that a site will remain live or that the content will remain relevant, decent or appropriate.

The publisher has made every effort to mark as such all words which it believes to be trademarks. The publisher should also like to make it clear that the presence of a word in the book, whether marked or unmarked, in no way affects its legal status as a trademark.

Every reasonable effort has been made to trace copyright holders, but if there are any errors or omissions, John Murray Learning will be pleased to insert the appropriate acknowledgement in any subsequent printings or editions.

Typeset by Integra Software Services Pvt. Ltd., Pondicherry, India.

Printed and bound by CPI Group (UK) Ltd, Croydon, CR0 4YY.

John Murray Learning policy is to use papers that are natural, renewable and recyclable products and made from wood grown in sustainable forests. The logging and manufacturing processes are expected to conform to the environmental regulations of the country of origin.

Carmelite House

50 Victoria Embankment

London EC4Y 0DZ

www.hodder.co.uk

For Noah, Evie and Nate

Contents

Learning about yourself as a student: *thoughts and feelings, experiences, circumstances*

Assessing your approach to study: *motivation, learning conditions, thinking styles*

Exploring the core study skill-sets: *self-management, task-management, people skills*

Entering the next stage of your studies: *academic thinking/behaviours/skills*

Focusing on your chosen course: *academic standards, skills development, risks/rewards*

Planning for success: *goal-setting, self-regulation, performance-management*

Starting to study well: *learning environments/habits/strategies*

About the author

Jonathan Hancock's fascination with study strategies began while he was still at school. The techniques he developed helped him to achieve top grades in all his exams, including a First from the University of Oxford and postgraduate qualifications in education from the University of Brighton and University College London. He has twice appeared in *Guinness World Records* for his remarkable feats of learning and, at the age of 22, he won the title of World Memory Champion.

Jonathan is a prolific author of books, courses and articles about thinking, learning and educational success. Following ten years as a teacher and school leader, he now advises universities on their teacher-training programmes, as well as working as a study-skills coach for a wide variety of organizations and clients. He is a Director of the Learning Skills Foundation, an advisory member of the *Learnus* think-tank, and the Founder of The Junior Memory Championship, through which he supports the achievement of teachers and students across the UK and Asia.

A former BBC presenter, Jonathan still appears regularly on radio and TV, writes a monthly column for *Reader's Digest* magazine, and has been the memory and learning consultant for all six series of the popular Channel 4 programme *Child Genius*.

Follow Jonathan on Twitter: @J_B_Hancock

Acknowledgements

My approach to higher-level learning has been shaped over the years by many extremely talented academics, particularly during my studies at Oxford, Brighton and UCL. For this book I have also received valuable support from staff at the University of Nottingham – particularly Sarah Speight, who offered thoughtful guidance from an early stage and gave me access to the university's wealth of resources for students. In addition, her colleagues Sarah Stubbings and John Horton contributed very useful help and advice. Gaye Conroy at the University of Brighton provided me with detailed insights into the work of Study Support teams and the issues they address. I am also grateful to Jon Chapman at the University of Oxford, and Tom Witelski at Duke University, for offering their expert feedback, and to the many other academics and students whose experiences and suggestions have become part of this book.

Special thanks go to two of my nieces, Maddie and Anna Clingan, for finding time within their own university studies to give me their detailed comments and excellent ideas.

It has been a pleasure working with the team at John Murray Learning. Publishing Director Iain Campbell championed this project from the start and provided vital input throughout. The finished text has also benefited greatly from the copyediting skills of Robert Anderson, the careful proofreading of Duncan Baylis, and the overall direction of Jenny Campbell, who has deftly guided the manuscript through each production stage.

As always, I am grateful to Caroline Shott and her colleagues at the Learning Skills Foundation for giving me such energetic backing for my work.

Finally, I am indebted to my family: to my wife Lucy, for her remarkable patience and unwavering support; and to my children Noah, Evie and Nate, who improve my understanding of learning, personal achievement and individual strength every day.

Introduction

Higher-level study is a serious challenge, but one that's well worth taking on – and this book will help you get the most out of it, every step of the way.

Beyond the pain barrier

Studying is hard – it has to be. It's a risky, confusing, gruelling, emotional, thrilling process of self-discovery and transformation. If you're not struggling with it, if it doesn't hurt sometimes, you're just not doing it right.

But – it shouldn't feel impossible. Energetic, but not frantic. In its toughest moments you should still know why you're putting yourself through it, where it's taking you – and what you've got to do to get there in good shape (even if that means going backwards for a while first). It's definitely not a straight path, and there are no easy answers – which is exactly why you're doing it.

When you choose higher-level study, you challenge yourself to think differently. It calls into question many of the things you thought you knew. It's like you're picking a fight with the learner you've been until now.

But on offer are fresh insights, priceless new skills, a different future. If you can stay well, hold your nerve and keep building your strength, the strain along the way will have been more than worth it.

I've written this book to help you – and, I hope, to inspire you. To show you why proper, grown-up study pushes you to the limit in just about every way imaginable, *and how that makes it pretty much the best thing you'll ever do.*

And if you're going to do it, put everything on the line like this, you might as well *give* it everything. This book is about embracing the challenge, taking on the fight, explaining all the strategies that got me through it in one piece, along with ideas and advice from students and academics who are grappling with it all right now.

I made a very good return on all the time, energy, money and raw emotion I put in to my own higher education. It was a love/hate relationship at times, but I'm so glad I kept going. I'll know I'll always benefit from the investment I made.

I spend a lot of my time now helping other people get the most out of their study – to get properly involved in the struggle. It's hard work – that's the point of it – but there are so many ways to maximize your efforts and drive yourself to make the greatest gains.

Buckle up

I'll keep returning to the theme of battle (and being battle-*hardened* – it will be the making of you). For many students, it's a battle fought on several different fronts, with social, cultural, language or learning barriers to be overcome. As you'll see from the Contents, I also like the idea of study being a journey – which, in my own case, was more than a metaphor, taking me hundreds of miles from home to a town that was *very* different from the one I knew. Maybe you, too, have a real journey to make for the next stage of your studies. But even if you're able to do it from your kitchen table, you'll still need to be in the mood for some serious travel.

Higher-level study takes you to entirely new territory, where the ground is uncertain, the culture complicated, the population diverse. You'll need to get to grips with a new language, new behaviour rules, a new set of standards and values. Sometimes you'll be able to work with others; sometimes you'll be in fierce competition. You're going to have to change – and keep changing, in many different ways – if you're going to survive.

Some of the landscape has been mapped before, but there's still plenty to explore. So, do your research, navigate carefully, find ways to make new discoveries – and take others with you. You really can make your mark here, maybe even start a revolution.

But you should also embrace just being in these new surroundings, get everything you possibly can from the experience, and come back with your eyes opened and your mind expanded. You'll be a changed person because of what you've done while you were away.

Enjoy the ride

Like the adventurous journey (or the well-fought fight; or the long-distance run – that will be another recurring theme), it's the difficulty of higher-level study that makes it so exciting, so much fun – and, ultimately, so worthwhile. You need to see evidence of your improvement and feel confident about the long-term benefits of your risk-taking. But I believe it's absolutely possible to revel in the struggle of studying. In fact, you have to, if you're going to stay committed for long enough to see real results and feel proper thrills. It's why you need to know how to study well: so that you put effort into the right things, get all the support that's on offer, and keep going long enough to enjoy everything else that makes student life so brilliant.

Love/hate

Studying at this level is meant to be emotional. There's so much to be excited about. You're choosing to do it. You have real independence. You pick a subject that interests you. You get the whole student lifestyle. And you do it all with *your* goals in mind.

On the other hand, the responsibility for success is yours now. You need to manage yourself through an increasingly complex range of tasks, making all the important decisions yourself, for years to come, adapting your approach to suit the needs of others, always having to do better to meet higher demands. *Your* ideas are questioned, *your* work held up to scrutiny. It's *you* that's really being tested here. And learning to handle the emotions of study is a big part of why you do it.

What it boils down to ...

... is this: how well you can learn to be a student, through the intense process of study.

That's the real test. By handling the workload, coping with the lifestyle, managing the emotions, wrestling with the ideas, getting better at it all over time, adapting, transforming ... you need to show that you can do your subject, and that you can do *studying*, really, really well.

Good study

This book is about everything you gain from good study – what you can *become* – and how it happens, in practice and over time: by doing more and more of the right things, all the way through your course.

There's no such thing as the perfect student. It's fine to make mistakes – especially if you learn from them – and it's important to be realistic about your development. This book is full of ideas to try, but don't think you need to be doing all of them at every moment. Start in areas where you know you need help, then gradually extend yourself in other ways. Give new techniques time to work. Use the strategies here to enrich your studying and increase your confidence bit by bit, aiming high but always allowing yourself to be imperfect – to be *human*.

We're born as learners, but studying is something different. You've done lots of it by the time you get to this stage, but just doing it isn't enough. (You have to be careful: doing lots of anything can actually make you *worse* – like some delivery drivers with their road safety, and some doctors with their handwriting.) Good study involves a wide range of skills, used and developed in the process of your studies. This handbook will show you how, and get you doing it. I've designed it to join up with all the resources and support available to you *from* your course, because that's where it all has to happen.

I'll show you how to apply all the best study strategies to the specific challenges you face. Courses vary wildly, and a big part of your job is to understand what's special about yours: what you learn there and how you learn it. If you're studying maths, or film studies, or physiotherapy, you'll be doing lots of things very differently from your friends who've chosen French, law or acting (and even from people doing a course with exactly the same name somewhere else).

But there are some very important aspects of higher-level learning that apply to every course, everywhere. Those things are the absolute focus of his book. Get them right and everything else will fall into place.

A pinch of salt

Grab all the advice and guidance you can get – that's a big part of being a successful student – but take it all with a healthy dose of scepticism (another key study skill).

Here's the case for listening to me. I was a student who came across some strategies that worked well for exams and got me good grades, but more importantly got me interested in study itself. I glimpsed some exciting, ancient memory techniques and adapted them to help me develop and demonstrate my understanding. A couple of teachers showed me new ways of making notes and exploring ideas. I loved running and I applied some of those training methods to my studies, too. The more it all worked, the more I looked for other ways to help myself do well – and I've carried on doing it ever since. I've loved (and occasionally hated) struggling with coursework, presentations, dissertations, exams. I've gone from a comprehensive school in the North East of England to Oxford University; channelled my skills into academic competitions; worked in primary schools, colleges and universities – and in publishing, radio and TV – to get as many people as possible excited about learning to learn.

I'm sold on the benefits of studying well. The qualifications are nice to have, and mine have helped me do some amazing things. But it's the academic and personal skills I've developed in the process that have driven everything I've done – and keep promising more.

Digging deep

Long-distance athletes often push themselves hardest towards the end of a training session. After they've put in the steady early miles and got to a point where they're starting to feel tired, rather than ending it there, they speed up. They 'dig deep', finding that extra something from somewhere, seizing the opportunity for intense, high-worth training in the last part of the run. They're still doing the same basic activity – running – but this version challenges them in new ways, and it asks different things of them, mentally and emotionally as well as physically. Like a student pushing on into higher-level work, they rely on all the work they've done before, and they have to trust themselves as they move out of their comfort zone. If they can embrace the difficulty, and make it transformational, they know that those tough later miles are where they'll find the most valuable opportunities for growth.

Moving in, moving on

The weekend before I started writing this book, I dropped my eldest son off at university to start his degree. It all happened quickly: he packed his bags, we loaded up the car – and suddenly he was leaving home, meeting new people, looking after himself, taking charge of his days, getting to grips with a completely new environment, starting to find out who he is when he's not with us and, among it all, facing an academic challenge that won't be like anything he's ever done before. What a challenge. What an *opportunity*.

Aim high

Higher-level study takes you to places where intense academic – and personal – development can happen. It's a challenge that can change the rest of your life.

This book will help you to hold your nerve, build your strength, and *use* your studies to become the student – the person – you deserve to be.

How to use this book

Use this book to prepare for or get started with higher-level studying – either by reading it from start to finish, or by dipping into particular sections – to build a strong, personalized approach.

Going up?

If you're interested in higher-level study (generally, the work done at the stage called 'higher education', in universities, colleges and conservatoires), then this book is for you.

You may be building up to it, taking courses that will qualify you for full-on higher studies (and these courses may already be stretching some of the skills you'll be using there). If that's the case, it's really useful for you to see what's on the horizon, and to start flexing some of the most important mental muscles so that you can begin developing the key academic skills. You'll boost your current efforts, and get yourself into great shape for when you do step up to the next level.

And if you're at that point now, about to start a course, in the middle of it, or even towards the end (and so probably squaring up to the toughest bits of all), then you'll find things here to help with every part of the challenge.

Welcome

Higher-level education is full of all sorts of people these days, and this handbook is designed for them all. It doesn't matter how old you are, where you come from, what your experiences have been like so far, where you hope to be going. I'm not assuming anything about you. But I'll get *you* to consider all these things and more, helping you to learn about yourself as a student and to see how *you* can get better and better at studying.

You're not alone

It's always useful to hear from fellow travellers, so I've included **Student Tips** from a wide range of helpful contributors, all with down-to-earth advice from the front line. There are also **Case Studies**: carefully chosen examples that illustrate the ups and downs of study, the real-life experiences of some very different students – and the rich learning that can emerge from the struggles of study.

So, whoever you are, however you've got here, I've tried to make this book as approachable as possible. Where I mention 'university', I know that you may be studying in a different sort of institution, and I'm aware that terms like 'tutor' and 'lecture' and 'dissertation' don't apply to everyone. But the *reasons* for writing about them matter to everyone studying at a higher level. I'll show you what it all means for you, and how you can adapt all the details as necessary.

To be clear ...

Every chapter begins with a **one-sentence summary** to set up the central theme in the pages ahead.

That's followed by:

- **What?** – the chapter's content and concepts
- **When?** – the best times to put the ideas into action
- **Who?** – the other people involved in making them work
- **Why?** – the range of benefits on offer
- **How?** – the way you'll be guided through.

And all the chapters finish with a **Ten-point summary**, a round-up of the ten most important points to take away, and a brief **Where to next?** signpost to the chapter that follows.

Throughout the book I've included graphics to give you an extra angle on the information. With the words, I've gone for a simple style, hoping it helps you to interpret, understand and remember some far-from-simple ideas. Academic terms are explained – and academics themselves appear throughout to share their experiences and insights. These are the professionals, the people working hard to support your studies (and the folk you need to impress), so look out for these valuable pieces of **Academic Advice**.

But sometimes even high-level academic activities are best described in more down-to-earth ways. It's easy to feel like a complete beginner when things seem specialized and unfamiliar, but very often we're already doing them without realizing. From an early age you've been analysing information, finding representations for abstract ideas, making complex arguments, exploiting the potency of language – and many of the most important academic skills are just extensions of behaviour like this. I want to give you the confidence to build on what you're already doing. You don't have to be fluent in the language to join in a very exciting conversation (but you will be, eventually, if you do).

Just do it

I want everything you explore here to have an impact, which will only happen if you get fully involved. **Note To Self** sections alert you when there's a particularly important action to implement, but on every page you'll see things to do, discuss, think about and try for yourself. The final chapter includes a practical plan for taking forward every key strategy explored in the book.

Good study is muscular and active. You'll get tired sometimes, but you can also *generate* energy by pushing yourself that bit further. The best learning comes when you're able to reach out and take all the things you need. Be prepared for plenty of activity (including the 19 different verbs that start the chapter descriptions in the Contents).

This is an interactive book that's designed to be kept alongside you throughout your work. You can read through it in order, carrying out the exercises and activities as you go. Or, you might feel the need to go straight to particular sections – elements of study you need most help with, or the things you're tackling *now*. Both approaches are fine. I've tried to make the structure and layout of the book as easy to get to grips with as possible, including a detailed **Contents**, **Part summaries**, an **Index** and **Go to** instructions throughout to help you navigate quickly and effectively. Sometimes I'll show you why you need to skip forwards or back to something, taking an integrated, layered approach. Sometimes you'll need to repeat an exercise or reassess yourself in the light of your real experiences. Remember, good study does not mean following a straight road.

But, as well as looking for the things you *know* you need, find time to read parts that might reveal aspects of your study that you didn't realize were an issue. Be honest with yourself: take a fresh look at what you're doing. It's all part of the reflective, self-aware, analytical approach that's at the heart of successful study. It's also what lets you mould all the advice into the shape that suits you best.

Ask Yourself sections will give you particular questions to reflect on – and advice on how to get something tangible from your response.

I'll also be urging you throughout to put this book to work *within your real studies*. I've coordinated closely with leading universities to make sure that the advice here matches the messages they want to send out, and it's all aimed at helping you get the very best value from the course you're on.

So, apply what you read and learn to the things you're doing every day. Use it to help you get the most out of all the teaching and learning opportunities you get, including any support materials and services you're offered from elsewhere. Discuss it all with other students. Tell them what you've found most useful, and see what insights they've got, what works for them, where they think you should go next. Make this book part of real, dynamic development from the start.

Part 1 helps you to understand where you're starting *from*: how to use key aspects of your experiences so far to help you to plan where you want to go. You'll explore some important thoughts and feelings about learning, taking an honest and open look at the personal factors that could help or hinder your progress – and what to do about them. By analysing your unique situation as a student, you'll be able to take on the task ahead with your eyes open, ready to do the right things from the start.

Part 2 focuses on stepping up to higher-level study in general – and into the particular subject you've chosen. It's important to know which skills are developed here, how it's done, and what's that's likely to mean for you personally. Prepare yourself for the processes of teaching and learning that go on, choose your personal goals, and check that your external and internal environments are set up in your favour.

Part 3 covers things that matter to all higher-level students: getting everything done well in the time you've got; researching, reading and recording information effectively, in print and on screen; developing your writing to deepen and demonstrate your understanding; and making yourself 'assessment-proof' from day one.

Part 4 explores thinking, and the complex processes that control your understanding, learning and memory. It also gets you thinking about yourself, developing the sort of reflective approach you'll need to engage fully with studying, and keep doing it better.

Part 5 looks at all the things you have to get done as a student – why you do them, and how you get the most out them – including teaching, independent tasks, shared projects, presentations, large-scale writing tasks, tests and exams.

Part 6, finally, is about keeping going from here, committing to building all your skills in the long-term, in context; learning what good study *really* means.

I've aimed to include plenty of thinking space, and to give you freedom to do everything at your own pace, with your own needs firmly in mind.

But there's no getting away from the fact that study is so valuable *because* it tests and stretches you – and demands so much from you. It's not a book that offers easy ways out.

What this book is *not*

It's not a set of instructions to follow (but it will help you to discover what works best for you).

It's not a remedial guide, trying to fix things about your approach, or about you. You'll need to develop from where you are, building a rich set of skills over time.

It's not a course to take before the real work begins. When you activate this advice in your studies, this *is* the real work.

It's not a race towards a finish line. Part of its job is to show you why academic development isn't like that, because the most valuable skills are continually being developed and enriched. However, it will help you to achieve qualifications, which are clearly much more than just checkpoints along the way.

What this book *is*

It's a handbook for you to use actively, so that you find out in practice what good study means for you. And you can't just *want* to do it. You need a *will* to study. I'm committed to helping you access all the energy and enthusiasm you need to grapple with the challenges ahead, and I'll guide you to get the most out of everything you put in.

If you haven't felt it already, I hope you'll soon experience the excitement of study – an occupation that offers risk, struggle, highs and lows, life-changing experiences, and the richest of rewards.

Part 1

Starting Points

Assessing where you are now in your academic journey, to help you plan the way ahead

Chapter 1 focuses on *you*, analysing your **thoughts** and **feelings** about learning, your **experiences** of studying so far, and the **circumstances** you're in as you prepare for all the challenges to come.

Chapter 2 explores your **motivation** to study, your ability to control the **learning conditions**, and your confidence to use the full range of **thinking styles** at your disposal.

Chapter 3 examines sets of skills that are vital for all students: **self-management, task-management, people skills**.

Chapter 4 explains the development of **academic thinking, behaviours** and **skills**, helping you to set yourself up for success.

Personal details

Make an honest assessment of everything about you that affects your studying, so that you can take charge of your academic development from today.

 ## What?

This chapter guides you through a process of **self-analysis** that's absolutely vital for success in higher-level study. To tackle the intensely personal challenge involved in this phase of your education, and to seize all the opportunities it offers to develop as a person, you need to see yourself clearly throughout. And the first thing to examine is what you're like now, all the aspects of you that are likely to have an impact on your studies, so that you can respond accordingly. Because it isn't just about reflecting. It's about *reacting*, doing everything you can to give yourself the best chance of studying well.

 ## When?

Self-reflection in its widest sense is absolutely integral to higher-level study. It features throughout this book as a key tool in the process of becoming a successful student, as well as one of the most valuable skills developed by studying like this.

The earlier you start, the better, and the questions asked in this chapter are particularly important to answer before you step up to full-on higher-level work. But don't worry if you're already deep in your course. These exercises will help you to strengthen your approach at any point. The sooner you appreciate the full range of factors influencing your studying, the sooner you can set up the best possible conditions, draw on all your strengths, head off future problems, and get used to working in ways that are right for you.

 ## Who?

Clearly, the most important person in this process is you – but others have significant roles to play, too. By talking to family, friends, fellow students and members of academic staff, you'll build up the richest possible picture of yourself – including pieces of the jigsaw that would be very hard to find on your own. You can also make these other people part of your responses to whatever you discover, harnessing their help at key moments and strengthening your ability to make studying collaborative and dynamic.

Why?

Good study is active and energetic. The exercises in this chapter will help you to reach out for what you need to be a success, and it's essential to have a clear sense of purpose (although you won't really know what you're taking on until you're in the thick of it). Higher-level learning is also an emotional business, requiring real strength of character, resilience, adaptability and a set of long-term survival skills. Self-analysis is a vital part of **planning** for the challenge and then **protecting** yourself throughout – ensuring that nothing gets in the way of your studying.

Ask the right questions and you'll reveal all the advantages you have, as well as any issues you need to address. You'll know what's likely to work, where problems could lie, the triggers to *use* as well as those to avoid. Crucially, you'll be alert to the signals that will tell you most about how it's all going.

You can't know everything about what's going to happen and how you're going to feel, and that should actually be a big part of why you're doing it. But you can make some sensible preparations, based on everything you know about yourself now.

 # How?

There are three strands to the process, and they all overlap.

Thoughts and feelings. First, look at yourself. Examine your opinions and beliefs about learning, consider what motivates you and what causes you concern, and reflect on how your emotional responses affect your study, thinking in particular about the things that *make* you react the way you do. You're looking for ways to harness your emotional energy and put yourself in the best possible place for higher-level learning.

Experiences. Next, examine your past to understand more about your approach to studying now. Mine it for clues about what the future might hold, but focus on finding ways to improve your outcomes.

Circumstances. Finally, make a broad sweep of your present position, exploring anything and everything that affects your study. The things in your favour will be exploited for all they're worth. Where potential threats emerge, you'll work out ways to minimize their impact or remove them altogether.

You'll be guided to get extra evidence for your investigations, and urged to be as honest with yourself as possible. Nothing here is black or white. Many factors have the potential to help or hinder. The things you find easy may offer less than you think. Threats and difficulties can add dynamism and richness to your work. Like your studies themselves, the grey areas are very often where the good stuff happens.

Within each of these three focus areas you'll be working through the '4Rs':

Reflect. Give yourself time and space to think openly about who you are, how you operate, and why. Consider pros and cons, strengths and weaknesses, and what it all means for your studies.

Reframe. See whether it helps to look at some of these things in a new way, emphasizing different aspects and viewing them in a more positive light.

Respond. Choose how you're going to use everything at your disposal, and deal with anything that threatens your success.

Resolve. Larger resolutions will emerge from the first three of the 4Rs as you clarify your understanding of what you're going to need to succeed. You'll know the areas to *stay* focused on from here, and the sort of committed, long-term approach that's likely to help you most.

Steps To Success

1 Take your pulse

Higher-level study is about *you* – which, for most people, means a mixture of excitement and fear, especially just before it starts.

You'll get to take control of so much of the learning process, make lots of your own decisions, manage your daily life, and have plenty of opportunities to express your opinions and ideas. But where's the line for you between freedom and responsibility? Do you enjoy decision-making, or need to be guided? How does it feel when you're outside your comfort zone? When does an 'opportunity to express yourself' become 'pressure to perform'?

It's important to be aware of how you're feeling about higher-level study now, and to monitor it throughout your course. Above everything else, it will help you to look after yourself. It will also play a vital part in developing your understanding of study, the 'studying to be a student' that's at the heart of this kind of work.

Start by pinning down some influential opinions and beliefs at this stage of the game. Give each of the following statements a score between 0 (completely disagree) and 10 (completely agree).	Score
Emotions have an impact on study.	
Studying is most effective when emotions are kept out.	
You need to be aware of how other students around you are feeling.	
Studying can improve your emotional health.	
Studying at a higher level is a frightening experience.	
Emotional awareness leads to more effective studying.	
Good study always involves difficult emotions.	
Higher-level study is emotional for staff as well as students.	
Students can become more confident through the process of studying.	
You can only study well if you're happy and relaxed.	

As well as giving you plenty to think about now, and providing valuable context for the other exercises in this chapter, your answers here are part of long-term self-analysis, developed throughout the whole book. See whether any of your responses change in the process.

 ## Ask Yourself

→ Which emotional factors are particularly significant for students?

Imagine a large lecture theatre. It's the first day of the first year for the hundreds of university students crowding in and taking their seats. You can tell just by looking at them that they come from a variety of geographic, social and cultural backgrounds. Some are considerably older than others. They're already betraying differences in behaviour and attitude as they sit down, unpack their equipment (or don't), talk to the people around them (or don't), waiting for the lecture to begin.

But what if you could also listen to their private thoughts and access their innermost feelings? What sort of things do you think you'd learn?

Spend a moment now thinking about (and maybe jotting down) all the emotional factors that are likely to be at play here. Remember to think about (potentially) positive emotions as well as (potentially) negative ones. It'll help you to consider whether any of these factors apply to you, and give you some useful insights to draw on when you explore the challenges of working with others later in the book.

 ## Academic Advice

'On the course I lead, and many others, there's something called a PDP: a Personal Development Profile. It's an ongoing record that the students fill in to keep track of their progress, particularly the aspects that only they really know about, like how interested, engaged and confident they are. We get them to update their file at key points in the course to help them adjust their working practices, get help if they need it, and plan their next steps. But we also show them how to use their PDP to build their self-awareness. If they're continually reflecting on their work – and responding to what they think and feel – they're getting to the heart of what higher-level study is all about.' **Sophie, university lecturer and head of department**

Student Tip:

'University is definitely a personal challenge, but it's also a chance to take a greater role in things beyond yourself. You get to see how your studies relate to global concerns, and there are opportunities to start participating on a new level – in democracy, human rights, public health … even the health of the planet itself.' **Parvinder, Pharmaceutical Sciences student**

2 Express your feelings

Why are you reading a book about study? What are you hoping to get out of it? Like every other reader, you'll be coming to it with a range of different needs, interests, hopes, fears ... based on how you're feeling about different aspects of the challenge ahead. Depending on how you address them, those feelings will have a real effect on how your studies go from now on.

Here are some of the big 'triggers' for students' emotions. Read them carefully, think about the positive and negative aspects of each one, and write down a few words or phrases to record how you're feeling now about these themes.

How are you feeling about ...

... **doing something new**: starting a course with working practices, tasks and assessments that are different from anything you've done before, explained in unfamiliar terminology, shared with a set of people you've never met – and very likely in a place you don't know at all?

_____

_____

... **specializing:** narrowing your focus to a particular subject and attempting to explore it at length and in great depth?

_____

_____

... **being a beginner:** grappling with difficult new concepts and practices that will often seem unconnected with the things you already know – and may even reduce your previous learning structures to rubble?

_____

_____

... **making decisions:** taking responsibility for when, where and how you work – as well as every aspect of your daily life?

_____

_____

... making judgements: gathering evidence, comparing, checking, analysing ... in order to reach conclusions and deliver verdicts – among a variety of different views?

_____

_____

... persuading others: being confident to stand by your judgements, and using various forms of communication to convince others to agree?

_____

_____

... making mistakes: revealing things that you don't know or can't do – sometimes because there aren't *any* right answers to aim for?

_____

_____

... getting feedback: doing intense, personal work, then standing back while it's discussed, unpicked, criticized?

_____

_____

... learning in teams: working with a wide variety of people, sometimes relying on them, sometimes competing with them?

_____

_____

... working with experts: coming into contact with leaders in their field – and having to meet them on their level, to their expectations?

_____

_____

… managing projects: keeping in control of large-scale, long-term work, getting everything done to a high standard while balancing the rest of your life and staying well?

_____

_____

… creating knowledge: starting to contribute to progress in your subject by doing real research, making discoveries, advancing new ideas, facing down challenges, keeping up to date … and adding to what's already known and understood?

_____

_____

Ask Yourself

→ Does the media affect the way you feel and study?

Think about all the different forms of media you consume: websites, podcasts, social media, radio, TV, film, newspapers, magazines … What sort of influence do they have on your emotions – and, crucially, how do those emotions impact on your studies?

- What do your news providers 'tell' you about **education**? (That it's exciting, irrelevant, transformational, expensive, easy, stressful?)
- What do your online services 'tell' you about **information**? (Is knowledge fixed or fluid? Who controls it? How is it created? Does it need to be checked, interpreted, critiqued? Do we need to remember *anything* anymore?)
- What do your social media applications 'tell' you about **communication**? (That it's safe, threatening, subtle, violent, valuable, throwaway?)
- What do your entertainment choices 'tell' you about **the world**? (Is it fascinating, dangerous, interconnected, lonely, beautiful, unfair, getting better, getting worse, full of problems, full of possibilities?)

Think about how your media use makes you feel in general, and at particular points in the day, week and year. Mental and emotional health are vital factors in higher-level studying.

- Are there points in the day (or night) when your media use has a particularly positive or negative effect on your feelings?
- What about over a whole year: are there times (like birthdays, seasons, festivals, holidays) when the media's effects on your feelings are especially strong?
- Which aspects of the media boost your confidence, motivation, energy and overall ability to study well, and which have the opposite effects?
- Do other factors play a part in the way the media impacts your emotions (tiredness, alcohol, other people's responses, how you were feeling anyway …?)

3 Find your purpose

Your feelings about studying are likely to be bound up closely with your reasons for doing it. Here's an exercise to explore what's driving you.

Below are ten of the key potential gains from higher-level study. Rank them in order, from 10, as the least important to you, up to 1, the most. I am studying to …	Rank
… add to my qualifications	
… strengthen my people skills	
… deepen my subject knowledge	
… develop myself as a person	
… improve my professional prospects	
… grow my personal confidence	
… increase my understanding of the world	
… stretch myself academically	
… enjoy new social and leisure opportunities	
… take my thinking and learning skills to the next level	

 Academic Advice

'I think it's important for students to have a mix of reasons for wanting to study. It helps you to engage with all the different bits of the challenge, stay motivated and build up your resilience and resolve.' **Maggie, university learning mentor**

4 Plan your attack

When you've examined your opinions, beliefs and feelings about studying – in general, and in direct relation to you – you can start focusing on what it all means. Where are the strengths here that you can draw on, the weaknesses you need to address, the opportunities to exploit, the threats to deflect? It's a classic SWOT analysis (Strengths, Weaknesses, Opportunities, Threats). It's a vital step in moving from *reflection* to *response*.

You're going to record the most important things that have come out of analysing your feelings about studying. You can then start choosing how you're going to respond to what you've learned about yourself.

Don't forget the other two Rs: *reframing* and *resolving*. Can any of the potential negatives be turned into positives here by the way you look at them? What sort of opportunities open up if you commit yourself to doing some key things differently?

Use the following themes to guide you. Think about each one in turn and write some thoughts about it in the appropriate space in the table below (or *spaces*; this task puts you into one of those magical grey areas, where decision-making is complex and rich).

Newness. Unfamiliar things – places, processes, people – can be unsettling and scary, but they also offer possibilities (I promise!). The unknown offers new threats but also new opportunities.

Change. If you do it right, you'll come out of your studying *different,* in lots of ways. To reap the rewards, you'll need to dismantle old understandings, adapt to new ways of working and thinking, and cope in a world where information and ideas are in a constant state of flux.

Independence. No one's going to tell you what to do or what to think. You'll have new freedoms and new responsibilities. How does this relate to the strengths and weaknesses of your character? How confident do you feel about going it alone?

Challenge. Higher-level study isn't just about 'harder' content. The work is more demanding on many different levels. It asks new things of you as an academic, and a person. Will that hold you back or spur you on? How much does it worry you, and how much is it exactly why you're here?

Exposure. There's no hiding-place. Your judgements will be sought, shared and scrutinized. You'll be asked to perform, collaborate, debate. In print and in person you'll need to communicate and justify knowledge, understanding, skill and personal points of view. The benefits and the credit will be yours, because the intense intellectual and emotional challenge will be yours too.

Pressure. Your course will apply pressure at key points, taking you out of your comfort zone with new tasks, encouraging you to ask more and more of yourself, stepping up the assessments, raising the stakes. What will this mean for your existing strengths and weaknesses? Are you feeling threatened, or can you see the opportunities beckoning?

Use these themes to guide you, read back through the chapter for ideas, and use the SWOT table to help you record and explore your thoughts.

STRENGTHS	WEAKNESSES	OPPORTUNITIES	THREATS

Case Study: Ellie

In the weeks before she left for university, Ellie had a number of conversations with her parents about her previous experiences of studying. 'I found it a bit annoying to start with, because they kept reminding me of things that hadn't gone very well for me before. It was quite painful actually. Some not-very-nice feelings came back. But after a while I started thinking more positively, about some of the things I could do differently this time. And it was good to talk to Mum and Dad because there were some practical things that they could do to help.'

---

5 Apply the 4Rs. Part 1: Thoughts and feelings

Think about what you've learned about yourself in this chapter so far: your opinions, beliefs and feelings about study; your reasons for taking your learning to the next level; your emotional reactions to the particular challenges involved.

Reflect

What are the most important things you've learned about *you*?

Reframe

Are there any factors here that could be reframed, to make them more useful to you now – negatives turned to positives, threats to opportunities?

Respond

How are you going to deal with any disadvantages, and make sure that you draw on all your strengths?

Resolve

Where do you need to direct particular energy, to be the most successful version of yourself in the future?

6 Explore your past

Although this book is very much about the present and the future, it's important to take a moment to go back in time … to explore experiences that could impact the way you think and feel about studying now.

Once again, you'll be *reflecting* first, in order to *reframe*, *respond* and *resolve*.

When you think back over your education, which experiences spring to mind – for positive or for negative reasons? Make notes in the spaces below as you reflect on the past; not just what happened or what people said, but what it could *mean*.

Positive experiences of education

How might these moments help you in the future? Think about their potential impact on your feelings, behaviours and your overall approach to higher-level study. Could they have any negative impacts, too? (Maybe they make you overconfident, homesick, risk averse?)

_____

_____

Negative moments

Could these events have any lasting impact? Are there threats here to being positive, confident, energetic, resilient? Are there any positives to be drawn from what happened? Does anything here actually *strengthen* your approach to study now?

_____

_____

Positive things people have said to you in education

What benefits can you take from conversations and comments you've had? Are any of these things also potential threats? Sometimes praise can actually be difficult to receive. Some outwardly positive words can make us anxious, complacent, demotivated.

_____

_____

Negative things

Do these words still have potential to hold you back? Or could they propel you forward?

_____

_____

7 Apply the 4Rs. Part 2: Experiences

Straight away, with thoughts about the past still fresh in your mind ...

Reflect

What are the most significant things for you in these reflections – about what's *happened* to you, and what's been *said* to you in the past?

Reframe

Which experiences or comments could possibly be viewed differently, to make them more helpful as you move on?

Respond

What will you *do* now in your studies, in response to what you've learned?

Resolve

Have you made any resolutions about your future, from looking at how things went before?

8 Know your place

What I loosely call your circumstances is made up of a number of factors. A few you have some control over, but most are just 'the way it is'. Being aware of them, and their potential impact on your studies, takes you another step towards shaping your strongest possible approach.

> Read each of the points below and think about *emotional* and *practical* impacts. How these things make you feel about your studying, as well as how they might affect it in more tangible ways.
> For each one, write down something mostly positive and something mostly negative. Notice which comes to mind most easily.
> Finally, decide which of the two points is likely to have the *most* impact, unless something changes, and put a tick in the relevant box.

Previous education. How well has it equipped you for the challenges you're about to face?

Positive impacts ☐

Negative impacts ☐

Non-study work. Think about the roles and responsibilities you've had so far in your life, paid or unpaid. What is there here that could go for or against you in your studies?

Positive impacts ☐

Negative impacts ☐

Family. Are you affected by what your siblings, parents, even grandparents did (or didn't do) in their education? What sort of impact might your family have on what *you* do from here?

Positive impacts ☐

Negative impacts ☐

Social/cultural/ethnic/religious background. Does it provide support, pressure, distraction, encouragement? How do its values match those of the academic world?

Positive impacts ☐

Negative impacts ☐

Age. Are you the same age as most of the other people on your course? These days, it's possible to be significantly older or younger than the people you're studying with – so what are the potential advantages and disadvantages of how old *you* are?

Positive impacts ☐

Negative impacts ☐

Geography. Are you close enough to live at home, moving to a new city, or maybe even travelling between countries?

Positive impacts ☐

Negative impacts ☐

Finances. What role does money play in your decision to push ahead with your studies? Will you have to combine paid work with academic work? Does money motivate or pressurize you? Help you or limit you? Make you feel safe or stressed?

Positive impacts ☐

Negative impacts ☐

Accommodation. How appropriate are your living arrangements for someone attempting higher-level study?

Positive impacts ☐

Negative impacts ☐

Wellbeing. Think about your physical, mental and emotional health, and factors such as diet, exercise, sleep, alcohol and drugs.

Positive impacts ☐

Negative impacts ☐

Close relationships. What impact will your family and friends have on your studies? Think about the practicalities of them looking after you, and you looking after them, as well as the emotional influences at play.

Positive impacts ☐

Negative impacts ☐

Special needs. There should be plenty of support available, whatever your particular difficulty. And remember: the things that challenge your learning sometimes benefit it, too, especially the long-term, multi-layered processes involved in learning at this level.

Positive impacts ☐

Negative impacts ☐

And ... anything else. Are there any other aspects of your personal situation that you know you'll need to take into account?

Positive impacts ☐

Negative impacts ☐

Academic Advice

'My university's good at providing support for students' wellbeing. There are lots of different services, all fairly well resourced and widely advertised – but it's frustrating because some students still seem to be reluctant to ask for help. Studying's tough, life can be tough. It's really hard to do your work if you're not OK. But we've got pastoral tutors like me, a medical centre, counselling services, student mentors, a chaplaincy team. They've all got specialist skills, but they can also signpost you to other people who might be more appropriate. So I always urge students to speak to someone if they've got issues, and to get in there early. It's all anonymous and often you don't even have to go anywhere – just do it online or over the phone. The help is there if people reach out to use it.' **Jackie, university tutor**

9 Apply the 4Rs. Part 3: Circumstances

There's a lot about our personal situation that we just can't change. But there's also plenty that we *can*, particularly when we choose the most positive reactions and highlight ways to make the best of the position we're in.

Reflect

Looking at your current circumstances, what are the most important things for you to bear in mind?

Reframe

Which aspects could become more favourable for you if you looked at them differently, maybe recognized some advantages on offer?

Respond

What are the key things you need to do to give yourself the best chances of success?

Resolve

What's the best resolution you could make, to get the most out of the position you're in?

> ### ✎ Note To Self
>
> If you're starting at a new place of study – and particularly if you're living somewhere different – make sure that the right people have all the right information about your physical, mental and emotional health. You'll be advised about registering with health professionals and accessing a range of other support services – so do. And check that all your records have been successfully transferred. Help the people who are there to help you. They need to know how you've been in the past, what's worked and what hasn't – and what to look out for in the future.

10 Stay alert

Don't end the analysis here. Keep reflecting on all the factors that influence your experiences and achievement throughout your studies. And keep thinking carefully about the most beneficial ways to respond. You'll be encouraged to keep recognizing the themes explored in this chapter throughout the book – and beyond. Part 6 will help you to build this sort of reflective and responsive attitude into your long-term approach, and there's always new information emerging.

Look. Alongside the activities in this chapter, keep your eyes open for any extra evidence. Old school reports, photographs from your education, the way your desk is arranged right now – there may well be some very visible indications of how you approach your studies, and why.

Listen. Talk to any likely witnesses among the people who know you, personally and academically. Find out what they have to say about the questions you're considering here – plus anything else they can add.

It's all about building up the most detailed picture possible, analysing its significance, and responding accordingly – so it also happens to be great training for the kinds of thinking you're going to be doing in higher-level study itself.

Ask Yourself

→ Is it right to get personal?

How much do you think someone's 'personal details' – their emotional landscape, past experiences, current situation – really affect their academic success? Which factors – if any – do you believe have the most impact? Before you read on any further, spend a moment thinking about your current thoughts and feelings about study in general. What sort of people do best? How much should anyone personalize their approach? Which makes more of a difference to your study: *who you are* or *what you do*?

Ten-point summary

1. Self-analysis is vital preparation for studying as well as a key part of the academic development process.

2. Find out what you think about the emotional aspects of learning in general and you'll get a better understanding of your own feelings about study.

3. Explore your reactions to the big challenges of higher-level work to help you plan a robust approach.

4. It's important to be aware of the positive and negative influences of the media, in all its forms.

5. Be clear about your reasons for studying. It's good to have a mixture.

6. Self-reflection helps you to unpick the complex collection of strengths, weaknesses, opportunities and threats in who you are – and to see the best ways to respond.

7. Learn from what's happened to you – and been *said* to you – in the past, to strengthen your approach for the future.

8. Every student's circumstances are unique, and almost everyone has difficulties to overcome – as well as advantages to exploit.

9. Studying is emotional, so it's vital to look after your wellbeing and get help as soon as you need it.

10. Stay reflective and self-aware, learning from new experiences and adapting yourself through the process of higher-level study.

Where to next?

Chapter 2 will get you fired up for learning and show you how to put yourself in control of your studies.

Ready for action?

You need to take an active approach to study to set up the right conditions for success, with flexible thinking skills and a clear understanding of which strategies work best for you.

What?

A word often used to describe learning at this level is *autonomous*. You're not on your own, but it does ask a huge amount of you as an individual, developing your abilities to think and operate **independently**, and offering some extremely valuable personal rewards. So much of what you get out of it depends on what you're ready to put in.

This chapter explores more of the personal factors that are likely to have a big impact on your experience and your achievement. It helps you to analyse how you **engage** with learning now, so that you can take steps to do it even better. It explores the core aspects of your **thinking** and **learning** that make you the student you are. And it shows you how to use this awareness to take an increasingly **active** role in the development of your learning from this point on.

When?

The sooner you know what leads to good learning in general – and *your* learning in particular – the sooner you can start doing the things that help. All kinds of habits are difficult to break, so it's important to start your new course as you mean to go on. But you can still benefit from this kind of reflection and resolution process at any point along the way – and it *should* be ongoing, regularly updated in the light of new evidence to make sure that you're putting the right energy into the right areas of your work.

Who?

As well as spending a lot of time inside your own head, you'll also be thinking about the people around you, and where *they* fit in to your engaged, active approach. You're joining a complex learning community. Good study here requires real connection with the others involved.

 # Why?

You need to be an aware and active learner. Remember: it's all about learning to *be* a student, developing the high-level thinking and learning skills that don't just help you achieve something – they *are* the achievement.

Much of your studying needs to be done very consciously now. The work you'll be doing explores how we get information, judge it, communicate it, remember it; why people think differently; what has to happen for understanding to be reached and knowledge created. So, you need to start thinking about thinking, ready to engage with the people around you who are doing that, too. It's how you engage fully with all aspects of academic life.

It's also how you do really well. You reach out for everything you need, put the right **conditions** in place, drive your development forward. Knowing your own mind becomes the secret of your success.

 # How?

First, assess your ability to take an active role in **skills development**. How committed are you to getting stuck in? Explore the best conditions for high-quality learning, your ability to achieve them, and the steps you can take to improve your studying from today.

Think about your thinking. How confident are you with the thought-processes involved in working well at this level? Which aspects of your **thinking style** will be most useful to you now, and which will need some extra work if you're going to develop next-level skills?

Finally, focus on how your thinking translates into *learning*: the **attitudes**, **preferences**, **abilities** and **habits** that affect how *you* learn, and the results you get.

 # Steps to success

1 Track your activity

This phase of education involves a very active process of skills development. How much enthusiasm have you got to give? And how engaged have you been in the past (because that's where you'll find the best evidence for how it's likely to go from here)?

Here's an exercise that explores your potential for becoming the sort of energetic thinker and learner who does really well at this level. It also gives you things you can do today to start investing more of yourself in your study.

Learning works better when you're motivated to do it

Motivation raises energy levels, improves concentration, strengthens stamina, fires the memory, and pushes you to give everything you've got. It can be about getting things (a scholarship, acclaim, self-satisfaction), avoiding things (redundancy, disapproval, feelings of failure) or just maintaining the status quo (staying on the course, retaining your certification, keeping your parents proud). Sometimes it's easy to tap into, sometimes it's hard to find – in which case studying gets really hard to *do*, because it takes real commitment at this level, sustained energy and drive and, without motivation, the game's lost.

 # Ask yourself

→ How *motivated* are you feeling about …
- taking on higher-level learning?
- studying your current topic?
- working through the course as a whole?

Grade … your **motivation** overall: ☐ % (to help you monitor and manage yourself from here on in).

Think about … your reasons for continuing with your educational journey.

Talk to … someone who's good at making you feel more enthusiastic about your studies: a friend, a relative, a member of academic staff.

Do something … that will make studying feel that bit more appealing – like putting up a poster that will raise your spirits, or just tidying your desk so that you feel better about getting down to some work.

Learning works better when it happens at your pace

It's like running again. Train too slowly and you lose interest, stop trying, gain very little. But join a group that's too fast and it's just as bad – you get left behind. Good study involves finding the right pace for understanding to grow and skills to develop. The pace changes. You can race through some bits of the course, while at other times you need to jog, or even walk back to the start for another go. Sometimes you get to control the speed you go at. The rest of the time you need ways to adjust to the pace as best you can.

 # Ask yourself

→ … about the *pace* of your learning:
- Do you notice times when the pace of learning is too fast for you, or too slow?
- Do you like following the same plan as others, or working to your own schedule?
- Do you know how to alter the pace of your study when necessary?

Grade … your ability to **pace** your learning appropriately: ☐ %

Think about … how you could take more control over pacing.

❯ *Go to: Chapters 8 and 9 to see how to plan and manage your time.*

Talk to ... students with working patterns that look different from yours. Why do they organize and pace their learning that way? Are there any elements in their approach that might work for you?

Do something ... *while* you're reading this book. As you go through the rest of this chapter, draw a pencil line down the side of the page to record your progress.

- If you're reading steadily, mark a continuous line alongside the text.
- If you pause (to think about something maybe, or to fill in one of the boxes), show that with a short horizontal line in the appropriate place (you could also add a quick note about how long you stopped for).
- If you look back to an earlier section to check something or go ahead to a later page, draw arrows and add reminders about what you did.

At the end of the chapter, look back at your pencil marks to help you reflect on your tactics, and to think whether there are other things you could be doing to extract the most learning from the study time you put in.

Learning works better when it's relevant to you

You're hard-wired to notice things that are connected to you in some way – like when your own name jumps out at you from a long class list. It's a survival instinct. The human brain pays attention to and remembers details that serve a clear, personal purpose. It also likes relevant information because it's connected to things that are in there already, accelerating and enriching the memory process. When learning feels important, useful, doable ... we tend to do it, and do it well. And when it doesn't? That's when the daydreaming begins.

 # Ask yourself

→ ... about the *relevance* of your current studies:
- Will this course help you to get where you want to go?
- Which will be more relevant for your future: the information you're learning, or the skills you're developing?
- Do you get any options within the course that could make your work more useful for *you*?

Grade ... the **relevance** of your current work to your reasons for doing it: ☐ %

Think about ... the opportunities you're going to have to focus on knowledge and skills that are particularly relevant.

> **Go to: Chapter 18** *to see how some writing tasks can be adapted to suit your needs.*

Talk to ... staff on your course if you ever doubt the relevance of what you're doing. Ask them to explain why certain things are on the syllabus, and what you could be doing to come at them with more of a sense of purpose.

Do something ... that fills in any 'missing links' between your study and your reasons for studying. For instance, if you'd lost the point about why you were exploring a particular physics concept, doing some extra research about wing design might show you exactly why it was relevant to your target job in the aerospace industry.

Learning works better when you find it interesting

Even if something is extremely relevant it can still be deadly boring. And if you lose interest, learning suffers. Our vigilant, restless brains are quick to find better sources of stimulation (or take the other option and just power down). You've chosen this course, so it should be interesting to you on *some* level. But even your favourite subject can leave you cold sometimes, and not every teacher knows how to bring every topic to life.

 # Ask yourself

→ ... about your levels of **interest:**

- How eager are you to learn about the subject you've chosen? All of it, or some parts more than others?
- Are you *ever* very interested in learning? Maybe you're more excited by the eventual benefits than by the work itself.
- Do you have any strategies for making your studying more interesting?

Grade ... your **interest** in your studies: ☐ %

Think about ... one aspect of your chosen subject that sparks your interest, then see where it leads.

> *Go to: Chapter 10 for research techniques that will help you make this the starting point for searching out new areas of interest.*

Talk to ... a passionate student of your subject, in the same building as you, in the wider community or somewhere online. See whether you can absorb some of their enthusiasm generally, as well as pointers to interesting questions, ideas and discoveries.

Do something ... now to prepare for a project you'll be doing later in the course. Base it on an area you're interested in, so that you're regularly reading and thinking about bits of the subject that you really enjoy.

Learning works better when the teaching is strong

Get ready for new types of teaching. Big lectures, small tutorials, unfamiliar things like seminars and workshops. You'll work with some teachers who are still students themselves, and others who are world leaders in their field – maybe even the authors of your textbooks. You'll need to learn new ways of engaging with them all, but you should still expect high quality – and know what to do if the standard slips. Even though independence is so important here, teaching – in all its forms – is still vital, and once again you need to be ready to take action.

Ask yourself

→ How well do you maximize the *teaching* you're offered?

- Do you know what you should be getting from different types of teaching?
- Do you ever take steps to get more out of it?
- Do you notice when teaching is effective, and when it's really *not*?

Grade … how much you feel you benefit from **teaching**: ☐ %

Think about … your own role: the things you could start doing to make teaching as useful to you as possible.

❯ *Go to: Chapter 15 for advice about getting the most out of all the teaching on offer.*

Talk to … staff members who can address any concerns or help you get support. You're probably paying a lot of money for this course, and you deserve to get full value for it. So, if you're not, talk to a member of academic staff you trust. Be respectful, specific, realistic – but also persistent if you don't think the problem's been solved.

Do something … to prepare for the next bit of teaching you get. Give yourself just five minutes with a notebook, the internet and some course information, and see how much you can find out beforehand that might intensify learning in the session itself. Who's teaching you (their background, specialism, likely teaching style)? What will they cover (is there any useful pre-reading/pre-thinking)? How will you get the most out of the experience (using coloured pens; typing notes on your laptop; even – with permission – recording the session on your phone)?

Learning works better when the environment is right

Where we are has a big impact on how we feel – and that can change the way we learn. Familiarity, safety, nostalgia, beauty and many other factors provoke emotional reactions, at the same time as the levels of comfort, warmth, light, sound and smell are having their own effects. Mix in the behaviour of other people in the same space, the equipment and resources nearby (or not), disruptions, distractions … *Where* you study goes a very long way towards shaping that study and determining its success. You've got work to do again.

 # Ask yourself

→ … about your *environment(s)*:

- What impact do you think your environment has on the quality of your study?
- Do you have a variety of workplaces to choose from?
- Are you in the habit of changing things if your surroundings are causing you problems?

Grade … the quality of your study **environments**: ☐ %

Think about … the advantages and disadvantages of the environments you tend to choose.

❯ *Go to: Chapter 7 for a guide to making good choices about where you learn.*

Talk to … a variety of people, on and off your course, about where they learn best and why. Be open to ideas that might be worth a try.

Do something … to experience something different. Try working somewhere completely new, then be honest with yourself about how well it went. Would it make sense to come back in future? Are there any clues here about improvements you could make to your regular spots?

Learning works better when you're actively involved

Like runners, wrestlers and travellers, students get on best when they're energetic and engaged. When you realize how important your role is, you start to understand what autonomous learning is all about, and you're ready to put the best conditions in place – so that you can learn at a good pace, with relevant and interesting stuff to get your teeth into, helped by strong teaching, in a place that feels right. There's a lot to handle, but *so* many chances to get stuck in.

 # Ask yourself

… how *active* you are in your learning – do you …

- read actively, asking yourself questions, making useful notes?
- play an active part in group tasks?
- make conscious improvements to the way you study?

Grade … your level of **activity** as a learner: ☐ %

Think about … how you could start being more visibly involved in your work.

> *Go to: Chapter 17 for advice on contributing to group work.*

How could you been seen to be more active, so that you *feel* more like an active player – and then maybe more opportunities for involvement start coming your way …?

Talk to … the clubs and societies you'd like to join (or get more involved in). You'll have to balance your time and effort carefully, but there are some exciting opportunities to be active and engaged during this part of your life – which can have a very powerful knock-on effect on your studies.

Do something … to show your active engagement *now*. Make sure that you do every activity and respond to every question you're asked in this chapter. Could you even go further and add questions of your own?

 # Ask yourself

→ What does this exercise reveal about your current approach?

How high are your ratings here generally? Where are the strengths and weaknesses? Which areas do you think you should concentrate on first? You'll be returning to this section several times to see how well you can learn to control these key conditions, and **Part 7** will help you take an active approach to *all* the learning you do from now on.

2 Think about thinking

Learning at this level involves – and develops – different types of thinking. It also gets you thinking *about* them.

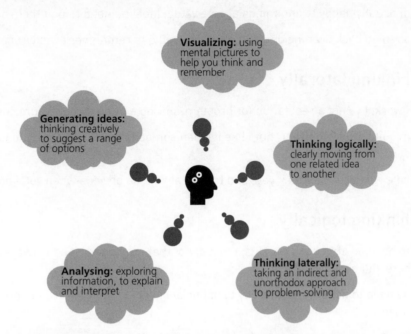

These modes of thought will need to be woven through all the work you do now, coordinated and combined in different ways. Your development as a student will involve learning how to use them confidently – and, when necessary, *consciously.* Knowing what thinking skills you're using and what impact they're having will be a key part of studying well at this level.

The following activity will help you think about your current abilities in these five intellectual areas. Read the responses under each heading, then highlight any that come close to the way you feel at this point.

Generating ideas

'When I'm asked what I think, my mind goes blank.'

'I'm a natural party-planner.'

'If someone else makes a suggestion, that inspires me to have ideas of my own.'

Visualizing

'Sometimes I can picture the layout of my notes – months after I've made them.'

'I find it very difficult to give directions to people: I just can't picture the places I'm talking about.'

'It always helps me to see plays for real because then I can "watch" them again in my head while I'm writing.'

Analysing

'My friends and I talk for hours about the films we watch, going into great detail about plots, dialogue, direction … and why we love them or hate them so much.'

'I'm usually happy taking things at face value; I feel no need to pull them apart.'

'I often go back over incidents in my head, trying to remember exactly what happened.'

Thinking laterally

'At work, I've got a reputation for problem-solving – often through pure common sense.'

'I'm quite a rule-follower, but I like it when someone says I'm allowed to follow my own instincts.'

'I hate riddles – they trick you, and they're always so obvious when you know the answer.'

Thinking logically

'I'm no good at Sudoku puzzles; I'm just not that methodical, and I always get to a point where all I can do is guess.'

'You need to listen very carefully to politicians. Very often their arguments have huge flaws in them.'

'I like games where you can plan ahead a little – but I also want to get on with playing!'

Use your answers here to start reflecting on the sorts of thinking you've been most comfortable with until now. All five of these themes will keep reappearing throughout the book, and you'll see how to draw on your strengths and address any weaknesses, developing a flexible set of thinking skills by using them all to grapple with the subject you've taken on.

Ask yourself

→ How do you see yourself as a learner?

Higher-level learning is driven by constant questioning, including some big questions for you to ask about yourself. Here are three (plus a supplementary one) to get you thinking at this stage – and to bear in mind throughout your course, because your answers may well change as your studies progress.

- What makes learning valuable?
- Do you like learning?
- How do you think others view your learning? (And how do you feel about *that*?)

3 Learn about learning

For whatever reason (your genes, your education, the way life's gone, the sort of person you are) you've got attitudes and preferences that guide how you think and learn. This book will help you to work with them, but also get you challenging them, trying out new things, opening up other options.

Read the following questions carefully. As you consider your responses, underline any words or phrases that you think describe your learning now.

- When you're dealing with new information, do you tend to focus on details first, then gradually take in more of the 'whole' – or do you start with an overall view and get into the details later on?
- Is your instinct to learn in sequence, from beginning to end, step by step, or to set off from somewhere in the middle and see where your investigations lead?
- Which helps you most: considering one idea at a time, or juggling several different concepts?
- Is it easier to learn when you're taught information directly, or when you get to explore it all yourself?
- Do you like being told answers or making your own discoveries?
- Are you more comfortable when answers are either 'right' or 'wrong', or when different interpretations can be valid?
- Do you prefer a clear, structured syllabus, or your own choice of what to study and how?
- Which is more important to you: knowing a little about lots of different things, or having in-depth understanding of just a few?

Questions like these take you another step further into *metacognition* – 'thinking about thinking' – and they can reveal some important aspects of your personal learning 'styles'. They can also help you compare yourself with some commonly used descriptions (but be careful they don't become labels).

- Perhaps you see evidence of *serialist* thinking in your preference for structured learning, or the *holist* approach in the way you like grappling with lots of ideas at once.
- Maybe you're into *deep* thinking, rather than *surface* thinking.
- Perhaps you have a clear tendency for *relativism*, valuing shifting interpretations more than 'easy' rights or wrongs.

Most likely it's a mixed picture, a combination of characteristics and behaviours. In practice, we can operate very differently depending on the subject matter or situation.

Academic Advice

'Sometimes simple is best. Studying at this level definitely requires deep thinking, gathering lots of different viewpoints, making personal interpretations, and being comfortable where there are no right/wrong answers … but there are also times when you need to work in a much simpler way: skimming for key words, breaking complex texts into more manageable chunks, not being afraid to spot the most obvious patterns. The trick is knowing which approach to take, when, and how to combine them in your overall approach. And sometimes you can confidently take what looks like a simple approach to produce very complex and rich results'. **Lars, English Literature lecturer**

It's always going to be complicated. The best learning combines information from a range of sources, in a variety of forms, exploring, analysing, remembering and using it in many different ways, and developing a rich mix of skills in the process.

We may have some natural preferences:

- for **visual** learning (seeing, watching, reading, visualizing)
- using **auditory** channels (hearing, listening, discussing, presenting)
- taking a **kinaesthetic** (doing) approach (handling, making, copying, experiencing).

But so much depends on what we're doing, how we're feeling, what we know works, and what we decide to try.

Metacognitive awareness helps you to make sensible choices about studying, including what to study and how to pick from the strategies available. To get the most out of your course you'll need to use your most comfortable learning styles to the full, but it's also good to experiment, trying out techniques that maybe don't come so naturally. Thinking differently.

You'll see that there's a lot to be gained sometimes from combining detailed knowledge with the big-picture view; from challenging views about 'truth' in different contexts; from choosing between surface and deep learning as the situation dictates.

Now that you've started thinking about thinking, keep doing it. It's how you'll make all the advice in this book appropriate for you: the learner you are now, but also the one you're turning into. Use your awareness to drive your activity. Take charge of your own development. Get ready to deepen your knowledge of yourself as a learner, and yourself full stop.

⑩ Ten-point summary

1. At this level it's more important than ever to be engaged in all aspects of study, including actively seeking out the best conditions for learning.

2. Motivation plays a big part in your ability to develop the skills you need.

3. Do everything you can to make the pace of learning right for you.

4. Take steps to make the work you're doing as interesting to you and as relevant to your needs as possible.

5. Be aware of the quality of teaching on offer, and what you can do to improve the provision if necessary.

6. Your environment has a significant impact on the success of your study.

7. Metacognition – thinking about thinking – will be a vital part of learning well at this level.

8. You'll need to use a number of different modes of thinking in your work, and it's important to know your current strengths and weaknesses.

9. Analyse the thinking behind your learning, to help you start taking control of your approach to study.

10. It's useful to ask yourself some big questions about learning – in general, and specifically what it means for you.

Where to next?

Chapter 3 will show you how to manage yourself, your work, and the people who can influence your success.

③ Test your strength

Your academic development depends on several different sets of skills, which you can analyse and assess to help you plan the best way forward.

 ## What?

Real success at this stage of your education involves developing a very wide range of identifiable skills – through the process of studying. In a sense they could *all* be called 'academic' skills: you use them academically; they're different at this new level of learning; they all play a part in your academic success.

However, some of these skills are *truly* academic, intimately linked to what makes higher-level learning so special. In particular, there's the set of thinking skills you use to explore and analyse complex information, reach judgements, make discoveries and begin contributing to the construction and communication of new knowledge. You'll explore those and other 'Academic-with-a-capital-A' skills in the next chapter.

But first you need to analyse the interconnected sets of skills that make all of that possible: **self-management skills**, **task-management skills** and **people skills**.

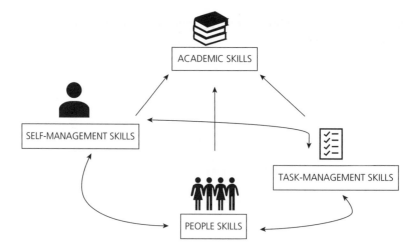

 ## When?

Like all the personal factors examined in Chapter 1, none of these skills can be 'sorted out' before you start, because they're all learned in practice and in context. But you can certainly learn *about* them before you begin your course, and there's a lot to be gained by assessing your **starting points** in each of the main skill areas.

If your new studies have started, that's fine; you'll already have some experience – and maybe some evidence – of what this skills development process is going to mean for you. You'll also be able to use examples from your course to help you reflect on the questions and engage with the exercises that follow.

But if you're 'in between' further and higher education, you're really in the ideal place – well positioned to understand the ongoing progression of skills, the similarities, as well as the significant differences, between how you've studied up till now, and the way you're going to have to work next.

 # Who?

You'll be doing plenty of thinking about yourself again (giving you plenty more opportunities to train your **self-analysis** and independent thought). But you'll also be looking at **collaborative** learning, dialogue and debate, and you'll see why the skills required to study well are best developed by working with and among other people.

 # Why?

You're studying to be a student, learning to learn. Skills development is the business you're in, and it's very much your own responsibility – so you need to know how it works. By seeing strengths to draw on, areas to improve, and ways to do both *within* your studies, you can be building a range of valuable skills from day one.

 ## Academic Advice

'I'd say that higher-level learning is a constant "test of strength". Analysing your own thinking is where it starts, because that teaches you how to start testing what everyone else is doing. It's all about seeing how strong a particular approach is when you hold it up to scrutiny – and always trying to find better ways of understanding your subject.' **Andrew, university tutor**

 # How?

You need to see the whole landscape of higher-level skills to be able to start locating yourself on the map.

In this chapter there are three *sets* of skills to explore – which, in combination, fuel the fires of learning at this stage of study. You'll be shown how to discover what each set means for you, by reflecting on your experiences with them so far, and on how you're *feeling* about them in the light of the new challenge you've taken on. You'll also assess your ability levels now, to give some clear directions to your development plans.

Lots will depend on your **opinions** about learning, which will be tested as well – along with some important aspects of how your **brain** works, and factors in your **background**, **personality**, **lifestyle** and **behaviour** that will also need to be addressed if you're going to get the best out of your studies.

Steps to success

1 Check your *self-management* skills

Studying well develops a wide range of self-management skills with far-reaching benefits:

Self-awareness: this is a theme that's developed throughout the entire book.

> *Go to: Chapter 1 if you haven't started this process yet.*

Skills-management: assessed here, and in the chapters on either side.

> *Go to: Chapter 2 for some exercises to get you started.*

Time management: this is explored in depth in Chapters 7 and 8.

Self-care: this is essentially a combination of all three of the skill sets above, helping you to understand what's going on, continually develop your abilities, and manage your life so that some very important aspects of your wellbeing are taken care of:

Physical health

- Doing your best to maximize diet, exercise and sleep
- Considering the effects of any substances potentially harmful to health, such as alcohol, tobacco and drugs
- Managing disabilities or times of ill-health, either short-term or long-term
- Finding the best ways to maintain your energy levels and general physical condition

Strengths to draw on:
Potential *weaknesses* to address:

Mental health

- Coping with a period of great change and intense personal effort
- Monitoring any existing conditions
- Being mindful of any previous issues, and vigilant for new problems emerging
- Making full use of all the resources available and the support services on offer

Strengths to draw on:
Potential *weaknesses* to address:

Emotional health

- Being aware of how your studying is affecting you emotionally
- Understanding the links between physical and emotional wellbeing
- Building resilience to cope with the highs and lows of student life
- Using your emotions to engage with learning (and have some fun doing it)

Strengths to draw on:
Potential *weaknesses* to address:

While you're busy developing self-management skills through the process of studying, don't forget to use all the *resources* at your disposal. These include **people** (friends, family members, staff on your course), **places** (home, university, placements) and **things** (equipment, materials, money). Together with your own abilities and attitudes, your experiences so far and the things you do next, the way you make use of these resources will have a very big impact on your success.

Use the headings below to record some of your most important resources, to help you realize just how much is already in your favour – and where you can turn for an extra boost if you need it.

PEOPLE

Who are they? How do they support you?

PLACES

Where are they? How are they helpful?

THINGS

What are they? How will they strengthen your study?

 # 2 Check your *task-management* skills

By this point in your education you'll be very used to completing academic tasks – so you should have plenty of evidence about how well you do it.

It's really valuable to think about what your experiences so far tell you about:

- how you approach different sorts of tasks
- what goes on in your thoughts and feelings when you do
- what sort of outcomes you usually get.

But there are lots of new tasks to cope with now, and all your thinking and learning has to be done at a significantly higher level, in an environment that will stretch you in so many different directions. You need to be ready to improve and adapt all your existing skills.

Below are boxed sections examining six key areas in this task-management skill-set.

Think about what they've meant for you up to this point, as you read how they'll *change* in the work you do next. Then fill in the three spaces to show:

- what you think you'll be able to *keep* doing now
- what you'll have to *stop* doing
- what could still work – if you do it *differently*.

Overall skill	MEETING STANDARDS
Differences in higher-level study	Established standards to meet within the academic community, including integrity, cooperation and the responsibility to stay up-to-date New academic practices to understand and follow (e.g. citing, referencing, avoiding plagiarism) Subject-specific standards in place – for evaluating evidence, presenting and testing interpretations, and advancing knowledge alongside others in the field Professional standards important during workplace visits, industry placements, etc. Assessment standards based less on knowledge, recall and explanation than on analysis, interpretation and deep understanding
Keep doing	
Stop doing	
Do differently	

Overall skill	FOLLOWING PROTOCOLS
Differences in higher-level study	Awareness expected of relevant protocols and behaviour Some aspects of work now covered by legislation Responsibility to follow strict ethical guidelines Protocols apply to a wider range of activities, including lab work, field research and clinical procedures Opportunities to analyse protocols and suggest changes
Keep doing	
Stop doing	
Do differently	

Overall skill	USING EQUIPMENT
Differences in higher-level study	More complex and specialized equipment used Less supervision provided More personal responsibility for checking equipment and managing health and safety Opportunities to use, combine or adapt apparatus in novel ways – even develop completely new tools Access to industry-standard equipment in professional settings
Keep doing	
Stop doing	
Do differently	

Overall skill	USING PROCESSES
Differences in higher-level study	More complex processes to carry out – in practical tasks and theoretical work Less direction and supervision Some processes carried out independently; others as part of a collaborative team Responsibility for completing all the stages of long-term tasks Involvement in adapting processes and developing new ones, then evaluating their effectiveness and wider implications
Keep doing	
Stop doing	
Do differently	

Overall skill	PROJECT MANAGEMENT
Differences in higher-level study	Larger-scale projects undertaken, often over a considerable length of time Greater responsibility for time-management in general Proposals may need to be agreed before work can start Strict ethical and safety standards apply More freedom to choose questions to investigate and methods of research Projects may involve other students, academic staff and members of the public Wider range of techniques used to collect information, including interviews and questionnaires Detailed information given to participants, and their consent obtained Established formats to follow for presenting written work Feedback available during the project as well as at the end
Keep doing	
Stop doing	
Do differently	

Overall skill	PRODUCING ACADEMIC WORK
Differences in higher-level study	More choices involved at each stage of the process Less direction from teaching staff Wider and more detailed research required Freedom to use personal note-making styles More subject-specific tasks (e.g. scientific reports, literature reviews) Some significantly longer projects (e.g. dissertations) Collections of practical work rather than individual pieces Self-reflection/evaluation an integral part of the process Critical analysis, interpretation and evaluation of evidence vital
Keep doing	
Stop doing	
Do differently	

🎏 3 Check your *people* skills

Higher-level study involves a heavy burden of personal responsibility. It means facing a range of intense individual challenges in pursuit of a qualification that will be yours and yours alone, and highly personalized skills that will be at your disposal ever after.

But it's also a very public place. Your work is open to wide scrutiny. You have to operate among, with and sometimes against a diverse group of students. You'll come into contact with a large and complex staff team. You may well end up dealing with members of the public, too, or entering busy workplaces. All the while you'll need to juggle many different relationships within your social and family life. There's a lot to cope with here, and a great deal to gain if you can.

The people skills you develop through your studies will enrich and improve so many different aspects of your life, including your journey onwards into employment or deeper into education. You'll do it by:

- actively contributing in groups
- giving presentations
- engaging in dialogues
- collaborating on tasks
- working supportively.

The exercises that follow are designed to get you thinking about any relevant experiences you've had – in and out of education – and what they reveal about your existing strengths and weaknesses. When you've tried these things before, how did it feel, and how well did it go?

It may be that you already know some of the steps you could take to start improving, making more of the opportunities to strengthen your skills – in which case, write those in the final space. You'll be coming back here to add more ideas later, but if you can already think of ways to prepare better, behave differently, or access useful support, make a note of them now.

People skill: ACTIVELY CONTRIBUTING IN GROUPS
Sharing ideas, taking on responsibilities, engaging constructively in whatever the group is trying to achieve – in person or online

When have you done it?

How did it feel?

What worked, what didn't?

How could you improve?

People skill: GIVING PRESENTATIONS
Sharing your knowledge, understanding and ideas, helping others to engage with the subject matter as you talk about, demonstrate and display it in a variety of ways

When have you done it?

How did it feel?

What worked, what didn't?

How could you improve?

People skill: ENGAGING IN DIALOGUE
Discussing and debating with other students and members of staff – including giving and receiving feedback

When have you done it?

How did it feel?

What worked, what didn't?

How could you improve?

People skill: COLLABORATING ON TASKS
Sharing responsibilities for different aspects of planning, producing and presenting work – with one other person or several

When have you done it?

How did it feel?

What worked, what didn't?

How could you improve?

People skill: WORKING SUPPORTIVELY
Creating positive, safe and fair conditions in which everyone is encouraged to participate and helped to do their best

When have you done it?

How did it feel?

What worked, what didn't?

How could you improve?

If you've done some or all of the activities outlined in this chapter, you'll have produced some very valuable information for yourself – about you *now*, and you *next*. Remember, it's not about you changing. You don't need to be 'fixed'. This chapter should have provided some very clear evidence that you've already got plenty going for you as you prepare to push ahead with your studies.

It's about *developing*: starting where you are now and gradually building your approach, so that you grow through all the opportunities that this next phase of your education has to offer.

Use all the exercises you've done here to start tuning into the challenges ahead. You can keep coming back to these pages (and, at particular points, you'll be reminded to). When it feels right, try out some of the ideas within the real things you're doing on your course. As you'll see from the next chapter, these skills lay firm foundations for the developments that come, when your studies demand that you take your thinking to the next level.

 Ten-point summary

1. Several sets of skills combine to support higher-level thinking and learning.

2. The skills you need to study well are only fully developed in the process of studying.

3. Managing *yourself* is crucial, and it's important to gauge your abilities early on.

4. Self-management includes being self-aware, coordinating a range of skills, organizing your time effectively, and looking after all aspects of your wellbeing.

5. Your task-management skills also need to be assessed – in the context of studying at this level.

6. Key areas of task-management include producing academic work, using processes, meeting standards, following protocols, handling equipment and controlling complex projects.

7. There are important differences to understand between the way tasks worked previously, and what they're like in higher-level learning.

8. Your abilities to work with people make up another set of influential skills.

9. Significant people skills include contributing in groups, giving presentations, engaging in dialogue, collaborating on tasks, and working supportively with others.

10. Mine your past for evidence of how well you've worked with other people so far, and what needs to change from here.

 Where to next?

Chapter 4 will help you to start adapting the way you think and work to match the new level of challenge you're taking on.

Higher ground

Higher-level study involves some specifically academic skills, developed through new ways of researching, exploring and communicating information – within a community that supports but also challenges every aspect of your work.

 ## What?

Advanced study is a judgemental business. Doing it well means developing highly tuned techniques for **analysing** and **evaluating** information, while also examining the strengths and weaknesses in your work, and everyone else's – as they do the same to yours.

This chapter explores the **key academic skills** you'll need to achieve this higher level of understanding – the skills you'll be judged on, increasingly, as you progress through your course. You'll learn how to prepare for the **emotional** strains that can come from stretching your thinking; to see how to make the most of abilities you've already got; and to find out what you can do to start adapting straight away to the new academic challenges you face.

 ## When?

These activities will play an important part in your long-term **academic development**, so you'll be returning to them at various points later on. The sort of self-analysis involved is particularly valuable as you prepare to step up to higher-level work, and as you're starting to get to grips with it (when it can feel very different from anything that's come before). There's also advice here about things that should definitely be done as early as possible – to give you the best chance of being ready to study well from the start.

 ## Who?

As well as examining your own abilities and planning your personal way forward, there are important preparations to be made for living and working within a complex **academic community** – plus key messages about knowing when and how to get help along the way.

 # Why?

Attempting harder, deeper thinking and learning can be a worrying prospect – but it needn't be. The exercises in this chapter will help you cope with your feelings about testing yourself in new ways – not just by analysing and putting them into perspective, but by addressing them quickly, so that the development's begun and you're on your way.

You'll need to use all the skills you've gained from your experiences so far – particularly your strengths in **literacy** and **numeracy** (which can be a cause of serious anxiety for some people when they get to this point). An honest look at your abilities in these areas is vital for you to plan how to develop them as essential academic skills, and to get any specific help you need.

It's also important to be thinking about **assessments** as soon as possible, so that, from the start, your studies are building the sort of academic strength that stands up to any kind of judgement.

 # How?

No one is born with academic skills. The people who succeed at this level developed theirs, through a gradual and sustained process of studying *at this level* – and you can, too. By using your **self-management**, **task-management** and **people skills** to the full, you'll drive forward your academic development as you gain the advanced abilities that take everything up a notch. These are what will make this stage of your education so special, so demanding and so valuable for the rest of your life.

First, learn about the defining elements of academic thinking and working. Explore how you feel about them, and start planning personal strategies for developing them all.

Next, see how this development is going to happen in practice, through research, analysis, communication, and by doing everything you can to match the exacting demands of your community. Gauging your literacy and numeracy skills will show you what you can use now, and what needs to improve, and thinking about your experiences with assessments will help you to start this phase of your studies with real confidence and purpose.

Finally, round off all the rich personal work you've done in Part 1 by choosing the areas you need to focus on now, from all the different sets of skills you've examined so far.

 ## Steps to success

1 Confront your feelings

Preparing to start a higher-level course can be nerve-racking to say the least. You just don't know what this kind of thinking and learning is going to feel like until you've tried it, or how well you're going to do. Are you 'clever' enough? Can you communicate at this very grown-up level? Can you behave like a specialist? Do you really deserve (or even want) to be an 'academic', a member of a community of thinkers built on curiosity and serious intellectual challenge?

It's important to explore how you're feeling about key aspects of study. It helps you to direct your own development, and to monitor it by knowing where you started from.

Here are some of the essential aspects of academic thinking you'll need to get to grips with. How comfortable do you feel about them at the moment?

Be honest. Choose a face to go alongside each idea, and put a date at the top of the column. You'll see that there are extra columns, too, so that you can return to this task later and record your reactions when you're further down the road.

Higher-level thinking involves …	Your reaction		
	☹ 😐 ☺ Date: _____	☹ 😐 ☺ Date: _____	☹ 😐 ☺ Date: _____
Joining in shared intellectual curiosity, as part of a dynamic learning community			
Moving away from generalizations, into complexities, contradictions, uncertainties			
Critically analysing information from a variety of sources			
Understanding how knowledge is constructed			
Constantly questioning data, concepts and methodologies			
Using the writing process to develop understanding			
Engaging in dialogue to stimulate thinking and challenge ideas			
Formulating theories and putting them to the test			
Arriving at new interpretations			
Considering the wider relevance of discoveries			
Achieving deep understanding of complex information			
Playing a role in the advancement of knowledge			

2 Know the development zones

You'll develop all the academic skills necessary to succeed at this level through:

* **researching**
* **thinking**
* **communicating**.

You'll also do it by engaging in **academic practice**, working to values and standards that should be visible throughout your learning community, but which can only be *fully* understood in the context of your chosen subject.

Here's an overview of each of these areas, with space to make notes about where you're starting from, and some ideas about how to start moving forward straight away.

Higher-level RESEARCH
Key skills:
<ul><li>Having a range of appropriate and effective ways of searching for information</li><li>Knowing how to evaluate the usefulness of both printed materials and online resources</li><li>Defining your task clearly in order to do useful and efficient research</li><li>Reading quickly and accurately, selecting your subject matter intelligently and using a range of skills to get full value from the information on offer</li><li>Making useful notes, improving your understanding, supporting your analysis and interpretation, and helping you to remember and reuse your research</li><li>Managing an efficient; flexible and creative research process: obtaining information from various sources; organizing and storing it; and being able to retrieve, combine and use it a number of different ways</li></ul>
Previous experiences; current strengths and weaknesses; thoughts and feelings about the challenges now:
Development ideas:
<ul><li>Look up the titles of research projects done by previous students on your course. Think about the sort of research techniques they might have used.</li><li>Explore a daily newspaper. What different sorts of research are represented here? How could you use them for your own research – and what would the potential problems be?</li></ul>

Higher-level THINKING

Key skills:

- Making careful, informed decisions about your academic development
- Analysing a range of information to judge its usefulness and its implications for your study
- Questioning everything: knowledge, theories, values, methodologies, working practices
- Deconstructing information to explore the component parts as well as the 'big picture'
- Using memory to store and organize information in the pursuit of deeper understanding
- Considering different points of view (and knowing why they exist), but always probing for flaws in arguments and information likely to mislead
- Solving problems creatively
- Synthesizing information from different places and in different forms, to deepen understanding and play a role in creating new knowledge

Previous experiences; current strengths and weaknesses; thoughts and feelings about the challenges now:

Development ideas:

- Look at Georges Seurat's famous painting *A Sunday Afternoon on the Island of La Grande Jatte*. Focus on the minute details – in the painting technique, and in the scene itself – but also consider the effect of this large picture as a whole. And if you could ask the artist one question, to help you understand his approach, what would it be?
- Watch a political discussion show on TV. Practise assessing each guest's point of view. What's likely to have formed it? Does it overlap with the outlooks of others? How does it help you judge the value of what they say?

Higher-level COMMUNICATION

Key skills:

- Varying your communication to suit different academic purposes
- Presenting information and ideas with clarity and precision
- Using both the structure and the style of your written and spoken communications to help you convey your messages
- Being aware of the needs of an audience, and the likely impact of your communication on them
- Understanding and following the rules of communication in different subject areas
- Acknowledging and referencing the sources of your information as required

Previous experiences; current strengths and weaknesses; thoughts and feelings about the challenges now:

Development ideas:

- Rewrite the story of *Goldilocks and the Three Bears* as a police report.
- Read an article, in a magazine or online, and think carefully about how informative and engaging it is. Focus on what it makes you think and feel – and *how* it does that. Then talk to someone else about the main points, highlighting important details, statistics or quotations, and discussing how significant or credible they seem to be.

Higher-level ACADEMIC PRACTICE

Key skills:

- Understanding the 'foundation' concepts within your field
- Basing all arguments on detailed, critical analysis of the evidence
- Offering up theories and interpretations for scrutiny
- Maintaining ethical awareness when planning, conducting and reporting on work
- Upholding the established standards of the whole academic community, including integrity, cooperation and respect
- Contributing to the construction of knowledge
- Working within subject-specific values, terminology and methodologies

Previous experiences; current strengths and weaknesses; thoughts and feelings about the challenges now:

Development ideas:

- To work in your chosen subject, what are the five essential things you need to know?
- Read through a journal article related to your studies. Highlight any terminology that you understand, but people outside your subject won't; and if there are any words or phrases that even you don't understand yet – look them up.

Academic Advice

'I talk to my students about PFI: the way you can build your skills over time through a cycle of PRACTICE, FEEDBACK and constant INSPECTION. You use the skills in your work. You assess your own success and get advice from other people. You keep monitoring your progress, adapting your practice in response … and on you go, developing personalized, long-lasting skills.' **Maria, university tutor**

3 Check your *literacy* and *numeracy*

You've been building your literacy and numeracy skills all your life, and that needs to continue now – even if these aren't particularly obvious aspects of your chosen subject. English and maths provide important tools for developing and demonstrating all the other skills required, and they're woven through all the key modes of thinking involved.

You'll sharpen your literacy and numeracy skills as you progress through your course. How that works and what it looks like depends a lot on your subject, and obviously some fields rely more on these skills than others. But everyone's development at this level involves using English and maths techniques and types of thinking in increasingly subtle ways, to help gather information, analyse and interpret it, discuss and present it – and keep on challenging the ideas that emerge.

So where do you start from with these skills? How ready do you feel to build on them? Will you need any extra help to use them effectively and make the sort of progress required?

Literacy

Think about your **language** skills – in reading, writing and speaking.

- Is English your first language, or an additional one?
- How confident are you with grammar, punctuation and spelling?
- How much do you rely on word-processing or translation software to correct your language use?
- Do you have any specific language difficulties?

How confident is your **reading**?

- Are you able to stay focused for a good length of time?
- Can you access key information quickly and effectively – and also read 'between the lines' to extract deeper meanings?
- How good are you at seeing what a writer is trying to achieve, and how they're using language to do it?

What experience do you have of **writing** in an academic style, presenting information and ideas clearly and precisely?

- Can you plan and structure your work to be readable, engaging and persuasive?
- Do you use writing to help strengthen your own understanding?

How good is your **spoken** English?

- Do you have the appropriate vocabulary to discuss and debate your subject with others?
- Can you vary the way you talk to suit different audiences?

> What gives you most confidence about your literacy?

What's the main thing you need to work on?

What would help you most with your literacy skills now?

 Note To Self

If you have difficulties with literacy, don't just assume that the staff on your course will know about them in advance, or notice them now. You need to let them know. Talk to your tutor, link up with any relevant support services, and check that you're accessing all the support available. There should be various kinds of help on offer. Some of the ways you're assessed may change in order to take your circumstances into account. And the sooner the course staff know, the sooner they can get on with adapting things to suit your particular needs.

 Academic Advice

'Don't be afraid to ask for help. Identifying weaknesses, and taking steps to overcome them, is a sign of strength and an extremely valuable way of leading your own learning. However confident other students appear, they're very likely to have their own worries, and many will be facing the same challenges as you to overcome their fears and get the help they need.' **Mei, learning support tutor**

Numeracy

What are your **numeracy** skills like overall?

- Do you handle maths well in everyday life, or rely on electronic help – or avoid it altogether?
- Do you think you have any specific difficulties with maths, such as poor 'working memory' or dyscalculia (a mathematical version of dyslexia)?

How confident are you with **calculations**?

- Do you understand how to extract the relevant numbers from among words and ideas (and other numbers), and then carry out the right operations with them to arrive at accurate, meaningful answers?
- Do you spot when the answers you get are unlikely to be right?

Can you interpret the **data** you see – in tables, charts, diagrams, graphs?

- Do you understand the ways in which information can be misunderstood, or even distorted, by the ways in which it's presented?
- How confident are you at reading very large or very small numbers?
- Can you use different sorts of average?
- Are you able to calculate probability?
- What are your abilities like with fractions, percentages, ratios and proportions?

What about **using** maths yourself?

- Does it help you to gather evidence, analyse and interpret it, and present your conclusions in a way that others can understand, scrutinize and challenge?
- Do you know a range of ways in which maths can enrich your work – whatever your field of study?

What gives you most confidence about your numeracy?
What's the main thing you need to work on?
What would help you most with your numeracy skills now?

Case Study: Angie

Maths was always Angie's weakest subject at school. She only *just* did well enough in her last maths exam to be able to stop studying it. Maths featured occasionally in her other subjects, and she kept scraping through. But it was when she was in the middle of a geography degree course, dealing with complex statistical information for her research, that Angie's old insecurities came back in force.

After struggling alone for a while, she asked for help from her tutor – who explained some of the straightforward maths that was hiding behind complex-looking data. The tutor also linked Angie to another member of staff who offered maths tuition, and three sessions took place: the first recapped some core maths principles and processes, while the other two used Angie's real work so that she could practise the maths in context. After the sessions she felt confident enough to return to working independently again.

4 Check your assessment literacy

It's time for more SWOT analysis, exploring your previous experiences of assessment to help you get the best possible results from the work you do now.

Certain things will look very familiar, but there are significant changes, too. Analysing how things have happened in the past can make you feel much more confident to face the new challenges ahead.

Assessments are likely to happen during your course as well as at the end of it, and to take various forms depending on your field of study. You'll need to demonstrate your abilities under a degree of pressure, in conditions designed to inspire energetic and intense thinking, and to test how well you can use and communicate the knowledge and understanding you've gained during your studies.

The period leading up to an assessment (which you should really see as the whole course) becomes a rich process of building subject strength and academic confidence. The assessment provides a clear focus and adds to its purpose – especially as it's the way you'll gain your qualifications and be able to move on. And, whatever it's been like before, the preparations involved are so much more than just practising or memorizing so that you don't get found out.

Assessment literacy means:

- understanding the role and significance of assessments
- knowing how to get the most out of them, as part of the reward for all your hard work
- seeing ways to prepare for them constantly, in the way you do all your study
- developing assessment resilience through careful use of self- and task-management skills
- using academic skills effectively in order to prepare for particular assessment tasks
- having a range of strategies for producing your very best work *when* you're being tested
- engaging with a long-term cycle: undergoing assessment, learning from it, and doing even better the next time.

Think about the assessments you've done so far: tests, practicals, written exams, performances, graded presentations ...

Which **STRENGTHS** have you shown – ones you'll be able to take forward and build on? Maybe you're calm under pressure, have strong memory strategies, or know how to learn from your mistakes.

Which **WEAKNESSES** need addressing? Do you struggle to motivate yourself for tests, get the timing wrong in exams, or find you've revised the wrong thing?

Where do your best **OPPORTUNITIES** lie – the resources at your disposal, the things on your side? Think about the quality of your note-making, the people who help you prepare, the practice apps you've found useful in the past.

And what are the **THREATS** to your success in assessments that you'll have to guard against now? Are they in your *feelings* about being tested, the *conditions* you try to work in, patterns of *behaviour* that are hard to break ...?

ACADEMIC ASSESSMENTS
STRENGTHS
WEAKNESSES
OPPORTUNITIES
THREATS

5 Know your priorities

As this first part of the book comes to an end, you should know a lot more about the challenge you've taken on: what's asked of you at this level, and what you'll have to do to achieve it. So much depends on your starting points: knowing your strengths and weaknesses, planning an approach that's right for you, and monitoring your progress so that your personal journey provides the most important learning of all.

To help you pinpoint the areas to work on in your studies, and to start taking charge of your own development, use the chart below to record some of the discoveries you've made so far.

- Alongside each of the skills and abilities named here, make some notes about where you are now, and what you'll need to do next.
- Comment on any bits of advice that seem particularly important for you.
- Make it clear which of these points represent your priorities now.

The information you compile here will help you to apply all the advice in this book to your personal needs. Follow the priorities you've highlighted as you try things out in your studies. The **Go to** details will guide you to sections of the book that apply directly to each of these key skills – which, together, reveal so much about what *your* academic development process is going to involve.

Abilities and skills	Notes	Go to:
Engaging actively in learning		Chapters 5, 7, 9, 13, 14, 15, 16, 19
Controlling the pace of learning		Chapters 5, 7, 8, 14, 19

Abilities and skills	Notes	Go to:
Maximizing the impact of teaching		Chapters 5, 7, 14, 15
Creating an effective learning environment		Chapter 7
Generating ideas		Chapters 10, 14, 18, 19
Visualizing		Chapters 10, 12, 14, 19
Analysing		Chapters 10, 14, 16, 18
Thinking laterally		Chapters 10, 14, 16
Thinking logically		Chapters 10, 14, 16
Completing pieces of academic work		Chapters 5, 7, 8, 9, 11, 16, 18
Using processes		Chapters 13, 18
Meeting standards		Chapters 11, 15, 16, 18
Following protocols		Chapters 15, 18
Using equipment		Chapters 15, 18
Managing projects		Chapters 8, 17, 18
Contributing within a group		Chapters 13, 15, 17
Giving presentations		Chapter 17
Engaging in dialogue		Chapters 13, 15, 17
Collaborating on tasks		Chapters 5, 15, 17
Working supportively		Chapters 15, 17
Carrying out higher-level research		Chapters 5, 10, 12, 13, 16
Engaging in higher-level thinking		Chapters 5, 7, 10, 13, 14, 16, 18, 19

Abilities and skills	Notes	Go to:
Communicating in an academic community		Chapters 15, 17
Meeting the requirements of academic practice		Chapters 5, 16, 18, 19
Using literacy skills		Chapters 10, 11, 13, 16, 18, 19
Using numeracy skills		Chapters 14, 18
Using assessment literacy skills		Chapters 5, 12, 14, 19

> **Go to: Chapter 1** *and see how you're feeling now about taking on higher-level learning.*

(10) Ten-point summary

1. Success at this stage involves a set of distinctly *academic* skills.

2. The step up to advanced study can seem worryingly big – but no one is born with academic ability, and many of the key skills are very familiar.

3. It's important to gauge your feelings about key aspects of academic thinking and learning.

4. Research is a powerful driver of many key higher-level skills.

5. Academic thinking is analytic, questioning, creative and constantly self-aware.

6. Key abilities are developed through communicating within an academic community.

7. Specific knowledge and skills are required to think, work and behave to established academic standards.

8. Numeracy and literacy are important tools on all higher-level courses, and it's important to get help quickly if you need it.

9. Strong assessment literacy is essential, to understand what's involved at this level of learning, and what you need to do to succeed.

10. Good study takes long-term management, involving continual reflection and ongoing improvement in all areas of ability and skill.

(▷) Where to next?

Chapter 5 will reveal what success is going to look like in *your* higher-level course.

Part 2

The way forward

Understanding the challenges of your chosen subject, and starting as you mean to go on

Chapter 5 examines your chosen subject: its key **academic standards, the skills development** required, and the **risks/rewards** of studying in this field.

Chapter 6 guides you through effective **goal-setting**, with advice on **self-regulation** and ongoing personal **performance-management**.

Chapter 7 looks at how to create the best **environments** for learning – and then get into good **habits** quickly, with a range of **strategies** to suit you and your studies.

Subject specifics

To get the most out of higher-level study you need to know how your course is structured, the way it develops relevant skills, and what it does to test your success.

What?

At this level you need to learn how to study the particular **academic subject** you've chosen. A big part of your job is discovering how information is dealt with, knowledge increased and understanding deepened within your field, so that you can engage with all of that yourself. So, once again, it's about being active, leading your own learning. Use this book as a very practical guide to understanding the specific challenges of the course you're on, and doing all the right things in response.

When?

There's a lot in this chapter that you can do before your **course** starts – and in its early stages, when you'll be getting a great deal of information about the work that lies ahead. It's also a good idea to use the guidance here when you're preparing to start a new module, or at key points in projects, to make sure that your approach to your studies is spot on.

But it's the **early work** that's particularly important here. You need to feel equipped to start well, with a sense that you can learn how to operate in this sphere. It's not about simplifying the challenge or softening this step into the unknown. You're choosing to do something difficult, and in many ways you *need* to be unsure, curious about what's coming up, ready to grapple with uncertainties and come out stronger at the other end.

Who?

You'll need to get the **right information** from the **right people**. The work in this chapter involves collecting documents you're sent, doing your own searches online, combining the details *everyone* is given with those that apply only to your course, and liaising with a variety of staff within the complex community you've joined. These are the people who create the context for your studies, and you can take a lot from watching the way they operate and learning to fit in. That's how you'll do your best studying – and, ultimately, how you'll ensure that they recognize and reward the progress you've made.

 # Why?

Your course should give you rich opportunities to develop in the subject you've chosen, and you need to seize them from the word go. As you learn how the experts in your field move their subject forward, you'll see the relevance of the things *you're* being asked to do in your studies. This will help you to work within the structure of your course and develop the particular skills that are valued there.

An active approach is as important as ever. You're grappling with much more complex learning at the same time as receiving much less direct help. The questions you ask in this chapter will help you develop the proactive, analytic, responsive approach that's so effective when you're studying. They'll also show you how to apply everything you do to *your* subject, so that you're developing the right skills in everything you do. That's also why you need to be so clued up about the assessment systems in use – so that they direct your efforts and help you come out with the qualifications you need.

 # How?

Start by considering some of the key differences between this kind of studying and the work you've done before. There are things that every higher-level student has to get used to (and get *using*), but the most important questions are about how the changes apply to you, your subject and your course.

Explore how that course is **structured**. Take a wide-angled shot first, showing which topics are covered when, how the **teaching and learning** is managed, what level of **group work** is involved, and when **key tasks**, **projects** and **assessments** take place.

Then examine how **academic development** works within your subject area, using its values, standards and practices to cast light on the thinking and working you'll need to do – as part of a general approach, and adapted to suit different activities.

Finally, choose some areas of your practice to focus on, so that the insights you've obtained can have an immediate impact on your studies.

 # Steps to success

1 Spot the differences

Change can be unsettling, but it can also be exciting. Higher-level learning actually uses doubt to energize thinking. It pushes you to reconsider some of the things you once relied on, challenging you to develop new kinds of confidence that help you *keep* coping with uncertainty and change.

But so much is new, all at once. For most students, almost every aspect of daily existence changes overnight. To keep some degree of control, it's important to recognize how and why the academic side of your life is different. That's what brought you're here and got you making so many personal adjustments, and it can really help to understand the kind of transition you're going through – including spotting the things that aren't changing at all.

In a strange setting, it's all too easy to overlook familiar challenges – things we've faced up to very successfully in the past. But studying well always involves building on what's come before.

Student Tip:

'It can take you a while to feel like you belong at university – it certainly did for me. You're dealing with academics who are completely immersed in their subject, and I can remember how hard it felt trying to start thinking and talking and writing like them. But you soon realize that's what you're there for, and you do settle into it after a while. Bit by bit you find out how your subject works – and how you join in. It takes time, and I don't think you ever really feel you've cracked it. But I'm glad I hung in there long enough for it to start making sense.' **Scott, final-year Geology student**

Use the following activity as a way into this new stage of your education. It involves looking carefully at the major differences that all students have to get used to, but also thinking about what they're likely to mean in your subject and on your course.

You'll need some detailed information to help you.

- Collect everything you've already got about the course you're taking, in print or online: handbooks, syllabuses, lecture lists, timetables, subject guides ... Some documents you'll have been sent directly; others will be there on a website or learning platform whenever you need them.
- See what else you can get your hands on. Make sure that you take any new course materials that are given out. Keep a record of all the important points you're told by members of staff. Students in the years above should also have plenty of useful information to share (but check that their information is up to date; things can change quickly).
- Use everything you know now to help you with this exercise – and add more details as they emerge.

For each of the six areas analysed below, think about what's going to be different now, and make some notes about:

- how these changes are likely to show up in your particular course
- what the key thing will be for you to do in response.

If this process highlights any significant holes in your knowledge, do some extra research as soon as you can to plug the gaps.

Teaching staff

In the previous stage of education ... Probably only one or two staff to teach each subject. Teaching usually delivered in whole-class lessons. Clear guidance given about any preparatory work required. Homework set and marked. Feedback usually direct and fairly detailed.

On a higher-level course ... Many more staff involved in teaching, including lecturers, tutors, graduate students and professional instructors. Teaching likely to incorporate a mixture of lectures, classes, seminars, tutorials, workshops and practical sessions. Some guidance given about preparatory work, but often left to students to decide. Specific tasks connected to some sessions, but students allowed more choice about what to do before and after. Feedback often through discussion. Detailed comments usually reserved for assessed work.

In the subject you're studying …

The key for you personally …

Class sizes

In the previous stage of education … Small- to medium-sized groups, usually with the same number of students attending each lesson. Any individual or small-group tuition likely to be for selected students, or organized privately.

On a higher-level course … Some significantly larger groups, into the hundreds for some lectures, but also some much smaller groups in classes, seminars and workshops. Tutorials may be for a very small number of students – sometimes even one to one.

In the subject you're studying …

The key for you personally ...

Session timings

In the previous stage of education ... Each lesson likely to be 45 minutes to an hour long. Balanced timetables with a very similar shape to each session and each day. Some sessions left free for independent study.

On a higher-level course ... Much more variety: some long sessions, up to several hours, allowing time for in-depth analysis or complex practical work; and some much shorter classes, tutorials, meetings, reviews and check-ins with academic staff. Usually some pattern to the timetable – for example, standard slots for lectures – but also plenty of variation in timings, and some opportunities for flexibility. Considerably more time allowed for working independently.

In the subject you're studying ...

The key for you personally ...

Study materials

In the previous stage of education ... Varied in complexity, structure, tone and style, with value placed on having a range of different types of content. Various techniques used to make information engaging, understandable and interactive, including illustrations, photographs and creative design techniques. Resources often coordinated as part of a published set, series or programme.

On a higher-level course ... Most materials match one of several formats widely agreed within the field of study. Emphasis on using consistent features to help determine the validity and usefulness of information. Design techniques often consciously avoided. Clear links provided between independently produced materials to help students navigate all the available resources.

In the subject you're studying ...

The key for you personally ...

Learning

In the previous stage of education ... Predominantly done by being told or shown something, then copying it or using it as a clear model. Processes often broken into separate, linear elements: when you can do this, you'll be able to move on to this ... An emphasis on acquiring knowledge from a fairly limited set of sources, building on previous work. Value placed on remembering and repeating.

On a higher-level course ... Information presented in ways that provoke thinking and discussion. Emphasis on independent research, critical analysis and the development of intellectual skills. Non-linear learning valued, building knowledge from a range of sources. Students encouraged to re-examine previously held ideas. Opportunities to learn from other disciplines. A focus on understanding, applying and innovating.

In the subject you're studying ...

The key for you personally ...

Assessments

In the previous stage of education ... Likely to involve numerous fairly low-key assessments, often on discrete aspects of learning, including tests, graded work and internal exams. Some flexibility possible in assessment arrangements. At the end of a course, high-stakes national exams taken, marked externally. Interim exams sometimes used to help staff decide whether students can continue on the course. Coursework may also be assessed, either by staff or external markers. Development feedback often unnecessary if a unit of work has been completed.

On a higher-level course ... Wide variation between different providers, particularly in the use of ongoing assessment compared with final exams. All assessments announced in advance, following strict processes and criteria, with little or no flexibility. Results of some tasks may contribute to an overall grade or accumulate points. Assessments usually show progress towards a final level, designed to help students as well as staff. (Results may affect students' own decisions about continuing.) Feedback often provided as part of ongoing development. Examinations, research projects and other assessed tasks set and marked by the university itself, and sometimes checked or validated by outside bodies.

In the subject you're studying ...

The key for you personally ...

A clear theme here is the variability of arrangements at this higher level – so, there's all the more reason to get to grips with your specific situation. The notes you've made should help you to consider what you know now about some important aspects of the course you've chosen, and to start addressing how you feel about them – but it's likely you'll have plenty to change and add as your experience grows. Keep thinking about what it all means for you, looking out for ways to address your personal priorities in your real work, and coming back here whenever you have new insights to record.

2 See the big picture

How much students know about their course as a whole often comes down to how much they've *found out*. Even if you're sent glossy brochures, given schedules on paper, directed to websites, or know that it's all there for you to check on a learning portal ... it really doesn't help until you've actually looked at it, and properly thought about it all.

As soon as you can, take a close look at the overall structure of your course, using all the information at your disposal. Don't expect anyone to remind you to do it. It's your responsibility at this level. And it has to be personal process because it involves your responses to what you find. Use the following questions to help you do this.

Key questions to ask	Tick
How is the **content** of the course organized – as a whole, over several years? Can you see how it develops? For example, does it recap previous learning and strengthen core principles before going deeper? Which aspects of the subject seem to be most important (and that doesn't necessarily mean they're given the most time)?	☐
Is there a pattern to each **year**? For example, times given over to theory and practice; group work/independent tasks; planning/producing larger projects?	☐
What are the different types of **teaching** involved (e.g. lectures, seminars, classes, workshops, tutorials, demonstrations, coaching)? Is it all face to face or is some done over the phone or online? How much will you have to teach yourself, using videos, websites or podcasts?	☐
What are the key **independent tasks** and where do they appear? Look out for research projects, presentations, dissertations, performances to give, events to stage, collections of practical work to deliver.	☐
How much is **group working** part of your course? Perhaps there are joint projects, paired placements, discussions, debates?	☐
Are there any **external placements** involved? How do they fit in to the work that goes before and after?	☐
What else do you need to find out about the course as a whole to help you do your best?	☐

Tick each box when you feel you've got enough information for this 'big-picture' view. Be aware of your emotional reactions to each point – for example, are you worried about online learning, or does it excite you that you'll be doing two placements? – and highlight anything you'll need to address (this will help with a forward-looking activity at the end of this chapter). It's all part of the ongoing process of learning *how* to learn at this level, reaching out for the things that will make it work for you – sometimes changing the situation, sometimes changing your approach.

✎ Note To Self

Print out an overview of your whole course, showing topics, modules, major assignments, exam periods – anything that helps you see the scope of the challenge you've taken on. If you're not provided with a sheet like this, do some detective work and make one yourself. Add extra details as you find them out. Use highlighters to make everything as clear as possible. Tick off each section when it's done. Stick it somewhere you'll see it every day – and take a photo of it so you can check it on your phone wherever you are. It's within this structure that your academic development will take place. Use it as a map to keep your learning journey on track.

3 Focus on the details

Once you've got a widescreen shot of your course, you can start zooming in. Important details can emerge at any point – for example, you might find out well in advance where your placement is going to be, or decide on the topic for your dissertation – so you'll need effective methods of storing and retrieving them. (You'll find much more about this in Chapter 8.) At this stage, you could add them to your printed-out overview, or start a computer file for each new aspect of your work (your placement, your dissertation, whatever else appears on the horizon), ready to be filled in with more information over time.

And when that time comes, and you can address all the details of a task as you prepare to do it … use the template below to help. It's a set of ten questions designed to draw out everything you need to know, pushing you to shape a personal response to key parts of whatever challenge you've been set. It's this kind of strategic approach that will ensure that you get full value from all the effort you put into your study.

Task-planning template

Summarize the task

What part does it play in developing my abilities in this subject?

How could it develop me as a student generally?

What's the timescale/deadline?

Are there other specifications to meet?

Is this task dependent on anything else?

Must/could technology be used?

Is anyone else involved?

How will my success be judged – and what are the implications?

Is there anything else important to know/find out?

4 Prepare to be tested

You'll soon find that understanding assessments is about much more than knowing when your exams are and working towards them. The concept of *assessment* itself is an important one at this level, as you learn to evaluate evidence, examine assumptions, test knowledge – test *everything*.

Good study is constantly reflective and responsive. Throughout your work you'll need to make the most of feedback to help you develop your skills. Any assessments of your abilities are there to *strengthen* them, as well as to guide the next steps on your journey – and to recognize your success officially at key points along the way.

So, as you explore the specifics of the challenge ahead of you, it's vital to see how assessments fit in. Brace yourself: it's absolutely natural to feel anxious when you see a test, practical exam or written paper flagged up in your course schedule. But the chance to perform under pressure is a big part of what makes these activities so valuable.

On your 'big-picture' plan, highlight the key assessments, using one colour for the 'one-off' challenges (maybe a particular exam) and a different colour for longer periods of assessment: a work placement leading to a formal report, for example, or a science experiment that you'll need to set up and run over several days.

So much of your success now will depend on maximizing your time and energy, so make sure that you know the relative value of the different assessments involved – not just in terms of the marks/grades/points/qualifications/opportunities they offer straight away, but also their potential to strengthen your abilities long-term. When you look at what they *really* give you, some assessments are much more valuable to you than others.

Academic Advice

'It's a good idea to get hold of some past exam papers early on, to glimpse the sort of thinking you need to master during your course. Look at the types of question that come up and the words that keep appearing (maybe 'describe', 'analyse', 'explain', 'evaluate'...) to start tuning your brain in to the thinking that's important in your subject. How does it challenge your knowledge? How does it test specific skills? Don't worry that you can't actually answer the questions yet; trust that your studying will train you to do this when the time comes.' **Mike, university course leader**

5 Live like a local

Epistemology is the theory of knowledge in a particular subject – so it's absolutely central to working *in* that subject. It shapes the values, standards and ways of thinking and operating that apply in every different field. Learning to work to its principles is at the heart of what you're learning to do.

One way to explore theories of knowledge in your subject area is to use the 'scientific method': a set of principles that's been around since the seventeenth century and still has a major influence on the way knowledge is developed in many different disciplines today (and not just the obviously 'scientific' ones).

Take some of its big ideas and ask yourself how they apply to studies – to your course as a whole, and to particular topics or tasks. Some of these principles may be very important in some aspects of a subject, but exactly the *opposite* of what's needed in others. See what the balance looks like in your own case, and use your responses to help you prepare and put into practice the most appropriate approach.

It's valuable to do this early on, exploring what you know so far about your subject – and then to keep adding to your analysis as you learn more through study.

Think about each of these questions in relation to key aspects of your chosen subject, and make some notes to show how much you know about it – at this point in your studies.

How important is it to be *objective*? Can you test your ideas against evidence? Or, maybe being *subjective* is more appropriate, sampling opinions and basing some of your judgements on common sense?

How accurate do your descriptions need to be? For example, will you be describing some things for other people to copy precisely? And what counts as accuracy in your field? Would metaphorical language make your work more or less accurate?

How testable are your ideas? Perhaps you'll be dealing with hypotheses that can be tested robustly – sometimes disproved, sometimes revealed to be workable theories. In some subjects that's simply not appropriate, and there are better ways to examine ideas.

How far can you control variables? This is a key part of the planning and thinking process in some subjects and tasks, but is irrelevant in others.

How important it is to replicate your results? Is it you repeating them, or others trying to get theirs to come out the same? Even if they *are* replicated, there could be other factors at play, so you'll need to evaluate all the information you generate very carefully. Then again, this might be an alien concept in your field of study, highlighting a very different approach to advancing knowledge.

How quantifiable is your analysis? Are you able to measure the change in one variable in relation to another? Or are the results of some (or all) of your research impossible to quantify? Maybe *qualitative* exploration is more valuable to you, looking at characteristics that can't be measured. Of course, it's quite possible that you're interested in both *quantitative* and *qualitative* research – maybe even within the same task.

To help you go even deeper into the epistemology, here are three other questions to explore as you investigate the priorities and values of your chosen subject. Again, start by making some notes under each one based on everything you know now. You can return later in the course to add more thoughts, and reflect on – and maybe rethink – these early ideas.

EXPERIENCE
Do individual experiences produce valuable insights, or put accuracy at risk?

INVOLVEMENT
It is important to reference yourself and your own role in the work, or vital that you don't?

GENERALIZATION
Are you looking for ideas that hold true everywhere, or the exceptions to the rules?

 Academic Advice

'Before you even open any of the books on a reading list, you can get valuable insights simply by looking at the titles. Try to look past the obvious information about coverage to see some of the important themes and focus areas; and, even beyond that, the different kinds of thinking and learning that are valued by your subject. Look out for words like "history", "manual", "perspectives", "applications", "reflections", "principles" … and weigh up the different approaches signposted – across different modules and your course as a whole.' **Ray, Ph.D. student and tutor**

❯ *Go to: **Chapter 1** and consider how you're feeling at this point about some of the core challenges of higher-level learning.*

6 Choose what's important

When you've investigated the course you're on, and the subject you're *in*, invest some time in planning some next steps based on the things you've found out.

The table below condenses everything you've explored in this chapter into 15 questions. Consider each question in turn – but, rather than writing down your answers, record some **reflections** about those answers: the most important thoughts they've provoked.

Add notes, too, about any specific **responses** that could help.

There's also room for any wider **resolutions** that might improve the chances of your ideas working. (If that simply means making them priorities, fine – just make that clear in your writing or highlighting here.)

It's all part of the ongoing process of developing *your* best approach to studying. It's valuable in itself because it involves some of the key skills required for higher-level learning. It will also play an important role in the goal-setting activities you'll be doing next.

Reflections, responses, resolutions to ...
What forms of teaching are involved? *(When you think of your answer to this question, what's the most significant discovery; how should you act in response; and does it inspire you to make any bigger resolutions?)*
How much learning is done with others?
What sort of tasks are you required to do?
What are the processes of assessment?
How objective do you need to be?

Reflections, responses, resolutions to…

How much do you write about yourself and your role?

What value is placed on individual experience?

How do you test out ideas?

Is it important to control any conditions?

How is accuracy judged?

Reflections, responses, resolutions to …

Are you looking to replicate results?

Is quantifiable analysis possible?

Is qualitative analysis involved?

How useful are individual differences?

How is the learning generalized?

 Ten-point summary

1. Good study means different things in different subjects, so you need to have a very clear understanding of the specific context you're working in.

2. Uncertainty is an important aspect of higher-level learning – but you can still prepare yourself for the challenges ahead.

3. Seeing how learning *changes* at this level helps you to recognize the skills you'll need to develop now.

4. Use all the information available to you to see the 'big picture' of your chosen course.

5. Find out as much as you can about teaching, group work, independent tasks, and the different sorts of support on offer.

6. Assessment is integral to higher-level learning, so it's vital to understand how it works as part of your course.

7. You need to explore the 'epistemology' of your subject: its theories about thinking, learning and the construction of knowledge.

8. The 'scientific method' is relevant to a wide range of subjects and can help you to unpick priorities and values.

9. To engage fully with academic development, you need to explore some key questions about the subject you're studying and the course you're on.

10. Identify your priorities for improvement and start tackling them straight away, in your study.

Where to next?

Chapter 6 will help you take a confident approach to mapping out the success of your studies from here.

Eyes on the prize

Understanding your motivations and setting clear goals will help you to plan your approach, manage your emotions, engage with advanced learning, and get long-lasting benefits from higher-level study.

 ## What?

One of the best ways to set yourself up for success as a student is to ask why you're taking on the challenge. Take the question seriously, give it some proper thought, and your answers will help to direct all the work you do – showing you which areas to prioritize, helping you to monitor your progress, and keeping you on track, with clear sight of the rewards on offer. They'll remind you of the need to be active, to do what *you* need to, to get what *you* want from your work. And, at this level, the process of properly exploring what you're getting out of learning is integral to the learning itself.

In what is an energetic book, this is a particularly active chapter. It's based on a set of activities that will strengthen your practice throughout all the work you do. There's **self-analysis** to find out how to tackle your course in the way that's right for you. You'll design a detailed **academic development plan**, and create a tool for measuring and refining your progress. It's about knowing your **motivations**, and making sure that they only get stronger from here.

 ## When?

All these activities build on the things you've done in the book so far. But things are moving on: there's a shift here from preparation to practice.

It's still very much the beginning of a developmental process, setting you up with tools to help you navigate a long journey ahead. So you'll need to keep coming back to this chapter to check your bearings, update your notes, and possibly alter your course a little before coming back again.

If you're already well into your studies, don't worry, there's still plenty to be gained from these exercises. But they're particularly useful if you're just starting your course, because your early sparks of energy and enthusiasm can be captured – and then used to keep the fires of motivation burning bright, lighting your way.

Who?

You're defining your personal purpose and setting up a highly individualized approach to study, but quite a bit of this chapter is about other people: the ones who make you want to study and help you do it well, and the ones who don't. You'll see that self-management has a lot to do with managing other people, too.

 # Why?

Studying at this level is a lengthy and challenging process, and your motivation's bound to go up and down – depending on what you're doing, how you're feeling, the way others are behaving, what's going on in the rest of your world ... Once you were probably encouraged just to get on with your work – but now your experience of learning is very much *part* of the learning. You'll need to engage with what you're going through, and see what it's telling you.

The activities here will help you get the most out of everything you do in the rest of this book. They'll also support whatever **Personal Development Plan (PDP)** process your university operates, enriching and adding to it with some extra ideas for ongoing self-help.

And the more you know what's driving you, the more you can turn your studying to your advantage, energizing your academic work and your personal development in a way that never really ends:

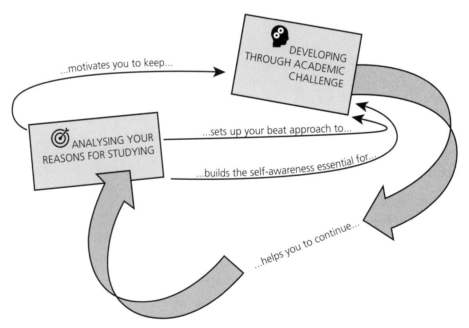

How ...?

In Chapter 1 you began thinking about reasons for stepping up a level in your learning. Start this chapter by analysing those in a bit more detail, using what you want to get *out* of your studies to direct the effort you put *in*.

Then, decide the importance to you of 20 essential aspects of studying. Assessing their potential benefits will help you plan a personal development process that matches your needs, covering all the necessary skills – in the most useful ways for you.

Put this plan into action, using it to guide what you do in your studies, and to keep you analysing and recording how it's all going, driving you forward, towards the goals you've set.

And to make sure that you get there, learn about the very practical things you can do – now and throughout your course – to stay positive, motivated and strong.

 # Steps to success

1 Ask yourself why

> ❭ **Go to: Chapters 1 and 2** *to remind yourself of any thinking you've already done about what motivates your learning.*

Then – look a bit deeper. Whatever the details of your individual circumstances, the forces driving your study will connect with the following five ideas, to a greater or lesser extent:

- Intellectual challenge
- Personal interest
- Official qualifications
- Professional development
- Self-improvement.

They're all ways that you'll benefit from your course, if you do the right things, but they all have some potential problems, too. For example, pursuing *intellectual challenge* might lead you away from the specific context of your subject or make you neglect collaboration. A drive to achieve *official qualifications* could tempt someone to miss out on the richness of the content, meaning that they struggle to stay interested long enough even to get to the exams.

So, see whether you can think of potential disadvantages, as well as clear advantages, in being motivated by these factors. Consider whether there are things here that you need to address, and highlight any points that seem particularly relevant to you.

Motivating factor	Potential ADVANTAGES	Potential DISADVANTAGES
Intellectual challenge		

Personal interest		
Official qualifications		
Professional development		
Self-improvement		

Ask yourself

→ **Do any of your motivations need to change?**

Even if you've had some very clear motivating influences in the past, maybe it would help you now if you could shift some of your perspectives. For example, if you've always been driven to make your parents proud, would it perhaps be healthier to emphasize other benefits, to avoid the risk of feeling too much family pressure? Or, if you're usually keenly focused on the qualifications you'll get at the end, could you temper that by boosting your interest levels, so that you don't miss out on the enjoyment of studying a subject you love?

It's healthy to have a range of motivating factors, and the balance can fluctuate – but it's an interesting experiment to try ranking yours at any given time.

So do it now. In the space under each idea in the left-hand column, write a number from 1 (the most important to you at this moment) to 5 (the least).

2 Plan your attack

You can get even more out of the things that motivate you (and strengthen your motivation in areas where it's weak).

Motivated by ... *intellectual challenge*:

- Focus on the thinking skills involved in the different tasks you take on.
- Do some research about the leading figures in your field, exploring the sorts of thinking they use or used – to see how you might take *your* thought processes even further.
- When you're selecting questions to answer or project titles to adopt, challenge yourself to write up mini-plans for the options you *don't* choose, too.

- Is there a learning strategy you find useful that could be shared with other students on your course – by making a video, creating a website or even putting together a simple app?

Motivated by ... *personal interest*:

- Keep thinking about what you already know about your subject, and how you can use it to enrich your own learning and help others.
- Read widely, finding titles that attract you – well beyond the limits of any book lists you're given.
- Look out for any competitions or challenges that might let you work in a favourite part of your subject, or develop your abilities in exciting ways.
- See whether there are any publications – like the university website or magazine – that might be interested in an article by you about something new in your field of study.

Motivated by... *official qualifications*:

- Whenever you start any kind of task, ask yourself how it will help you with an assessment, somewhere down the line.
- Get hold of past papers and mark schemes early, and make sure that everything you do moves you closer to the criteria for success.
- Find data about the qualifications given out by your university over the last few years. Analyse any trends. Are people becoming more or less successful in your subject? Do some parts of the course seem to be harder to do well in than others? Think about any strategies you might need to employ in response.
- Research the latest revision apps to see whether there's one that helps you with your exam preparation – even when you're on the train.

Motivated by... *self-improvement*:

- In any processes you use to analyse your progress (like PDP, or the learning journals explained later in this chapter) put extra emphasis on the personal skills you'll still have long after your course is complete.
- Choose leisure activities that will enrich your academic work in some way and let you put your developing skills to use.
- Talk to other students on your course about their personal journeys up to this point, and share your own reasons for taking on the challenge.
- Seize any opportunities to help 'sell' your course at open days or other public events.

Motivated by... *professional development*:

- In your PDP and learning journal (see below), pay particular attention to skills required by your future profession, collecting evidence of relevant experiences and achievements. (However, it's absolutely fine if you don't have much – or any – idea about your career. Many students only start thinking about work options in their final year of study.)

- Use social media to look into the educational background of some of the people doing the jobs you're hoping to get. As well as the qualifications they achieved, what else did they do to move themselves towards their chosen profession?
- Are any of your projects relevant to things happening now in the profession you're targeting? Seize opportunities to contact people there who might be interested in offering advice or getting involved in the research somehow, setting up useful links for the future.
- If you want your career to take you further into academia, find out if there are ways to be part of current research work within your university, or to help with teaching students in the years below.

3 Test your commitment

You've seen that your success as a student depends on developing a range of interconnected skill-sets, in the context of the subject you've chosen. And motivation plays a very important role here, influencing the areas you're likely to put more time and effort into, and those that could be neglected – if you're not careful.

But you *are* careful: you're already getting used to thinking about your thoughts and feelings, weighing up opportunities and threats, applying your findings to the ways you direct your studies... So, put all of that to use in this next exercise. See how easy you find it to spot benefits – personal and professional – in some of the key skill areas. And consider what *that* shows you about the pieces of the puzzle that interest you most.

Skills developed through study	PERSONAL benefits	CAREER benefits
Organization		
Creativity		
Problem-solving		
Numeracy		
General literacy		
Research		
Reading		
Note-taking/making		
Learning from teaching		

Skills developed through study	PERSONAL benefits	CAREER benefits
Group work		
Giving presentations		
Writing		
Completing academic work		
Meeting academic standards		
Analysis		
Evaluation		
Memory		
Exam preparation		
Exam performance		
Self-reflection		

4 Lead your learning

This is what this chapter has been leading up to: a performance management activity that harnesses all your insights into the things that motivate your academic development – and turns them into a practical plan, with self-assessment and rich, integrated learning built in.

This is your Core Development Plan. It's designed to help you engage with all the work you do in this book, and to put it into action in your studies.

Don't try to address everything at once. It makes sense to try the first five sections as soon as you can, as they're all things you've already examined in this book – and as you'll have plenty of real-life experience to draw on.

Start thinking about the others whenever you want to, though it's a good idea to have a look at the headings now. You'll be sent back to tackle them at relevant points in later chapters – marked by this symbol 📖 – by which time you should find it much easier to see what they mean for you and the progress you need to make on your course.

For each of these 20 ability areas:

- Summarize any thoughts you've had so far into a personal **priority** rating: low, medium or high. (Even if it changes as your course goes on, you'll always be able to use the current rating to help you prioritize your efforts – including putting energy into different parts of this book.)

- Then assess your **starting strength**. As this grows, you should get a nice boost to your motivation from seeing the progress you're making.
- Note some **success criteria**: how you'll know that you're improving. (It's fine to leave this and any of the sections below it blank until you know more.)
- Make some **improvement plans**: ideas for helping yourself get better at these skills (this book is full of them).
- And, in the final box, record any evidence of development. What happened? What worked? Add dates to your **progress notes**, and use this section to report on your strengthening abilities.

Come back to these pages any time you want, to get ideas for particular aspects of your work, to add new insights and reminders, or to record the steps forward you've made in any of these key areas of your study.

It's all great preparation for life *after* your current course, too. Everything you learn through this process will be extremely valuable when you're applying for postgraduate studies or preparing to enter the world of work.

Core Development Plan
Skill: ORGANIZATION
Priority: [Low/Medium/High]
Starting strength: [with date]
Success criteria:
Improvement plans:
Progress notes:

Skill: CREATIVITY
Priority: [Low/Medium/High]
Starting strength: [with date]
Success criteria:
Improvement plans:
Progress notes:

Skill: PROBLEM-SOLVING
Priority: [Low/Medium/High]
Starting strength: [with date]
Success criteria:
Improvement plans:
Progress notes:

Skill: NUMERACY
Priority: [Low/Medium/High]
Starting strength: [with date]
Success criteria:
Improvement plans:
Progress notes:

Skill: GENERAL LITERACY

Priority:
[Low/Medium/High]

Starting strength:
[with date]

Success criteria:

Improvement plans:

Progress notes:

Skill: RESEARCH

Priority:
[Low/Medium/High]

Starting strength:
[with date]

Success criteria:

Improvement plans:

Progress notes:

Skill: READING

Priority:
[Low/Medium/High]

Starting strength:
[with date]

Success criteria:

Improvement plans:

Progress notes:

Skill: NOTE-TAKING/MAKING

Priority:
[Low/Medium/High]

Starting strength:
[with date]

Success criteria:

Improvement plans:

Progress notes:

Skill: LEARNING FROM TEACHING

Priority:
[Low/Medium/High]

Starting strength:
[with date]

Success criteria:

Improvement plans:

Progress notes:

Skill: GROUP WORK

Priority:
[Low/Medium/High]

Starting strength:
[with date]

Success criteria:

Improvement plans:

Progress notes:

Skill: GIVING PRESENTATIONS

Priority:
 [Low/Medium/High]

Starting strength:
 [with date]

Success criteria:

Improvement plans:

Progress notes:

Skill: WRITING

Priority:
[Low/Medium/High]

Starting strength:
[with date]

Success criteria:

Improvement plans:

Progress notes:

Skill: COMPLETING ACADEMIC WORK

Priority:
[Low/Medium/High]

Starting strength:
[with date]

Success criteria:

Improvement plans:

Progress notes:

Skill: MEETING ACADEMIC STANDARDS

Priority:
[Low/Medium/High]

Starting strength:
[with date]

Success criteria:

Improvement plans:

Progress notes:

Skill: ANALYSIS

Priority:
[Low/Medium/High]

Starting strength:
[with date]

Success criteria:

Improvement plans:

Progress notes:

Skill: EVALUATION

Priority:
[Low/Medium/High]

Starting strength:
[with date]

Success criteria:

Improvement plans:

Progress notes:

Skill: MEMORY

Priority:
[Low/Medium/High]

Starting strength:
[with date]

Success criteria:

Improvement plans:

Progress notes:

Skill: EXAM PREPARATION

Priority:
[Low/Medium/High]

Starting strength:
[with date]

Success criteria:

Improvement plans:

Progress notes:

Skill: EXAM PERFORMANCE

Priority:
[Low/Medium/High]

Starting strength:
[with date]

Success criteria:

Improvement plans:

Progress notes:

Skill: SELF-REFLECTION
Priority: [Low/Medium/High]
Starting strength: [with date]
Success criteria:
Improvement plans:
Progress notes:

Case Study: Paulo

Whatever your personal mix of motivations, it's also possible to slip into self-sabotage if you're not careful. Paulo was in the second of his three years at university when he realized that he was starting to make little or no progress in his studies – and that he was his own worst enemy. He tried to work when he knew he was tired. He left assignments until it was too late to do a good job, even when he stayed up most of the night. He refused offers of help, talked himself down to his friends – and, in the end, it was one of them who pointed out that he seemed to be plotting his own downfall, sabotaging his own success.

Paulo knew it was true, and wondered why he was doing it. Could it be something to do with his background – as the first person in his family to go to university? Maybe he wasn't really sure that he wanted that title, or deserved it. Perhaps part of him was looking for a way out.

He wasn't quite ready to talk to his family about it, but his friends were helpful – as was his tutor, who reassured Paulo's about his abilities and his absolute right to be there, and set him up with a student mentor from the year above. Together, they worked on breaking the self-defeating habits he'd developed. Paulo also started using a learning journal as part of this fresh approach, and found it boosted his confidence to manage his feelings and make better decisions about his studies. The more he saw the benefits, the happier he felt about pushing on and aiming high.

5 Build a portfolio

Personal Development Planning, or PDP, is a well-established feature of higher education, and there are various different ways it can be done.

You may be given a set of documents – either on paper or online – to fill in at various times in your course, guiding you to reflect on your experiences and the development of your skills, perhaps with several checkpoints for you to discuss your PDP with a member of staff.

In other places, opportunities for examining and recording progress are built into particular parts of the course, and students have more flexibility about how they document their development.

Some approaches to PDP focus on career planning, emphasizing skills required in the workplace – professional life in general, or in a relevant field or specific role – and some are firmly fixed in the academic process, used to develop self-awareness and metacognition in order to enrich the learning itself.

Engaging with your version of PDP is part of learning to operate within the academic community, but it's still important to make it work for you. Treat it like everything else: as an opportunity that you should be able to take *something* from, even if it's uncomfortable sometimes (which it will be if it's challenging you to think hard, be honest, maybe change what you're doing).

See how much you're allowed to do it your own way. Spot practical benefits: for example, many PDPs provide a manageable system for collecting evidence for projects, accreditation processes or job applications. Maximize the parts of the process that seem to be benefiting you most, and see whether it's possible to drop the ones that aren't helping. You can also *add* to it, to make it even more effective; for example ...

6 Record your thoughts

... with a personal learning journal – which is completely under your control. It's a private collection of reflections on study, either on paper or in a computer file, and many students use it to support the PDP process. It's also a powerful way of integrating your personal journey with your academic development, charting your experiences of grappling with the way your subject works. Those experiences can feed back into your practice to create a very rich, dynamic, self-aware approach.

Sometimes, writing about an experience is the best way to understand it – and then to talk about where it leads, using the journal as a guide to discussions, especially during check-ins with staff.

Here's a useful format for reflecting on your learning activities. Try it out a few times, adapting it as necessary, experimenting with different ways of analysing your experiences and building up a learning journal that feels right for you.

- What was the activity? (Give a very brief description, mostly to remind you later.)
- How did you feel: before/during/after? (Be succinct, but precise.)
- How successful was it? (This should be on your own terms as well as according to the 'official' criteria.)
- What did you gain? (Think about personal development as well as subject ability.)
- What will you do differently in future? (This could be in similar work or when applying this learning to other tasks.)
- How will you *know* you've learned from this task? (This covers all areas of your development from this point on.)

 # Ask yourself

→ **Do you ever fall into the trap of acting like you're studying, without actually studying?**

Maybe you carry on reading when you're really tired, so that you can tick off another hour on your schedule, but nothing's actually going in. Do your sometimes find yourself making long notes (even copying whole sections) to fill up your book and amass pages of information – when it would actually be better to spend less time but be more selective? Or have you ploughed on with your work alone, getting nowhere, rather than linking up with others, as if independent study somehow beats group work?

Monitor your effectiveness closely, using activities like the ones in this chapter to keep improving your self-management. At this level it's never about how studying looks; always about how well it *works*.

7 Keep on keeping on

Even with a clear understanding of your motivations and how to maximize them, and detailed plans of action for a range of key skills, your resolve can waver. Feelings fluctuate, life gets in the way, work gets really hard, or boring, or pointless, and maybe you're tired, or ill, or just can't remember why you thought this would be a good idea ... So here are some ideas for active self-regulation, helping you to rediscover your mojo and get back on track.

Systems. When you're feeling demotivated, directionless, sometimes a clear, step-by-step way of doing things can reassure you that you *do* know what you're doing, and it *is* worth your while.

> ❯ *Go to: Chapter 8 to see how a strong system for time-management can make your work seem much more possible.*

Supporters. Who are the people you want nearby when you're in need of a boost (and who should you avoid)? As you go through your course, you'll find out who are the best motivators and supporters of your study. It's also useful to think about the people – maybe some you've never even met – who motivate you through the things they've achieved or the trails they've blazed.

❯ *Go to:* **Chapter 17** *to see how working with others can energize your study.*

Reminders. Advertisers know the power of bold statements and eye-catching imagery, and the mood-changing influence of ideas seen or heard repeatedly. Tap into those effects yourself: make posters, desktop backgrounds or phone home-screens that remind you, simply and persuasively, of what you're doing here, and why it's important to keep going. Find quotations that motivate you, choose pictures that inspire you, and keep them in clear view.

❯ *Go to:* **Chapter 6** *to remind yourself about the wide-ranging benefits of your studies.*

Triggers. Stay alert to the things that boost your mood and keep you going – and those that bring it down and turn you off. Your learning journal is a good place to record your personal 'triggers' and spot patterns of behaviour. Does a certain lecturer always leave you feeling disheartened? At what point in tasks do you feel most positive? When you've worked with a particular group of friends, why do you come away feeling so good?

❯ *Go to:* **Chapter 1** *to explore whether some of your emotional triggers are connected with your media use.*

Rewards. It's important to focus on the long-term rewards of your study, and to enjoy your academic development and personal growth as rewards in themselves. But it's also good to treat yourself a little when you deserve it, setting up short-term prizes to aim for and linking successful studying with happiness, satisfaction, gain. Make it part of the way you organize your work: a long bath when you finally finish that bibliography; a takeaway after passing the practical; festival tickets when the research project's complete. You don't have to spend any money (or any *more* money than you would have done anyway) if you simply link the things you *enjoy* doing to the things you have to get done.

❯ *Go to:* your Core Development Plan in **Chapter 6** – *whenever you think you've made progress in one of the key skill areas; record it; and then think whether there's something simple you can do to reward yourself for winning this particular fight.*

⑩ Ten-point summary

1. Exploring your reasons for studying strengthens your academic work – giving you even more tools to manage your development and accelerate your personal growth.

2. Analyse your motivations carefully: the things that drive you can also threaten your success.

3. Use *why* you're studying to influence *how* you study, focusing on activities that interest and inspire you to energize everything you do.

4. Consider the full benefits of building higher-level skills, extending beyond your academic life into personal and professional development.

5. Plan how you're going to develop all the skills you need, including the ones that interest you the least.

6. Work out what improvement will look like in each key area, so that you can keep monitoring how it's going.

7. Address any self-sabotage: underlying reasons for tempting failure.

8. Engage with the approach to PDP that's on offer, but use it in the most appropriate and effective way for you.

9. A personal learning journal can enrich the PDP process, improving your chances of learning in, and from, your course.

10. Use a range of practical strategies to keep your motivation strong.

 # Where to next?

Chapter 7 will show you how to make the best possible start to this new phase of your education.

The right foot

As you begin your course, put the right conditions and behaviours in place straight away, so that you're living and learning well from the very start and setting yourself up for long-term success.

What?

With plenty of preparation under your belt, and an exciting challenge ahead, this chapter is about taking your first steps into higher-level study – carefully, but with real confidence.

It's vital to start as you mean to go on. Habits quickly become ingrained, and it's all too easy to do things early on that cause problems – and then never get around to doing anything about them. Before you know it you'll be really busy, with many new aspects of daily life to manage as well as the competing elements of your academic work. Learning happens fast now, and you need to get the right **conditions** and **behaviours** in place as soon as possible so that you don't struggle against unnecessary barriers, or get left behind completely.

You can still enjoy the excitement of stepping into the unknown, and make a few things up as you go along. But taking an active approach to getting things right for you will let you get so much more out of everything that happens from here.

When?

The more of this advice you can take with you as you start your course, the better. That doesn't mean that your first moves will be unchangeable. You can always return to this chapter and make improvements to your approach later on – and in fact it's vital that you do keep reflecting on what's working and what's not. You'll need to *develop* the styles of living and learning that work best for you, just as all your other abilities need to grow over time. But that's so much easier if you get some big things right from the start.

Who?

It's important to think very carefully about what *you* need to do well. You'll still need to consider the wider situation you're in, living and working among a range of other people with their own ways of doing things. But a *small* streak of selfishness is an asset, especially at the start, when the best choices will bring long-term benefits for you *and* those around you, and potential problems with others can be dealt with early on.

Why?

You're here to learn and grow, to enjoy the process and to make the most of all the opportunities you've won (and paid for). For that to happen really well, some important factors need to be in your favour – and you have the power to control them, especially if you get in quick. Sorting out your **learning environment**, making sensible decisions about your **lifestyle**, getting into good **working habits** at the start of your course; all this will boost your chances of getting everything you want from this new, intense, fiercely exciting stage of your studies.

 # How ?

Start where you are – the location(s) of your learning. Think about the things that help people generally, make an honest assessment of what *you* need to study at your very best, then start working out how to adapt your environment to suit.

Next, your lifestyle: how can you get the balance right between work and play, activity and rest, healthy living and having fun, safety and striking out into the unknown? If you make the right choices, you'll find that it's possible to study well *and* seize life (and that you really do need to do both).

Then look at how you operate day to day, organizing yourself and getting started. Like any traveller in an unfamiliar land you'll have to adapt to the things you find – but you can still set off prepared and well equipped, alert to threats but open to making the most of the journey ahead.

 # Steps to success

1 Make space for study

The places where you work have a *huge* impact on how well you do. Their influence is clearly seen in your ability to learn, but they affect your achievement in many other ways: how likely you are to get started; how long you can focus; what *types* of learning you do; and whether you're just meeting the requirements of a particular task or developing lasting skills and a love of learning that's going to keep growing.

In a way, it's extremely simple. *The best place to work is the place where you work best.* There are no hard-and-fast rights and wrongs, because we're all different, and we all have to do a range of activities that suit some spaces better than others. It's important to feel like you've designed an environment for study that's the one that you want.

But ...

Be brutally honest. Forget about what you'd like to be true, the sort of learner you'd like to be. However attractive something might be in theory, there's absolutely no point studying in surroundings that don't help. And it's not just about avoiding threats to success (and there are plenty of very tempting ones). It's about realizing that working at this level is a seriously big challenge, and you'll have to get extra support from every direction you can. Your surroundings can't just be *fine*; they need to contribute directly to your success.

So, maybe you'd *like* to be able to work completely alone, with others around, with music on, in the park, in a coffee shop, only using beautiful notebooks, only online, in the middle of the night … You need to get over your image of what *would* be good, and focus firmly on what really *is*.

Academic Advice

'Research shows that most students these days have many different study spaces to choose from. So they've got choices – which can be tricky, as the nearest or most relaxing or best-equipped place may not actually be the right place for a particular type of work. Most locations have something going for them, but it's important to choose carefully, weighing up the pros and cons – and, after a while, learning from experience. If you're reflective and honest you'll soon know where you learn best, or work fastest, or think most creatively, or collaborate easiest … all depending on the details of the work you're doing.' **Mo, learning support tutor**

❯ *Go to: Chapter 3 to consider some of the most important resources – people, places and things – that you already have at your disposal.*

Here are five key questions to ask about the places available for your study. As you consider your answers, think about the pros and cons of each location generally, and in relation to some of the specific tasks you're required to do.

1. **Is it practical to use?** Is this place conveniently located, bearing in mind where you'll be coming from to get there? (Remember, convenience can be dangerous too, if you go to the wrong places just because they're easy.) Do you have easy access – all the time, or only sometimes? Is it physically suitable for all the activities involved in your studies?
2. **How does it make you feel?** Do you want to be there – and stay? (And maybe it makes you feel too happy, too relaxed …?) Think about physical factors that affect your emotions – such as décor, furnishings, warmth, light, smell, comfort – as well as more subtle things like associations and memories.
3. **How well equipped is it?** This depends very much on the tasks you're considering. There are general things like desks and chairs, internet access, toilet facilities, food and drink. There are also the specific things you know you'll need, such as particular sorts of stationery, research materials, hardware and software, and specialist tools.
4. **Does it help you to concentrate?** *Honestly*, do you concentrate best with or without music, other people nearby, technology, background chatter? Personal preference is vital – as long as it's rooted firmly in the truth, and matched to specific types of study. If you're exploring early ideas for a project, or doing some long but fairly functional preparatory task, you may well benefit from the buzz of the cafeteria. But that probably wouldn't be the best place to do deep calculations, memorize details or write your final thesis.

5. **Does it suit the way you like to learn?** Again, depending on the learning in question, you may do it best with plenty of visual stimulation around you, a variety of sounds, things to touch and work with, freedom to move around; or with blank walls, silence, minimalism, stillness. Crucially, does this place let you have any control over the factors affecting learning? Part of your job now is seeing the significance of different elements of the study process, and playing an active part in controlling them, based on your developing understanding of yourself, and of the way thinking and learning works.

2 Check the conditions

To help you start taking that sort of control over your environment and your studying, go back to the key conditions for good learning explored in Chapter 1. Use them to get some extra insights into the choices you make about where you work, and to think about practical things you could do for the better.

Learning works better when you're MOTIVATED. Which of your potential study locations motivates you most for which types of work?

What three things could you change, to make you more motivated to study there?

1. _____

2. _____

3. _____

Learning works better when it happens at your PACE. How do different places influence your ability to go at the right speed? Do you have to rush to get finished before closing time, or maybe get so relaxed that you get really slow?

Write a different academic task on each of the lines below; and alongside it, the place that's most likely to let you do it at the right pace.

1. _____

2. _____

3. _____

Learning works better when it's RELEVANT. Which places are best at focusing you on the work you came to do, giving you access to appropriate research materials, the right equipment for the task at hand, and the best conditions for the thinking involved? Where can you get up-to-date information, check that you're on the right track, and make sure that the new learning builds on what you already know?

Write down three specific ways in which one of your study spaces could help you to do relevant learning.

1. _____

2. _____

3. _____

Learning works better when it's INTERESTING. Where do you feel most excited about your studies, and where do you tend to switch off? Is it the way a place makes you feel in general, or how well it helps you (or doesn't) to *make* your work interesting?

Write down three ways you could change your study spaces to keep you interested – and help you *pursue* your interests – in the different types of work you do.

1. _____

2. _____

3. _____

Student Tip

'I really got into geology because of a set of books I got for Christmas – as a ten-year-old! In the second year of my degree, I suddenly remembered them, and thought: why are they just sitting at home? So I got my parents to send them, I put them on my desk – and I can't tell you how helpful it's been to have them nearby. Even at degree level they're surprisingly useful for checking details, and I've got some of my best ideas from just flicking through a few pages. They get me excited again – remind me why I've always been so interested in this stuff.'
Ali, Geology undergraduate

Learning works better when it's TAUGHT well. So, which places help you to access the different forms of 'teaching' available to you: textbooks, podcasts, recordings of lectures, class notes ...? Some locations can feel very separate from the teaching elements of the course (which can actually help, on occasion, if your thinking needs to be original, rebellious, disruptive). But others are great at keeping you connected to the information, instructions and advice you need to use.

Write down three things about your places of learning that help you to benefit from teaching, even when there's no actual teacher anywhere near.

1. _____

2. _____

3. _____

Learning works better when you do it ACTIVELY. What this involves in practice varies greatly – between different subjects, and different types of student. Your active involvement may require particular resources or equipment, or need the room to be physically suited to your work. But, whatever you're doing, your styles of thinking and learning will also dictate different forms of activity – maybe creating colourful notes to loud music, or performing energetic mental calculations with your eyes closed, in absolute silence.

Write down three ways you study actively – and, alongside each one, something in your place of study that helps.

1. _____

2. _____

3. _____

3 Look after yourself

As well as *where* you're working, plenty of other things influence how well your study goes. People's circumstances can vary wildly, but everyone benefits from looking at some key aspects of how they're living, and trying to make good choices early on that benefit their work (or at least don't get in the way).

This is meant to be an exciting time of your life. You need to meet new people, try new things, widen your experiences, develop yourself. Higher-level learning requires leaving your comfort zone and building strong, independent thinking skills – so it's hugely valuable to be *living* like that, too – taking on new responsibilities, making decisions for yourself (and sometimes learning the hard way).

Living unpredictably can build resilience. Having fun is one of the things that will keep you going. But, throughout it all, bearing a few important things in mind will help you to *keep* enjoying the whole experience, and end up feeling that it was time well spent.

There's a lot to think about. Talk to family and friends, get advice from experts, and start your course by making the best decisions you can about the following factors (and keep adapting, depending on what happens next).

Safety

You need to feel safe to study well. You're making a big investment, over a considerable length of time, so you want to get to the end in one piece. Minimize any risks to you enjoying yourself and doing really well, and help the other people you're living and learning with feel supported and safe.

- Which aspects of your **safety** are most significant for your studies?
- What do you think you should *stop* doing?
- What could you *start* doing to improve your chances of success?

Student Tip:

'Freshers' Week was mad. So much fun, out every night – making friends for life, I hope. One thing we did in my flat – which I'm sure avoided lots of problems – was to agree that no one ever travelled anywhere on their own. We sorted a different plan every night, and everyone bought into it. It was a new city for all of us, and I know that lots of us were glad we had someone making sure we got back OK.'
Corinne, politics undergraduate

Health

When you're working hard, and playing hard – and especially if you're living away from home – looking after all aspects of your health is vital if you're going to thrive in this phase of your life. Make sure that you sign up with a GP, know how to access dental care, and use all the health support provided by your university – which should be paying great attention to your wellbeing, and which will have resources and systems in place to help with every kind of issue. Get advice as early as possible: worrying about your health can be as damaging to your studies as actual health problems. Be as active in nurturing your physical and mental health as you are in your academic development, and pay attention to the things that have a particular impact on your study – such as diet, exercise, sleep, alcohol and drugs.

- Which aspects of your **health** are most significant for your studies?
- What do you think you should *stop* doing?
- What could you *start* doing to improve your chances of success?

Finances

Loans, student bank accounts, overdrafts ... get them all sorted as soon as possible so that you're free to concentrate on your course. Work out which technologies suit you best for managing your money. Automate as much of the essential stuff as possible – accommodation payments, subscriptions, utility bills – helping you to keep a close eye on everything else. Use the thinking skills you're developing in your academic work – such as organizing, analysing, evaluating – to help you keep control of your finances, quickly learning from your experiences and using money to enrich rather than restrict your life.

- Which aspects of your **finances** are most significant for your studies?
- What do you think you should *stop* doing?
- What could you *start* doing to improve your chances of success?

Spend some time now reflecting on the other important aspects of life listed below. How could they affect the quality of your development – personally and academically?

For example, travel can be a great time for creative thinking, enriching your understanding in geography, giving you ideas for psychology experiments, even letting you test theories in maths. Or it can cost you a fortune, make you tired and stressed, and cause you to be late for all your lectures. It all depends on seeing the links between your lifestyle and your learning – and then making some sensible choices as a result.

So, based on previous experience and the work you've already done in this book, what will you need to avoid doing, and what could you do, consciously, to get the following factors working in your favour?

Accommodation (what will you have to cope with, what can you change?)

Significant factors for your study

Something to avoid

Something to do

Food (choosing, buying, storing, cooking)

Significant factors for your study

Something to avoid

Something to do

Belongings (what to bring/not bring, where to keep it, how to protect it ...)

Significant factors for your study

Something to avoid

Something to do

Cleaning (dishes, clothes, flats ...)

Significant factors for your study

Something to avoid

Something to do

Travel (different options, costs, time)

Significant factors for your study

Something to avoid

Something to do

Technology (think about fun *and* functional uses)
Significant factors for your study
Something to avoid
Something to do

Leisure time (resting, as well as embracing cultural, sporting and social life)
Significant factors for your study
Something to avoid
Something to do

Student Tip

'I tried lots of different ways to organize my life when I left home – apps, spreadsheets, to-do-lists … In the end, the thing that worked best was really simple: just having one place – the Reminders function on my phone – and putting everything there. That was so much better: I only had one place to remember to check! It backs up automatically to the Cloud, so I can't really lose anything. There are different tabs for different sorts of lists, all colour-coded if that helps you. But I just use it as one list, where I can store the sort of stuff I need every day – shopping lists, jobs, travel details, money I owe … and delete something when it's done.' Cameron, first-year Sports Medicine student

4 Get ready to learn

As you prepare to put all this into practice and take your first steps into your new life, here's a final activity that draws together all the ideas in this chapter, focusing them on *learning* – the reason you're here.

Learning is often split into different activities:

Access Record Organize Analyse Remember Use

Ask yourself

→ What might this approach to learning look like in your studies?

You might access information from a history book, record notes about it, organize your ideas into key themes, analyse their significance, remember them to discuss in a tutorial, then use them as the basis for writing an essay or giving a presentation to your class. After that you'd *keep* using the information you'd gained in other activities, enriching and strengthening the learning.

Described as recognizable 'steps', this model of learning might look fairly straightforward. But there are six overlapping and interconnected parts here, each one complicated in its own way, and they all need to be performed well for good learning to take place.

In the context of some of the large-scale academic tasks you'll be exploring in the chapters to come, that's a lot of scope for things to go wrong.

But when they're done well, this is a plan for pulling off the sort of learning that can take you far. From day one of your journey you'll need to make strong choices about how to study well. Questions about where you'll do it, and how your new life will support it, are the perfect place to start.

Think about practical ways to support each of the component parts of learning, noting down some of the positive choices you could make about your *environment* and your *behaviour*.

ACCESSING information (gathering new ideas – by reading, researching, watching, listening, experimenting …)

Environment choices	*Behaviour* choices

RECORDING information (in its original form, a different format, or in your own notes)

Environment choices	*Behaviour* choices

ORGANIZING information (so that you can find it again, and to help you understand and explain it)

Environment choices	*Behaviour* choices

ANALYSING information (to make sense of it and start deciding its importance and potential)

Environment choices	*Behaviour* choices

REMEMBERING information (to make it part of your own knowledge and understanding, ready to be tested and put to use)

Environment choices	*Behaviour* choices

USING information (practically, intellectually, logically, creatively; to strengthen the learning, give it a purpose, move it on ...)

Environment choices	*Behaviour* choices

(10) Ten-point summary

1. Get into the right habits early – start your student life as you mean to go on.

2. You can be well prepared for this new part of your life – and still have fun stepping into the unknown.

3. The places where you study affect the quality of that work in many different ways.

4. Most students have many study spaces to choose between.

5. Be honest with yourself about what *really* helps you to study well.

6. Workplaces shouldn't just be neutral: at this level they need to contribute to learning.

7. Different places are suited to different types of academic work.

8. Study spaces can be chosen, or adapted, to support the key conditions for learning.

9. All aspects of your wellbeing impact on your academic success.

10. Choices about *where* and *how* you work affect every part of the learning process.

(▷) Where to next?

Chapter 8 will prepare you to cope with a new level of responsibility for managing your time.

Part 3

Student skills

Developing the skill-sets that all higher-level students need

Chapter 8 reveals the implications of **independence** at this stage of education, requiring a high degree of **organization** and a strong approach to **time-planning**.

Chapter 9 shows you how to maintain high levels of **engagement** in your work, developing the **stamina** required to study well throughout each session – and the ability to do other things, too, for a healthy **work/life balance**.

Chapter 10 looks at how you get hold of the information you need for your work, involving advanced skills in **research**, **reading** and a variety of **note-taking/making techniques**.

Chapter 11 analyses the **planning**, **construction** and **presentation** involved in successful academic writing.

Chapter 12 explains how to use assessments to drive your success as a student, through effective **revision strategies**, careful **exam preparation** and powerful **memory techniques**.

On schedule

Planning your time well is an essential part of successful study, helping you to meet all the requirements of your course – and, in the process, to develop important academic and personal skills.

 ## What?

This chapter and the next explore one of the biggest higher-level challenges of all: making the most of your time. Not just getting things done quickly or ticking them off a list, but very actively using all the time you've got in the richest ways you can.

This chapter is about planning your time. The next one is about using that time to the full.

As a *dependent* student in your previous phases of education, you were mostly reliant on teachers to tell you what to study, where, how and when. Now, as an *independent* learner, the vast majority of that is up to you. You've got lectures to go to at particular times, classes, tutorials, specific events. But you'll also find you have a vast amount of independent study time. And how well you use that will go a long way to determining the success of everything.

Studying is a full-time job. If each credit on your course equates to around 10 hours of learning, and you're aiming at 120 credits a year, that works out at nearly 40 hours a week. That's a lot to do – alongside everything else you want time for, and *need* time for, in your new life. You'll have short-, mid- and long-term **deadlines** to cope with (and they'll often compete with each other). You may well have paid work to fit in too, and family commitments, and all the unexpected issues that life throws your way. Every day of your course – and even when you're back home for the holidays – managing your time will be crucial for your wellbeing, your happiness and the quality of your learning.

 ## When?

In Chapter 5, you took a look at your course as a whole. That's the first step in planning your use of time – a process which happens at particular points (the start of each year, each term, each week, every single day) as well as being a continual part of your practice. To be successful you'll need to adapt to changing circumstances, cope with new calls on your time, and keep looking backwards as well as forwards, constantly monitoring the effectiveness of your approach so that the *next* choice you make is the right one.

Who?

Time-planning at this level is very much about knowing what you can and can't control. There's so much that you *can* control, when you know yourself well and see all the options open to you. You can develop a highly personalized approach to directing your time. But you can't change deadlines or alter the systems you're operating in, and you have to be alert to other people's time constraints. With some people you'll be helping to manage *their* time – fellow members of a group project, for instance. With others, you'll be negotiating time, especially if you end up juggling paid work with academic life. And, of course, a lot of your decisions will be affected by the appeal (or necessity) of spending time with other people, and how *their* diary's looking.

 # Why?

Higher-level courses are *long* – to cover a lot of ground, but also to give you enough time to develop a rich set of skills. To do that you'll need to share out your time wisely, then use each bit of it to the full. And by organizing your life, you'll be continually developing your ability to *think* in an organized way.

Careful time-planning allows you to pace yourself and keep studying well over a long period, **balancing** work and rest. It helps you to meet key academic standards, operating professionally and punctually and completing tasks on time. It also lets you get the most out of all your *non*-academic activities (which will fuel your studies if you use them in the right way).

Intelligent scheduling gets easier with experience. As you learn to maximize your efforts – discovering when to study, how to get started, what to do to keep working well – you feed that knowledge back into your planning for the next parts of your course.

The way you go about studying increasingly reflects your understanding of how your subject works. It's a vital part of studying to be a student – as well as building skills that are essential in the workplace and endlessly valuable for life in general.

 # How?

Start by looking at your current behaviour. What are the strengths and weaknesses in the way you do things now?

Organization is essential, so pull together everything you need to take control of your time, and get into efficient habits early on.

Then there's the **planning** process itself: mapping long-term work as well as weekly and daily activities, and producing plans for specific aspects of the course. Learn how to use different tools to make time-management responsive and dynamic.

Steps to success

1 Test your time-management

Studying well always relies on knowing yourself. This book is about you learning how *you* can study well, based on the sort of person you are and the particular situation you're in. All your development has to start with where you are now, and is has to be right for you in the long term. So, feel free to try anything, but also do your best to be honest: to recognize the things you probably can't change (or don't *want* to change) as well as those that you should, and can.

This is especially true about time-management, which takes you into some very emotion-sensitive aspects of study. So much of your approach to organizing your life and using your time comes down to how you feel.

As you consider the following questions, explore memories from your studies so far and try to think up a representative example for each one.

To what extent do you ...

... feel organized?

Do you know what you have to do and when? Do you have a range of techniques and practical strategies for organizing your time? Do you usually have the right equipment with you? Do you have efficient ways of sorting and retrieving documents and resources?

Have you ever noticed yourself spending too much time planning, and not enough *doing* the important things? Are you ever *too* organized – so you find it hard to adapt to changing situations, or miss opportunities to be spontaneous?

For example: _____

... *look* organized?

Do you arrive on time, prepared for the task at hand? Do you deliver finished work that looks organized and satisfies all the requirements set? Do you give people confidence that you've got all the information you need to operate accurately and efficiently?

Are you sometimes so concerned with looking organized that you don't ask for details to be clarified? Have you ever put too much effort into the neatness of notes or assignments, and not enough into the quality of the thinking and learning involved?

For example: _____

... need deadlines?

Do you find it hard to motivate yourself until a deadline is looming?

Maybe you delay your work just long enough for the deadline to focus your mind and make your thinking intense and sharp?

For example: _____

... put work off?

Do you ever plan a date for starting work on a particular task, but find yourself pushing it back in your schedule? Do you have to wait to see how you're feeling before you know if you can start as planned?

Maybe you trust in your instincts, and waiting until you're completely ready helps you to do your best work. While you're getting around to the really challenging parts of the learning, do you use the time to do some of the functional bits that have to be done anyway?

For example: _____

... struggle to start?

Do you suddenly find different jobs to do, or let other things get in the way of making a start – even when you have a clear plan, and no real barrier to getting going?

Maybe you make the most of this trait, using the time before you're ready to begin to get your materials and your thoughts in order.

For example: _____

... get distracted?

Do you find your mind wandering away from the task at hand – to other subjects, or maybe to areas of the topic that interest you but aren't relevant to *this* piece? Do you lose focus easily if your study's interrupted? Do you have a habit of disrupting it *yourself*?

Some students rely on moments of daydreaming to achieve their best thinking. Perhaps you get distracted – but use that to tell you when it's time for a break.

For example: _____

... task-shift?

Do you often get one part of your work going, then feel the need to swap to another before it's properly finished? Do you take small steps back in your learning every time you return to part of the task you left hanging?

Maybe task-shifting is what keeps you studying for long periods – perhaps it even helps you to see links between different aspects of the subject, or to combine styles of thinking in valuable ways.

For example: _____

... try to be perfect?

Do you work slowly, or take a long time to do anything because you're determined not to get anything wrong? Do you worry that any imperfections early on will stop the rest of the task from developing as it should? Do you miss out on the learning that can come from making mistakes?

Perhaps you've found this is the best way for you to get high-quality results: setting the highest standards for yourself from the start and putting extra effort into getting things right first time.

For example: _____

... continue for too long?

Do you ever carry on working when you're no longer working well? Do you need to get to the end of every study session you've planned, whether you're really benefiting from it or not?

You might still get some useful work done during this time, especially if you can switch to more administrative or mechanical elements. Perhaps you even find yourself switching on again and studying productively after doing lower-level work for a while.

For example: _____

Questions like these highlight attitudes, preferences and personal characteristics that can have a big impact on organization and time-management. But it's clearly a complex picture, and there are advantages and disadvantages in each of these nine areas. So, thinking about your responses, and the way study has gone for you in the past ...

- What are the main **strengths** in your approach to time-management – things you'll be able to build on?

_____

_____

_____

- Can you spot any **negative** aspects that are worth trying to eliminate, or at least minimize?

_____

_____

_____

- And is there anything here that's less than perfect, but not worth changing because it's just part of **who you are**?

_____

_____

_____

2 Get organized

Being organized doesn't mean that you have to become a robot, obsessing about every detail and planning every aspect of your life. Some people may want to become more organized generally, while for others that's the last way they want to see themselves. But all students need to be *able* to organize (and to know what to organize), so that they can achieve the levels of working and thinking required at this stage.

First, get together everything you need – which is part of the work involved in creating a truly effective working environment.

> *Go to: Chapter 7* for a detailed guide to setting up your study space.

Make sure that you've got all the following things close by, organized well enough to let you work efficiently and to help you feel prepared and calm:

- **Information:** everything required to plan what to do and when, including term and holiday dates, course schedules, timetables, assessment arrangements ... plus as many details as possible about the things likely to fill up the rest of your time, such as trips away, sporting fixtures, family commitments and social events.
- **Materials:** the stationery (paper, ruler, pens, pencils, highlighters) and the technology (computer, printer, mobile phone) that *you* need for creating and updating the sort of study plans that work for you.

Start thinking early about the best systems for managing the large amounts of information you'll be gathering during your course, in both physical and digital formats. You'll need good strategies for storing, retrieving and using a wide range of materials, to support all the different types of thinking, learning and academic working you'll be involved in. Being organized helps you to access information efficiently and logically, but also to work creatively with it, making connections, seeing patterns, combining ideas in new ways.

Student Tip

'Make a conscious decision about every document you're given, whether it's on paper or on screen. I used to be terrible at just sticking handouts in a drawer or letting emails pile up in my inbox, but now I force myself to decide whether to deal with it right away, throw it away, or file it somewhere I can find it again when I need it. It's made a very big difference to how organized I feel.' **Marcie, postgraduate student**

3 Plan for success

The way you plan your study has to suit you. Among all the general principles there's plenty of room for personalization, to create an approach that gets you doing your best work, and helps you to manage all the other people involved in your studies.

Planning is a great driver of success at this stage of education, and many of the most successful students learn to plan on several levels simultaneously:

- Some plans show them what they need to do, and are based on aspects of the course that they can't change.

- Other types of planning represent how they've decided to organize their time to get it all done.

- They create plans that outline their strategies for using time in the long-, medium- and short-term as well as for specific elements of the course.

- They can access relevant planning wherever they are, adding or updating things as required.

- Crucially, they get all these different pieces of planning working together, creating an interconnected, dynamic structure that supports their study.

Students like these use the fixed points of their course to help them get things done, but they also make their own choices about managing their time (and then managing themselves when they get down to work). They take a very active approach, leading their own studies, learning as they go and continually improving their ability to:

- know what has to be done and when
- decide how long different tasks are likely to take
- weigh up priorities, spotting activities that require more time and effort
- notice when they have to work on several things at once
- think carefully about when to do particular tasks – and how to coordinate several of them
- match different sorts of work to different times in the day and week
- react to changing circumstances
- balance academic work with everything else they need and want to do
- get the very best out of all the time they put in.

Good planning is the key to all of this. Remember, there are different ways of doing this. As you learn more about your course, your new life – and yourself – keep reflecting on what's helpful, appropriate, and realistic – for *you*.

The key layers in higher-level planning are:

Long-term planning

Whole course plan: this is the overall map showing what's covered and how it's arranged, and highlighting where key components such as projects and placements fit in.

> *Go to: Chapter 5 to see how to put this together yourself, and why it's so important.*

Year plans: produced at the start of each year, these include dates for terms, holidays, particular units of work, and special times such as placements, study weeks or exam periods.

Assessment plan: this is a very important guide to all the different forms of assessment involved in your studies, showing how they're interwoven with the rest of the work you're doing, and exactly when each aspect of assessment takes place.

Medium-term planning

Term plans: these include the dates and times of lectures, seminars, classes and so on; reminders about important pieces of work, group tasks and assessments; details of relevant events within your university, such as visiting speakers or careers fairs; and, increasingly, your own notes about *when* the work for all these things needs to be done.

Project plans: these are schedules produced as part of the planning process, noting important dates, mapping out the different stages, and showing how you can give them all enough time.

Short-term planning

Diaries: whether in book form or on your mobile phone, these can be used to hold details of where you have to be and what you have to do there (in both your academic work and your life outside the course). They need to be portable so that you can check and update them wherever you are.

Week plans: these are based on medium-term planning and any other standalone plans. They're related to what happened the previous week and should be coordinated closely with your diary. Draft them at the start of each week to show all the things you need – and want – to do, and how much time you're allocating to each one.

Day plans: these take any relevant information from any other form of planning to give you a clear, prioritized schedule for the day ahead. Outlining all academic work along with details about all the other jobs, tasks and activities you're hoping to get done.

Week beginning: __/__/__	Morning	Afternoon	Evening	Additional tasks
Monday				
Tuesday				
Wednesday				
Thursday				
Friday				
Saturday				
Sunday				

An example week plan. Use this as it is or adapt it to suit your needs. If you create it as a digital document, you can add regular events or commitments to save you having to write them in each week. It might also help to use colours – to link different topics or tasks, or to emphasize particularly important slots.

Date: __/__/__	
07:00–08:00	
08:00–09:00	
09:00–10:00	
10:00–11:00	
11:00–12:00	
12:00–13:00	
13:00–14:00	
14:00–15:00	
15:00–16:00	
16:00–17:00	
17:00–18:00	
18:00–19:00	
19:00–20:00	
20:00–21:00	
21:00–22:00	
22:00–23:00	
Other plans:	

An example day plan. Again, feel free to adapt it to make it work for you.

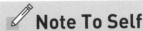 **Note To Self**

In your week and day plans, use different colours to highlight things that are essential to do, and those that are valuable to do if possible – to keep you focused on the top priorities and always pushing to get as much as you can out of your time.

Student Tip

'I've found that having a plan for the day ahead, backed up by medium- and long-term planning, really helps me to protect my time, because I can be clear with other people about when I can and can't do certain things – and why. I'm pretty good at sticking to my own timetables, but I know I have an even better chance if I've set the scene with other people first and headed off as many disruptions and distractions as possible. As the course goes on I'm starting to show more and more people my actual plans, as it only ever seems to make them more supportive.' **Kyle, Journalism undergraduate**

Specific planning

Task plans: these are drawn up to help you complete all the stages of a particular piece of work.

> *Go to: Chapter 5 for a generic template for academic tasks, and Chapter 11 for an example format for written work.*

Note To Self

Find out what the word limit is for your next assignment – particularly if it's a big one. See what that amount of text looks like in practice, with the font size and line spacing you'll be using. When you come to plan your work, note down an estimated number of words for each section. Then, as you write, keep checking the word-count, so that you don't waste time editing a finished draft that's way over the limit. It can be really hard choosing which information to take out once you've written it, so keep the word limit in sight throughout the process and you'll leave yourself with a much more manageable editing job at the end.

Exam timetables: these are often given to you ready-made, so that you just have to add notes, highlight important details and so on.

Exam preparation timetables: these are the detailed plans you make for yourself, based on your developing knowledge of how long you need to get ready for particular assessments and exams, and how you can best work on several subjects at once.

> *Go to: Chapter 19 for a full guide to this important type of planning.*

Placement schedules: these are sometimes provided for you, and sometimes left to you to compile yourself. They include information about where you'll be, what you'll be doing, and other pre-planned details (you can add more as they emerge).

Keep your **whole course plan** permanently visible in your main study space, alongside the relevant **term plan** and any **specific plans** that are relevant at a given time (doing a project, revision for exams, *doing* exams ...).

Put your **day plan** up as soon as you make it (and replace today's with tomorrow's when it arrives), but also take a photo of it on your phone. In fact, it's a good idea to have photos or electronic copies of all your other plans so that you've got them whenever you need them.

Your **diary** should also be with you at all times, ready to check, change or add information, and you can use it to keep all your other plans up to date. That's how you manage to work within the fixed structures of your course and still react to anything you need to add or change, using an approach to time-management that's systematic and robust, but also dynamic, responsive and right for you.

There's advice throughout the book on how to go about deciding how much time to allocate to different aspects of study, when it's best to do certain things, and why it's so important to coordinate tasks carefully. All the way through your course you'll be juggling long-term projects, very short-term tasks, and everything in between, and having a multi-layered planning process is essential for doing them all, and doing them well.

So much of the decision-making also depends on what you learn about yourself and your subject as you progress. There's clearly a lot to get to grips with in an approach like this, even when you refine it to develop the system that's right for you. But it *needs* to be this sophisticated because it's helping you to do sophisticated thinking. You'll use it in more and more subtle ways as you learn how to operate well in your chosen subject, and as you get an increasingly clear picture of what good study at this higher level entails.

⑩ Ten-point summary

1. When you move from *dependent* to *independent* learning, you take on new responsibility for managing your time – with great significance for the work you do.

2. Find out what your past experiences and current behaviours tell you about your approach to time-management, to reveal strengths to draw on and weaknesses to address (or accept).

3. At this level, organization is central to effective working and high-quality thinking.

4. Make sure that you have all the information you need to help you structure accurate and appropriate study plans.

5. Your approach to planning needs to be highly personalized, to suit your emotional responses to studying as well as your thinking and working styles.

6. You need to know – and display – the 'big-picture' map for your course as a whole.

7. Use medium-term plans to start deciding how long to spend on each aspect of your work, when to do it, and how to coordinate different tasks.

8. Short-term planning involves weekly and daily schedules, kept up to date by using a physical or digital diary.

9. Extra plans can be developed as necessary to help you manage particular pieces of work, larger projects or distinct periods of study.

10. A strong time-management system lets you manage your commitments, talk honestly with others about your work, and help *them* to help *you* stick to your plans.

 # Where to next?

Chapter 9 will show you how to use your time well, so that you're ready to make the most of all the opportunities on offer.

On task

As well as planning your time, you need to prepare to use it well, with a range of strategies for managing your feelings, maximizing your work, and adapting your whole life to support consistently strong study.

 ## What?

After a chapter about the importance of planning your time, this one explores how you *use* that time – because planning out your days is only part of the story. When you've structured your time to match the needs of your study, and you know what you've got to do and when, the even bigger challenge is to use that time *well*.

Good study is always about the **quality** as well as the quantity of time spent doing it – particularly at this level, with more complex work required and so many other things going on. In this chapter you'll explore all the choices you have to make, and the practical steps you can take, to avoid wasting a moment. And you'll learn the importance of **balancing** your life, so that *all* your time is used well, and everything you get up to supports your academic development as well as your personal growth.

 ## When?

You need to start working at full capacity as soon as your study plans are drawn up. Your day-to-day efforts will depend very much on what you're aiming to get done. The long- and medium-term plans shape everything and are always accessible if you need them, but the strongest direction comes from your short-term schedules. Every week, and particularly every day, you'll have a plan of action, designed to match your needs and support your development – if you can carry it out well.

You'll need to stay in control of competing calls on your time, know the risks and benefits of them – now and in the long run – and make strong choices about how you use all the time you've got, particularly when circumstances change. More than ever, continual reflection will be the key to getting everything you want out of the effort you put in.

Who?

As with the last chapter, how well you use your time will depend a lot on how you manage other people. These strategies will help you to get learning partners and fellow group members working in ways that benefit you all. They'll allow you to play a supportive role within your **academic community** and guide you to make strong choices about your **social life** and any **paid work** you want or need to do. They'll also ensure that you can protect yourself when other people threaten to disrupt your study.

Why?

It's all part of the struggle of higher-level learning: the long, complex and deeply personal challenge to understand how to study well in the field you've picked. It has to be hard, to forge high-value skills, but you still need to be able to engage with it over a significant period of time, and get enough out at each point to keep motivated, keep up with your course – and keep getting better.

Studying is different at this higher level. You need to be prepared to learn new ways to do it well. The stakes are higher, and the threats to learning are, too – but so are the benefits of developing an active and ambitious approach. There are plenty of general, real-life gains to be made, but the techniques in this chapter are integral to study. Engaging with the quality of your learning gets you closer to understanding how your subject works, and the sort of academic and personal development it demands.

How?

When your plans are in place for when to do what ... focus on *how*. Think about the **emotions** that affect the quality of your study, and develop a personalized approach to getting started quickly, staying focused, getting the most out of your time and maximizing your learning.

Self-monitoring strategies will help you make strong choices and keep improving, especially as you learn to meet the **deadlines** dotted throughout your plans.

Then, see how techniques for planning and managing your time can help you to balance all the different parts of your new life: paid work, socializing, leisure activities, family commitments, resting ... and, central to it all, consistently good study.

Steps to success

1 Address your feelings

Even when you have clear study plans in place, your emotions can play a big part in what happens next. Often there seem to be many more questions than answers:

Good study involves finding the right answers for you – based on knowing yourself, and understanding more and more about how learning works.

In response to the six questions above, here are six aspects of study in practice, all of which are impacted by your preferences, habits, attitudes – and feelings that can quickly change. As you consider each one, think carefully about what you know about yourself as a learner, and write down one thing that could help you to get better at this part of the process. (And bear in mind all the people you'll be collaborating with in your learning, as the choices you make here can affect how well they do in their parts of the work.)

Getting ready

A few minutes spent clearing up your desk or arranging your materials can save a lot of time, and dramatically improve the quality of your work. Remember, honesty is the best policy: you may *want* to be the sort of person who can work in a laid-back, messy environment – but are you really doing your best there?

You don't need to become a different person. Just get into a few housekeeping habits that help you think and work well.

Action: _____

Getting going

You've spent time making plans, so do what they say. They're not arbitrary. You've structured them carefully to support the best possible study, with a clear view of your long-term needs – so stick to them (even if the final deadline is a very long way off). If you intended to start work at 4pm, start at 4pm.

See whether 'rituals' help, such as sitting in a particular chair, turning on your desk lamp or always drinking from a particular mug. Some people find rituals very useful for switching on to studying, getting them into the work almost without realizing it.

Having everything ready and waiting for you makes it easier, too – like runners who lay out all their kit the night before to make early-morning training that little bit easier to face.

Action: _____

Case Study: Luke

Luke realized that he was deceiving himself about study – so he developed a trick of his own.

'I'd got into the habit of finding "important" jobs to do instead of the things I should be doing for my course. I had it all planned out in detail, but when the time came to start, there was always a load of washing that needed to go on, or a present to buy, or a phone call to return. I was being busy – just not the right sort of busy. And I knew getting started was the problem. Once I eventually got going, I was fine.'

Luke's solution was to blur the lines about when the task actually began: 'Instead of sitting down to start (which had become something to avoid) I put the kettle on and stood there with my work while the water boiled. Then I kept standing there working until the coffee was cool enough to drink – so, by the time I eventually sat down, I'd already started studying.'

Breaking in

As well as getting started quickly, good study also involves getting *into* a piece of work in the most effective way (and not necessarily by beginning at the beginning). That could mean finding a part of the process you can do straight away – or maybe starting with an element that's difficult, but which helps to shape the rest of the task.

Some people follow their interests, letting curiosity dictate where they start unpicking a problem or investigating an issue. Others prefer to begin near the end – reading the summary section of a document, for example, exploring how a play finishes or preparing the structure of a final report – to help them see where their work's headed, and to make it feel more manageable.

And if you're held back by worrying about mistakes, try agreeing with yourself that you can write *anything* to start with, to help you get going and to see what you're thinking – in the knowledge that you'll have a conscious editing stage at a specific point later on.

Action: _____

Breaking up

Throughout this book you'll see the importance of splitting up academic tasks (and integrating everything at the end). Your time-planning will guide the way you divide different processes and projects over days, weeks and even months, but each individual study session also needs to be cut into manageable chunks.

Agree with yourself how long you'll concentrate before you get up, stretch your legs, have a drink, shift your focus for a while. Don't shift it so far that it's hard to get back (you can use your learning journal to find the right balance), but use short breaks to keep you working well for a good length of time, helping your brain to catch up every so often and consolidate new ideas.

Action: _____

Working smart

Studying has to be emotional, driven by your interests and passions, relying on your personal responses. It also requires a high level of strategy – often in order to *deal* with emotions and make sure that good study prevails. However important it feels to study *now*, or in a certain way, or just to keep going, it's essential to draw on objectivity, analysis and common sense. Are you too tired to be productive? Is this really the best time to be working? This activity looks very virtuous – but is it?

Experiment with your effectiveness at different times of the day or week. (Your learning journal will be really useful here, too.) Think about a variety of sessions, successful and unsuccessful. What might have happened if you'd done them at different times?

Do parts of your study (or the rest of your life) clash? Are there intelligent ways to move things around in your schedule so that study works better? For example, you might find you're always better at analytic tasks in the morning, or creative thinking after being around other people. If you struggle to start a new essay at the start of the day, try doing it in the evening next time, when decisions might seem less weighty.

Does it help to spend a whole session – even a whole day – doing the same type of study, or is the opposite true for you?

Action: _____

Ask yourself

→ Are you missing easy ways to save time?

Always be on the lookout for simple things that can save you lots of time and effort. This is a key part of successful study: by understanding the value of different parts of the process and allowing yourself to do some things quickly, you'll save your energy for the important bits.

Think about the functional elements of learning, such as writing up your notes. Do you ever write them by hand, then type the same notes later (perhaps to start structuring an essay or to give a copy to other members of your group), when you could have done it digitally the first time around?

Instead of copying out quotations from books you own, what about just marking them with coloured sticky notes?

Technology often provides valuable time-savers. Speech-to-text software might save you from transcribing research interviews. There are websites that turn lists of book titles into perfectly formatted bibliographies. Delegate mechanical tasks whenever you can so that you can concentrate on developing higher-level skills.

Keeping going

You'll need stamina to study well. That doesn't mean working all the time (although there will be spells when you have to put in longer hours – and make them effective) but it does require you to give it everything when you do, learning with energy and focus, day after day.

Your physical health is significant here. Monitor the effects of different foods and drinks on the quality of your work, and make sure that your study's not being sabotaged by a lack of sleep. When you do get tired, see whether it's possible to stay productive by switching from higher-level thinking to lower-level tasks.

There'll be days when you can decide to keep going longer than usual if things are going well (maybe your lecture starts later than usual in the morning), and others when you need to be particularly strict about stopping.

Notice what distracts you, and keep it out of reach. If you're honest, will your phone really help you with this work, or is it more likely to get in the way? What impact is the radio having? These things might be more valuable as rewards instead. Half an hour of high-quality study equals five minutes on social media, say, or keep going until ten o'clock and then listen to the whole of the sports news.

As much as you can, use study as its own reward. Remind yourself why you've taken on this challenge. Emphasize the interesting bits. Use your learning journal to record the pride you feel when you've completed a session particularly well. Remember where it's taking you in the long run.

Action: _____

 Note To Self

Use your learning journal to help you monitor the quantity and quality of your study. Add specific notes about time-management, alert to insights that could improve your work in the future.

- What was the activity? **And how long did you plan to spend on it?**
- How did you feel: before/during/after? **Did time have any influence on your emotions?**
- How successful was it? **Did you get started quickly and concentrate well throughout?**

- What did you gain? **Include any new insights into schedules, motivation, deadlines, stamina ...**
- What will you do differently in future? **Was this the right time for this particular task? What would have helped you to get started faster and stay focused longer?**
- How will you *know* that you've learned from this task? **What improvements to your time-management do you hope to see as a result?**

2 Beat the clock

However well you plan, however good you are at studying, things happen. Real life doesn't pay much regard to the deadlines you're working to. You're bound to have to withstand some blows along the way but, with the right defence, the resilience you develop will play a big part in your success – at university, and long after.

The better you are at planning, the more you can adapt to new circumstances. You can see the implications for your work, and you have much more chance of plotting new ways of getting everything done on time.

It's also easier to get help, since you can demonstrate your situation to friends, family and the powers that be, and get a realistic response about the flexibility or support on offer.

Set your own deadlines ahead of the real ones, to give you breathing space in case problems arise. Include some contingency planning in your whole time-management approach. What if the questionnaires don't come back by then? What if the final draft carries on into next week? What if they decide to have the wedding *that* weekend ...?

Academic Advice

'Students often complain that we don't give them enough time for their assignments, and that there's no flexibility built into the system. But they have to realize that things like marking and moderation take time, and there are official processes going on that they don't see. Moving deadlines would create big knock-on effects. My advice is always for the students to build some wriggle-room into their work. Give yourself time to solve any problems – which is impossible if you work right up to the wire.' **Tom, university course leader**

3 Balance your life

We're all trying to sort out the right balance in our lives, between activity and rest, other people and ourselves, home life and travel, paid work, family, friends, community, health, learning, culture, sport ... and any number of other things that matter to us. It's a lifelong challenge, but it has particular significance when you're studying.

This is because you need to secure enough time for your learning and to make the progress required to pass your course – as well as to leave room for the things *outside* your course that enrich your studies, prepare you to excel at work, and release the full power of the skills you've developed.

Student life can seem overwhelmingly full, with enough possibilities to make your head spin. It's all part of the wonderful challenge it offers. If you make the right moves, it's what makes studying at this level so special and rich.

Here are some of the key things to think about:

Paid work

Before you agree to anything, make sure that it's going to work alongside your studies. You may need the money – but is this the right job? (And if you're already *in* work and preparing to take on new studies, think very carefully about the commitments required on both sides.)

Get as much information you can about what the job entails. Are the hours regular, flexible, unpredictable? Will the job change at different times of the year?

Be open with both prospective (or current) employers and academic staff. Either side (or even both) may need to give their permission. And the more they know about each other, the more they'll be able to help you combine these two big parts of your life.

Add **paid work plans** into your overall planning system, so that you take them into account when organizing your study.

Look for links between paid work and study. Can the work be accredited in any way and go towards your academic qualifications? Could you learn skills and attributes that would feed into your academic life? Might your experiences provide good subject matter for assignments? Is this a place to do useful research? There could be significant benefits all round (with the right agreements in place). Some employers even support staff in their studies – financially, or by allowing them time off – and many educational bodies are very keen to reach out to the world of work.

Sporting activities

You should have plenty of choices here, so make them wisely.

Look for activities that will keep you happy, enrich your social life and contribute to your personal growth.

Consider the benefits (and weigh up the risks) to your health and wellbeing. You'll think and learn better when you're feeling good, and sport can improve your aerobic fitness, core strength and flexibility, as well as responsiveness, coordination, decision-making ... Maybe you know it will push you to have a better diet or sleep regime. Or are you likely to be too exhausted to work? Is the risk of injury one that you're prepared to take?

Think about the practicalities. When are the training sessions? How far in advance will you know about the days, times and locations of fixtures? Are the important times in a particular sport's season well matched to the overall plan of your course?

Social life

An accurate and responsive time-management system is vital for enjoying a rich social life while you're studying.

Your diary lets you check your availability when opportunities arise, and then record your plans so that they don't collide with other things.

Use your medium- and long-term planning to keep sight of the big picture, remembering the need to pace yourself. Be alert for pressure points on your course, when the workload is heavier and the stakes are higher – when *some* socializing might be vital, but too much could be disastrous. Say 'no' when you need to (even if it's just for now), but have the confidence to manage your time creatively and make room for the things that really matter.

> ### Student Tip
>
> 'When I was at university, I saw so many people who didn't know how to say "no" to social activities, and their studies suffered as a result. I think there's a real pressure to justify any time you're not spending with other people, so planning your time carefully also helps you communicate your needs to others, to protect yourself and your work.' **Maddie, Master's student**

 # Ask yourself

→ How can extracurricular activities help you to study?

You certainly need to be mindful of the risks when you're weighing up how to prioritize your time. But it's also important to recognize the benefits on offer, especially when they apply directly to your academic work.

Look out for the activities that:

- improve your memory for processes and techniques
- strengthen people skills, such as collaborating on tasks, engaging in dialogue and working supportively
- stretch you to learn how to operate – and how to learn – in new environments
- develop your communication skills, including giving presentations and teaching others
- challenge you to practise organizing, analysing and evaluating information, and putting it to use in new ways.

Seize every opportunity do things that interest, challenge, entertain and excite you – *and* enrich your studies in the process.

> **Student Tip**
>
> 'Keep a notebook handy, to jot down any ideas you have or useful things you come across. You can get insights from the most unexpected places. It also gets you into the habit of thinking about your work whenever you've got some "dead" time, like standing in a queue or waiting for the train. It's amazing how creative you can be when there's nothing else going on.' Rachel, History undergraduate

(10) Ten-point summary

1. Good study happens when you plan your time intelligently, then use it effectively.

2. Learning can be disrupted – or stalled completely – by a range of negative emotions.

3. Successful students know how to get organized, start quickly, stay energized, and concentrate for long enough to achieve high-quality results.

4. Look for simple ways to make it easier for *you* to study well.

5. Learning journals are useful for developing time-management skills.

6. Improve your ability to meet deadlines by giving yourself room to manoeuvre, and by asking 'What happens if …?'

7. Paid work and higher-level study can benefit each other, if you're open and honest, plan your time carefully, and consider the risks as well as the rewards.

8. Choose sporting activities that boost wellbeing and strengthen study.

9. A well-managed social life can have a very positive impact on your learning, helping you to develop some essential higher-level skills.

10. Good time-management helps to balance and enrich all aspects of student life.

 Where to next?

Chapter 10 will help you to develop the new research skills you'll need to study successfully at this level.

Take what you need

Good study involves gathering relevant information from a wide range of sources, knowing where to go and what to do to extract everything you need for your work.

What?

This chapter takes you to the heart of **active study**, exploring parts of the learning process that set academic development in motion – and which are particularly visible features of higher-level tasks.

Access Record Organize Analyse Remember Use

To get the ball rolling, you have to access information (the right sort), by knowing what to look for, how to find it, and how to get *into* it to take out the things you need. There's theory here (how to know what you're looking for, whether what you find is any good, which bits you need to collect ...) but also lots of highly practical behaviour: getting hold of key materials, exploring them effectively, and recording some of the contents, to use now and in your work to come.

The first stage of *accessing* is getting to the information sources you need, to read, watch or listen to them. But this learning model is an overlapping one. *Recording* – done properly – is part of accessing, collecting sections of the information or making your own notes about it in order to access it better, understand it more, incorporate it properly into your learning. And then *organizing* blurs with that, as your recording helps you to make sense of the ideas you've obtained, rearranging them in ways that support all the other parts of the learning process.

For higher-level students, three particular skill-sets are involved in getting the learning process off to a good start: **researching**, **reading** and **recording**.

It's important to examine these three together. In practice they often look like linear steps: you work out what to read and find it, then you read it, and after each section you make some notes. But they're also interconnected, and it's vital that you know how to integrate them; because you need to read well to be able to research, and note-making happens during reading – and often guides where your research goes next.

Gathering is a word that appears a lot in this chapter: the active, selective, strategic acquisition of all the information required for the task at hand. Your studies will help you develop the confidence to do it well, whatever the activity – whether you're sitting in a lecture, scrutinizing a document, doing research for an assignment or working towards an exam. It's a core academic ability, with a range of specialist applications – all made possible by knowing how to access and engage with whatever *you* decide you need.

When?

You can start the information-gathering process before your course begins. Even if you haven't been given a reading list (and not every course provides one anyway), the strategies here will help you to gain valuable background knowledge, see the 'lie of the land' in your subject – and get into good study habits early.

Then, when you're officially up and running, this active approach will be essential for building the foundations of your subject knowledge, preparing you to begin interpreting, evaluating and challenging it as your understanding increases and your own judgements emerge.

You'll need to use all these strategies during independent study as well as in taught sessions and group work, adapting your approach to suit particular tasks – aware of what different parts of the activity require you to do. Sometimes you'll be consciously focusing on one skill (finding relevant articles online, reading a report in depth, making notes to structure an essay) but very often you'll be integrating all three.

The skills you're developing will be vital throughout your studies, but they'll also equip you well for everything you go on to do in the complex, information-rich world beyond.

Who?

These are core skills in independent study, requiring your active involvement and careful personalization. Your attitudes will have a significant influence on which strategies you choose and how well you use them, and there are plenty of practical things that will help – but only if you do them. The responsibility is now yours alone.

But other people are still involved: as potential sources of new knowledge and better understanding (writers, teaching staff, other students), and as fellow members of an academic community that needs a constant flow of quality material to keep the fires of learning alight.

Why?

You're here to learn how to work with the information and ideas that are important in your chosen field. Using them to drive the learning process will be at the heart of your development as a student. You'll also gain thinking and working skills that will help with everything else you do.

Gathering information effectively is vital for engaging fully with your course, and staying with it as it moves. *Why* you do it changes all the time: to get a specific detail; to access general information on a subject; to pull together a range of different perspectives; to learn about how those perspectives came to be ...

It all merges into a very rich process. You learn what other people have discovered, and how – on their own, and by challenging each other and moving knowledge on. And that helps *you* to get better at discovering and challenging and moving it on yourself.

There are also some clear and immediate benefits. You learn to research efficiently to save time and stress. You make reading more effective and enjoyable. You use your notes to produce successful assignments – and, eventually, to do brilliantly in exams.

Learning begins when you get hold of things that are new to you, and start finding out what they mean. The information you gather – and the way you gather it – has a major impact on everything that happens next.

How?

Start by analysing your current approach to **research**. Exploring your existing attitudes and strategies will help you to understand how to develop the advanced skills you'll need for your course.

Do the same thing for **reading**. Examine the many different parts that make it work, and consider what it needs to *do* for you at this level.

Finally, focus on how you can develop your techniques for **recording** information: to be efficient and accurate, but also to boost understanding, creativity, and embed long-term learning.

Steps to success

1 Analyse your approach to research

Start your assessment by returning to some questions you've already answered.

> **Go to: Chapter 4** for some valuable background information.

Then tackle six more – designed to let you look into some key aspects of higher-level research. Make a few notes under each one, to help you reflect on different parts of the process generally, and to understand more about your own research habits.

- How much information do you need before you start researching something?

_____

_____

_____

- How do you know what will be a useful source of information, and what won't?

_____

_____

_____

- How do you decide where to look for research materials?

_____

_____

_____

- How do you go about searching for the things you need?

_____

_____

_____

- Are you good at working efficiently and getting the most out of your time?

_____

_____

_____

- How organized are you with the information you collect?

_____

_____

_____

2 Develop higher-level research skills

Research can be a confusing concept. At this stage it's tempting to think of it as a very specific part of the academic process – several days of research for a major project, for example – or as a particularly advanced level of learning in itself, as if you work up to a point when what you're doing suddenly becomes 'official' research. Yes, some research does carry more weight than others (and you'll need to learn why, and how to spot the clues). But all academic tasks involve research of some form, and you'll find that you're doing it all the time. In fact, often without realizing it, you've been doing it for years.

 ## Ask yourself

→ How many different forms of research can you think of?

If checking bus times, looking for creative ideas in a magazine and watching a video connected to your course are all forms of research ... how many other kinds do you do?

Bear all those activities in mind now (along with your answers to the six questions in Step 1) as you consider the following pieces of advice. Think about how you could use the ideas below to strengthen your current approach, and to develop your skills further through the research you'll be doing for your course.

Be focused

You have to know what you're doing it _for_. That doesn't mean you know what you're going to find, and you can still be curious and open to considering whatever emerges. But you've got to know the purpose of your research.

- Define your research task – precisely. Look very closely at the wording of questions you're trying to answer. Exactly what are you trying to find out? Will it be possible to do that from one source, or can it _only_ be done by examining several?
- Check the 'boundaries' for your search. Have you been given instructions or guidance to work within particular timeframes or subject areas?
- If you're researching in order to produce a specific assignment, use the word limit to influence how much information you collect, and the levels of detail and complexity you reach.
- If there's any marking guidance available to you, read that carefully to find out what your research priorities should be.

Development steps:

_____

_____

_____

Be realistic

In the past, it's likely that your approach to research tasks was often influenced by practical considerations: how long you had, which topics had the most material about them, which sources were the easier to get hold of.

Now you'll need to look past questions like those if you want to get deeper answers – but don't disregard them altogether. It's still important to be realistic about your working practices – and you can even use the same questions to do some higher-level *thinking* about research.

- Be clear about how long you have to do the research – among everything else you need to do. You won't be able to read everything relevant to your work, so you'll have to prioritize carefully – and you can only do that if you know how much time you've got. (You may find that you actually mention this in your work, if you reflect on your practices and suggest next steps in your own research.)
- Find out early in the process what you can actually get your hands on (physically or virtually) when you need it. Higher-level courses move quickly. You might not be able to hang around for a key text to become available at the library, or to sit on a waiting list for a particularly popular set of documents. What are the best choices you can make from what's *actually* available?
- It's definitely worth looking into areas of the literature where lots of research has been done. These are likely to be the important ones – but not necessarily, so weigh it all up carefully, and always consider *why* certain aspects may have had more or less focus. Questioning the way research is done is a key aspect of higher-level study.

Development steps:

_____

_____

_____

Be discriminating

Research is one of the many aspects of your work where both quantity and quality count. The amount of information you need to gather depends on the task, but the quality always has to be high. If you discover lots of poor-quality material about something, that may well reveal something interesting in itself – but even that comes from being discriminating about your sources from the very start of the process. You haven't got time to waste on inferior information, so make clear, conscious decisions about what to include in your work. To help you do this, think about:

- recommendations: is it on any of your official reading lists, or has it been mentioned by academic staff?
- references: does it link to other credible texts, and is it referenced *by* any other works you've used?
- reviews: to what extent has it been 'peer-reviewed' – scrutinized by academics and other respected people in the field?
- reputations: is it written by a qualified author – and published by a company you recognize?
- responses: as you scan the information to see whether it's worth going further, does it read like the coherent, up-to-date academic writing you're getting used to?

Development steps:

_____

_____

_____

Be efficient

You demonstrate your ability to study well when you work within the systems set up to manage information, using them smoothly and intelligently. You save on time and strain, too – but the greatest gains come from being able to locate high-quality materials.

It's about tracking down particular items or running searches that provide a wealth of appropriate information. Finding key details within large documents. Using one resource to get to another. Setting yourself up well to *continue* working efficiently when you get into the reading and recording phases of research.

- Make sure that you learn where the books, journals and other documents and resources relevant to your work are stored. (If your course draws on research from different fields, you may have to go to completely different libraries.)

Academic Advice

'Make the most of everything your university's library has to offer. It's designed to support your studying – to get the resources you need, when you need them. Too many students miss out on some really valuable help, and there's no excuse really. Most libraries have online guides and tutorials. They offer tours and talks – and the staff are experts. I tell all my students to sort out their registration and access arrangements as soon as possible, then use them. You can take lots of the stress out of research just by reserving books, getting resources sent from other places, even using other libraries' collections. And it's not just free; you're already paying for it in your fees, so get your money's worth!' **Alison, university tutor**

- Use all the virtual libraries you have access to. There's a wealth of academic literature available for free online, and your university may also have bought into subscription services – general databases of academic research or specialist collections.
- Learn how to use advanced search terms when you're gathering information online. Don't leave everything to the algorithms: you can quickly learn to be so much more proactive and precise. For example:

  - Add " and " around search terms when you know the exact word or phrase you're looking for (for example, **"data analyst"**) ...
  - ... and use the word NOT when you're clear what you need to avoid (**analyst NOT manager**).
  - Put AND into your search to narrow the focus and see where information overlaps (**"data analyst" AND "data manager"**).
  - Use OR when you want to widen your search, deconstruct ideas and head off in some new directions (**"data processor" OR "data controller"**).

Development steps:

_____

_____

_____

Be creative

Good research is efficient, strategic, logical, but also highly creative, laying the groundwork for equally rich *reading* and *recording*.

- As well as university libraries and academic journals, where else could you look for useful information? Are there professional publications that could give you up-to-date, real-world perspectives? How does the media report on the subject matter you're exploring? As well as text-based materials, what about videos, TV shows, podcasts ...?

- Experiment with new ways to track down high-quality information. Be open to new directions *into* your research – finding credible references in non-academic publications, for example, or on reading lists from other disciplines with some shared interests.
- Pick up trails that start inside the research you've already done. Go to the sources used by the writers you value most, looking for insights in other topics they've written about, or taking some of the specialist words they use and trying them out as search terms online.

Development steps:

_____

_____

_____

> *Go to: Chapter 7 to see how to adapt your **environment** and **behaviour** to improve the quality of your research – accessing, recording and organizing information.*

 Note To Self

There are lots of apps and online tools to help you manage your research. Some give you new ways to store the information you collect. Others record the processes you use – for instance, letting you create annotated trails through all the websites you visit. There are also ways to leave virtual sticky notes on those sites, as you mine them for valuable material and use them to develop your ideas. See which systems and services the staff on your course recommend.

 > *Go to: Chapter 6 to check/update the **research** section in your Core Development Plan.*

3 Think about how you read

First, think about your literacy in general.

> *Go to: Chapter 4 to explore your previous experiences and your current levels of confidence and skill.*

Focus on reading: how you approach it and how effective you are.

> *Go to: Chapter 6 to reflect on the benefits of developing your reading skills.*

❯ *Go to: Chapter 6* *to see how **reading** fits into your Core Development Plan.*

Then pick a real, recent example from your own studies.

- What were you reading?

_____

- What were you trying to find out?

_____

- Did you have a clear purpose for reading and strategies to do it well?
- Before you started reading did you scan any general information – such as front/back cover text, chapter headings, document abstracts?
- Did you consciously predict what you might find?
- Were you sceptical about the information, asking questions about meaning, relevance, significance, validity ...?
- Did you mark or highlight the text in any way, to help you engage with it and record your responses?
- Did you do anything to check your understanding as you read?
- Did you feel the need to go back and read any of the information again?
- Were you able to concentrate well throughout?

Now, do that all again, thinking about a time when you read something that *wasn't* part of your studies – with a very different purpose in mind.

- What material were you reading here?

_____

- What were you trying to get out of reading this time?

_____

You can learn a lot by comparing your responses to these two reading experiences.

- Which one was easiest? Most enjoyable? Most effective?
- At the time, were you aware that you were reading for different purposes?
- In what ways was your *approach* different – if any? Did your reading speed change? Did you read more words in one task (proportionally) than the other? Did you explore the texts in any different ways?

✎ Note on digital texts

Even if you're not doing distance learning, many universities now deliver a great deal of reading material in digital form – which can take some getting used to if you're more accustomed to textbooks or handouts.

There are some clear advantages to reading from a screen. You don't have to wait for someone else to be finished with the original resource. You can dip in and out of documents without having to buy or store them yourself. You can use technology to highlight and annotate texts, to help you engage with them now and to use them again later. You might even be able to use search tools to navigate the information, or follow links within the text to reach other documents.

But there are disadvantages, too. Some students miss the reassurance that comes from reading a physical book, which isn't going to stop working if their internet goes down or their laptop runs out of power. Others prefer to know exactly how much they still have to get through; to be able to flick back and forward through the pages by hand; and to read wherever and whenever they want (even in the bath). And if your memory benefits from picturing information on particular pages in a book, on-screen texts might feel like real barriers to your learning.

If you find digital texts difficult, try to pinpoint *why*. When you have choices about how to access reading materials, do what's best for the quality of your study. And when it's a case of screen or nothing … do what you can to improve the experience:

- Check you can see how far through the text you are at any point, and make sure you understand the controls that let you navigate it efficiently.
- Think about how quickly you're scrolling through the lines or clicking between pages.
- Check that the screen resolution and text size are right for you.
- Consider having an eye test to find out if you'd benefit from some extra help when you're reading from a screen.

4 Learn what academic reading means

> *Go to: Chapter 5 to consider why the materials you read are different at this level, and what that might mean for you.*

It's no coincidence that people often talk about 'reading' a degree subject. It's an absolutely essential skill at this level, where you need to …

- access a wide range of varied information quickly and accurately
- understand the significance of the things you read
- use the facts and ideas to increase your knowledge and strengthen your understanding
- use the *process* of reading to develop key thinking skills.

It's also part of the reason why higher-level learning can feel like such a struggle. It's great to grapple with the ideas you extract from all the different materials you get your hands on – but …

- there's just so much of it to get through
- it uses specialist terminology
- the structure and style of the writing can seem complicated and unwelcoming
- you're assumed to know certain important aspects already.

Academic Advice

'Reading's a funny thing at university. You need to be good at lots of different aspects of it, and it's a problem if it's a barrier to your learning – but it's also meant to feel quite difficult. Even at my level I'm reading slowly, chewing over the ideas, rereading bits, deciding what does and doesn't make sense. Reading gives you a chance to use the writer's ideas and think with them for a while, which is intense and problematic even when you're doing it right!' **Kerry, PhD student**

Throughout this book you'll be developing reading skills required for higher-level study in general, but also ones that match particular aspects of your work. Here are some of the key skills you'll need to master if you're going to meet all the challenges of academic reading head on.

Learn to focus

> **Go to: Chapter 7** *to consider the impact your environment can have on your reading.*

Pay particular attention to the quality of light, so that you're not straining your eyes or likely to get a headache from a flickering bulb. When you're reading from a screen, make sure that all the settings are adjusted to suit you, and that your desk and chair allow you to see as well as possible. And if you have any concerns about your eyesight, get it tested sooner rather than later.

Being an active reader (see below) will also help, but there are plenty of other things you can do to stay focused and engaged.

Learn to prepare

Get into the habit of tuning in to your material before you start reading properly. Scan the cover, contents page, chapter summaries – anywhere you can find easily digestible clues about what you're going to be reading, and how you'll need to read it.

Check that you know something about the author(s). If there's not enough information about them within the material itself, do a quick online search. What qualifies them to write this? What's their likely purpose, viewpoint, argument? Does knowing who they are help you to engage with what they're writing, and to judge its significance and usefulness to you?

Learn to question

Questioning is a powerful way of engaging with what you've read, and how it's been created. Asking questions before, during and after reading boosts understanding and learning, and also paves the way for whatever you're going to do with the information next.

- What's the overall argument? What are the big ideas? What sort of influences have shaped the writer's views?
- Is this information familiar to you? How does it fit in with the other things you've read? What does it lead you to look at (or go back to) next?
- What kind of evidence is presented – and is it possible to challenge it?

You're questioning the information and the author, but you're also questioning yourself. Are you interested in what you're reading? Do you understand it? Does it seem reasonable? Does it convince you? How well does it match what you were looking to find out, and how helpful is what you've discovered? Has it changed anything for you?

Learn to predict

Your predictions can become increasingly specific as you read. If you're constantly asking what topic the author is going to turn to next, what the next point in their argument could be, even what example they might be about to use, you're checking your comprehension of what you've read so far, and you're integrating that into your wider knowledge and understanding. You're engaging with the way the author thinks about this topic – which doesn't mean you have to accept it. In fact, you're constantly testing whether or not you agree with the direction the writer's going as you walk in their shoes.

Whether your predictions are right or wrong, you learn something. Your memory is strengthened either way. Your interest is maintained – to keep following the trail or to find a way to get back on it. You're continually exploring the way different connections can be made, all the while improving your understanding of how learning works.

Learn to comprehend

Academic writing is precise and compact, often dealing with abstract ideas and using words and phrases that are rarely seen elsewhere – including some highly specialist terminology.

If you don't know what something means, *find out* (from a glossary, dictionary or online search) and then do something *with* the definition. Highlight it in your notes, put it into a search engine or add it to a personal list of useful terms (to start experimenting with in your own writing). Sometimes you'll have to stop reading and find out what it means there and then, because your understanding and engagement rely on it. But, if you can, keep your flow going – but make a note to get the answer later.

Learning moves from the general to the specific. So, start with an overall sense of what a piece of writing is about, its purpose, subject matter, central arguments – then go deeper from there, reading about some of the difficulties involved, more complex ideas, maybe different views. It's likely to get harder to understand as you go on, but that's only because you're thinking in more and more subtle ways, and it's taking you to places where things are no longer clear cut.

 # Ask yourself

→ How deep do you need to go?

Sometimes you'll be taking a fairly surface view of the material, especially if you're already secure with the basics. You'll read quite quickly, not necessarily in a linear way, using the signposts in the language and layout to help you get enough information to suit your needs.

At other times you'll need a much more *deep* reading style: probably slower, reading many more of the words, in the order they're written.

At this level you're going to need to work flexibly between these different reading styles.

Learn to check your success

It's essential to be able to spot when you've lost 'contact' with the material in front of you. Continual monitoring is vital. You still need to review the whole process at the end, so that you can go back and reread any parts that might need a second look, and make informed decisions about where to go next – but that's no substitute for checking your comprehension all the time you're reading.

- Are you following the thread so far?
- Can you summarize that last point?
- Is this making sense, in the light of things you already know?

There'll be times when you don't understand what you're reading – when it challenges you with new and complex ideas, and gets you to reconsider things you thought you knew. You can keep going for a while if you feel confident there's clarification coming. But when you're not sure where the writing is headed, can't see *where* your understanding broke down, and don't feel like there are answers on the way any time soon ... *that's* when you've lost contact, and you need to do something to get it back.

❯ *Go to: Chapter 6 to see how a Learning Journal can help you monitor the quality of your study.*

Analyse reading tasks from time to time, to record your progress and reflect on the things you still need to improve.

Learn to help yourself

Be prepared to get stuck. Get into the habit of rereading sections or looking ahead for guidance later in the text. Which other resources might cast some light here? Would drawing a diagram help, talking yourself through the argument out loud, or discussing it with other students or academic staff?

> **Student Tip**
>
> 'If you're reading something that's really hard to understand, don't be afraid to put it to one side for a while. You can come back to it later, so you're not giving up – just giving yourself time to find the information or develop the skills you need to get something out of it. My course uses several texts that were impossible when I first saw them, near the start. Now I'm in my final year and they make a lot more sense – but then I'm a very different student.' **Lisa, Economics undergraduate**

❭ *Go to: Chapter 6 to check/update the* **reading** *section in your Core Development Plan.*

5 Assess the way you record information

You've already had a chance to explore some very relevant attitudes, habits and skills.

❭ *Go to: Chapter 6 to look at the benefits of having good recording techniques.*

Consider the following materials. What sort of note-taking/making techniques would you use if you were reading …

- a list of sources in the back of a textbook in the library?
- a persuasive article about environmental change?
- several online articles about a key topic in your field?
- a detailed scientific report?
- two opposing viewpoints about human rights?
- a book on a complex topic that's related to your work?

Ask yourself

→ How would you describe your current approach to taking/making notes?

Are you always aware of what you're trying to achieve? Can you recognize times when it has been effective, and times when it hasn't? Do you have a range of different recording techniques, or does one size fit all?

6 Develop your note-taking/making skills

Like the *researching* and *reading* parts of the 'gathering' process, *recording* is done for a number of different reasons.

It can be as straightforward as copying a document, or even just keeping hold of it. You might decide to photocopy part or all of a journal article; download and save an online report; or copy out a section of text word for word. You've made choices about what to select, and you'll need to decide next how to store it and for how long, but you haven't engaged in much *thinking* about it – which, in some circumstances, is absolutely fine.

At other times, however, recording has to be about much more than that: taking ownership of the information in order to enhance your understanding, activate your memory, and let you process it further in a variety of ways – logically, analytically, creatively. It can still be note-*taking*, picking out particular words and phrases, but it also needs to encompass note-*making*, constructing something out of the things you read: something more manageable, more memorable, more meaningful.

Notes represent a zone somewhere between the content of your sources and the processes going on in your head, and that can give them real dynamism. They can generate the energy required to drive forward any kind of academic activity.

To improve your note-taking/making, you need to consider ...

Why you're doing it

It could be ...

- to collect bodies of information, for use now or later
- to extract particular details: facts, ideas, points of view
- to understand the information better by simplifying aspects of it (or by discovering more *complexities* in it)
- to let you use it in some way – maybe to compare it with another source, to write about it or to discuss it in a group
- to help you remember it: key points, important themes or overarching ideas.

Knowing what you're trying to achieve means that you can make strong choices about your approach, and be active, ambitious, realistic and reflective as you carry them out.

How to do it efficiently

All forms of recording should be efficient (even if they're also exploratory and creative) but some can be extremely straightforward, simply copying the original material.

If you've decided that all you need to do is 'capture' the information, to use straight away or bring out later, or because you just don't know what you're going to do with it yet, you could:

- **photocopy it** (but consider the cost, especially if it needs to be colour, and check that you have permission)
- **photograph it** (your mobile phone can be an extremely useful recording tool, allowing you to video or audio-record non-text sources, too)
- **borrow it** (and just refer to it when you need it, then send it back – but spare a thought for others in your community who might be waiting for it)
- **mark up the text** (with pencils or pens if you own it; with bookmarks or careful sticky-notes if you don't)
- **copy it by hand** (which is fine for small amounts of text, but quickly becomes unmanageable for anything more).

Other ways to be efficient in your note-taking/making:

- Consider the **layout** of your notes. Depending on what you're trying to achieve, will it be most effective to make one long list of points or several? Within that, will it help to number them, group them or categorize them in some other way? Or would more creative note-making styles actually be more efficient for this kind of information?
- Use **abbreviations**, especially if there are certain long words that keep appearing. Initials, symbols or shortened forms of the original words can save you lots of time – maybe even help you to see connections and patterns. It might be useful to create a 'key' chart to remind yourself what each abbreviation means and put it up where you work.
- **Reduce** the number of words you use – but be careful not to miss important details. Quotations need to be exact, and many concepts are easy to misunderstand if key words are left out. Resist the temptation to use single words as the context is usually vital. Reviewing your notes will help you check they all still make sense, but will that still be the case next month, next year?
- Always record the **sources** of your notes, in enough detail to find your way back to them if necessary (so just writing the author's surname or a book title probably won't be enough). This will be a big help if you need to include citations and references, or even a full bibliography as part of your finished work.
- Think about ways to **connect** notes in different places (and different *sets* of notes) – to help you find them easily and use them cohesively. Colour-coding can be good for this, helping you to spot themes running through lots of different pages. You could put a coloured heading on particular collections of notes (maybe coding all the pages about anatomy red) or use highlighting to link information intended for a specific purpose (green, for example, for things that looked useful for your next essay).

How to make it interactive

Record your thoughts on what you're reading – and your feelings, too.

Engaging with the information helps you to grapple with its meaning and significance, remember it, and take the next steps in your research. You're left with notes that direct you clearly to the important bits and capture the personal processes at work.

- Add notes that are also questions. 'Pope excommunicated Henry/Cranmer – ever done before?'
- Use markings to show your reactions: double underlining for importance, exclamation marks for surprise, even emoji-style faces when you want your notes to reflect your uncertainty, disbelief or delight in what you're reading.
- Make notes about some of your thinking processes as you go. Reading about the pros and cons of wind farms, you could be lining up the two sides of the argument against each other visibly in your notes as you're doing it.
- Mark sequences/connections/similarities/contrasts/comparisons ... circling sections, drawing arrows and using any other strategies that make your notes clear and rich.

How to be creative

Note-taking/making can be creative while you're doing it, *and* help you to be creative with the information later.

The interactive techniques above are a good start. Even colour-coding very straightforward details can help you to see existing patterns and prompt you to explore them in imaginative ways.

Some research lends itself particularly well to creative note-making techniques. If you're examining different perspectives on a single topic, for instance, it can help you to notice similarities and differences and maybe shape your own judgements. When you're trying to unpick complex information, it can strengthen your understanding. With information you're studying for an exam, it can make it a great deal easier to remember.

- Think about the layout of your notes overall. Consider how their positioning on the page could make them more meaningful – to show patterns, different groups of ideas, similarities/differences, or how one thing relates to another.
- Will pictures (even just quick doodles) help with what you're trying to achieve with these notes?
- As you make each new note, think about how it fits in with the ones already there – and show that in a creative way, using colours, symbols, arrows.

How to make it work for *you*

At this level of study, it's important to have a variety of different formats for your notes, to use flexibly depending on the particular work you're doing. You can also combine them to great effect: a logically ordered list of play titles, for example, within a set of creative notes about the big Shakespearean themes, or a precise flow-chart among descriptive notes about an engineering task.

Which activities in *your* studies might benefit from the note-making styles below? Which formats would be effective for gathering the sorts of information you work with – and match the ways *you* need to explore, analyse, innovate, communicate, apply and remember it?

Lists: collecting key points, possibly grouping or ordering them in the process

- Use abbreviations whenever possible.
- Write phrases and short sentences rather than individual words.

- Add numbers if that helps you to organize your ideas.
- Colour-code individual points or mini-lists to reflect any patterns or connections you've seen.

Possible uses: _____

Grids: sorting and categorizing different aspects of the information

- Label the grid squares clearly.
- Use columns and rows to categorize your ideas if appropriate.

Possible uses: _____

Timelines: allowing you to link information to the passing of time in different ways – including planning when you're going to *use* that information (for example, showing the points in a project when you're aiming to try out particular things)

- Draw a vertical or horizontal line, to suit your information – and the way you think about it.
- Label the scale in the best way to show the chronology, and its significance.

Possible uses: _____

Flow-charts: involving clear sequences of ideas or processes

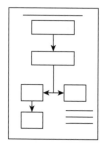

- Draw boxes or circles around separate parts of the pattern.
- Write notes alongside any arrows that need explaining.
- Include background details or further information as required.

Possible uses: _____

Concept maps: exploring how different aspects of the information relate to each other, and what this might mean

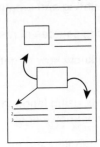

- Show how specific points can be drawn out from a central idea.
- Use arrows or connecting lines to explore and record connections anywhere in the notes.

Possible uses: _____

Creative notes: deepening understanding of themes, connections, problems, possibilities – now, and when you use these notes in the work that comes next

- Use images to represent key ideas.
- Draw arrows, connecting lines and other marks to show patterns of information, emerging themes, and relationships between different elements.
- Include colours to help you explore, organize and remember the information.

Add any other creative touches or techniques that make your notes more effective for you.

Possible uses: _____

> *Go to: **Chapter 7** to see how your environment and your behaviour can be adapted to help you **access**, **record** and start **organizing** the information you need for your studies*

> *Go to: **Chapter 6** to check/update the **note-taking/making** section of your Core Development Plan.*

As this book goes on, you'll be testing out all the note-making ideas here in relation to the key academic tasks you face.

⑩ Ten-point summary

1. Learning is driven by gathering (researching, reading and recording) information – ready to move it forward through your study.

2. Research, reading and note-taking/making are overlapping sets of skills which need to be coordinated to produce the best results.

3. To research well you need to be clear, realistic, efficient, discriminating and creative.

4. Active reading skills are essential, for *selecting* as well as *exploring* sources of research.

5. Careful preparation helps you to 'tune in' to academic texts, and know how to get the most out of them.

6. Higher-level writing is often dense, complex, compact and precise, using language in highly specialized ways and assuming a significant amount of prior knowledge.

7. Questions and predictions boost engagement, strengthen understanding and provide insights into how writers are thinking.

8. Keep testing your comprehension – not expecting to understand everything immediately, but always 'in contact' with the flow of information and ideas.

9. Note-taking/making is an important part of active reading, helping you to collect, understand, remember and develop the information you study.

10. Choose the form of recording that suits the task you're doing – and your own learning preferences – using your notes to provide rich material for every aspect of your work.

▷ Where to next?

Chapter 11 will set you up for success in all the written work involved in your chosen course.

Good on paper

Learning how to write at this level develops a range of key academic and personal skills, helping you to work productively within your subject and allowing your abilities to be assessed.

What?

Writing is another universally important aspect of higher-level study. Like reading, it challenges you in new and difficult ways, but it, too, will accelerate your academic development if you approach it well. You need to understand what's changed at this stage, what each part of the process involves, and how you go about building the skills required to tackle a variety of different writing tasks.

You'll explore some specific types of writing later in the book. This chapter explains the common challenges – and opportunities – to help you begin your course with the confidence to get stuck in actively, committed to developing your skills as you go. You'll see why it can get tough, but you'll also know why it's worth giving it your all.

When?

You develop higher-level writing skills by *doing* higher-level writing – if you engage with it fully and use the process to adapt the way you think and work. You'll have many chances to practise, all the way through your course. The advice in this chapter will help you to start as you mean to go on, but you'll also need to come back to it at times, to check your general direction and to consider specific tasks in the light of these core ideas.

Who?

Writing at this level is intensely personal and extremely public. Your individual abilities are held up to general scrutiny. You're in control of the process ... until you're not. There's a great deal of self-management involved, as well as the ability to engage closely with a whole community.

Your role is a complex one. You'll grapple closely with **evidence** and **ideas**, developing a variety of skills as you shape the material into *your* version of it. Sometimes you'll write about yourself and your experiences, but always you'll need to consider your own values and viewpoints, and know how to manage yourself through what's often a long and testing process.

But in other aspects of your writing you'll be trying to be as *impersonal* as possible, not letting opinions or beliefs, hopes or concerns cloud your judgement. You'll reveal your personal approach only when it helps your readers to evaluate the quality of your ideas.

You need to be acutely aware of who's reading. Feedback is essential, and academic writing is designed with that firmly in mind. As you progress through your course you'll see why the academic community needs you to write in a certain way, and how it can teach you the rules.

 # Why?

Writing like an academic is one of the best ways to learn how to think like one. After hearing and reading about the ideas that matter in your subject, now you get to use them – and find out what you really know and understand as you try to make sense of them on paper and present your work for scrutiny. It's a risky business but, if you go into it ready to learn, you'll show your developing skills in every piece you complete, and grow as a writer every time.

 # How?

To get ready for all the new challenges at this stage of education, it's important to look at your experiences so far. Reflect on the different sorts of writing you've done up to this point, and on your confidence with the key skills required to work at this level.

There's a clear emphasis on preparation in your work, too. Explore the steps in the process leading up to starting your first draft. Find out how to match your **note-making** and **planning** styles to the particular task at hand.

And when you're ready to write, see how to shape and express your ideas so that your work develops your understanding and skill. By meeting some important standards, you can produce writing that also offers something useful to the academic community at large.

 ## Steps to success

1 Reflect on your writing so far

> *Go to: **Chapter 4** to see what you can learn from experience.*

> *Go to: **Chapter 6** to see how **writing** fits into your Core Development Plan.*

There's lots to learn to write well at university, but it's important to remember that you're not starting from scratch. You've had plenty of experience writing for a variety of purposes, and in the process you'll have developed many of the skills you need to do well now.

To see *which* skills, here are ten questions about the writing you've produced in the past, looking for evidence that you've already practised some essential academic techniques.

For each one, write down any examples that come to mind. Think about the different sorts of written work you've done – not just in the subject you're studying now, but in any areas of your education, and in your life outside.

Audience awareness

When have you had to think very carefully about your readers, and adapt your writing accordingly?

_____

Finding your voice

When have you focused on the tone of your writing: for example, to be reassuring, persuasive, formal, clear?

_____

Sampling views

When have you taken information, evidence or opinions from elsewhere and incorporated them in your writing?

_____

Weighing up

When have you used your writing to compare and contrast different viewpoints, findings or ideas?

_____

Quality control

When have you evaluated the strengths and weaknesses of information, perspectives and processes?

_____

Seeing the problems

When have you written honestly about weaknesses or inadequacies in your own work?

_____

Making your case

When have you had to put together a persuasive argument?

_____

Following the plot

When have you had to guide your reader through different ways of looking at something?

_____

Pulling it all together

When have you had to combine ideas to create new perspectives?

_____

Coming to a decision

When have you had to write about something in order to present a clear decision?

_____

Use the examples you've come up with to help you with the next part of the activity. With your past experiences fresh in your mind, consider how you're feeling about some of the essential elements of academic writing. Think about your overall confidence, as well as any particular strengths and weaknesses you can see in your current approach.

Key SKILL: Writing according to specific standards and values

Current CONFIDENCE:

STRENGTHS to draw on, based on ability and experience:

Potential WEAKNESSES to address:

Key SKILL: Writing in an emotionally neutral tone

Current CONFIDENCE:

STRENGTHS to draw on, based on ability and experience:

Potential WEAKNESSES to address:

Key SKILL: Writing about information and ideas from a range of sources, and acknowledging them all clearly and accurately

Current CONFIDENCE:

STRENGTHS to draw on, based on ability and experience:

Potential WEAKNESSES to address:

Key SKILL: Writing about comparisons and contrasts observed within the subject matter, and making the *thinking* involved in this clear

Current CONFIDENCE:

STRENGTHS to draw on, based on ability and experience:

Potential WEAKNESSES to address:

Key SKILL: Writing about judgements on the material that are based on clearly defined criteria

Current CONFIDENCE:

STRENGTHS to draw on, based on ability and experience:

Potential WEAKNESSES to address:

Key SKILL: Writing about the complexities and difficulties in the question – and any problems encountered when trying to answer it

Current CONFIDENCE:

STRENGTHS to draw on, based on ability and experience:

Potential WEAKNESSES to address:

Key SKILL: Writing a carefully structured argument

Current CONFIDENCE:

STRENGTHS to draw on, based on ability and experience:

Potential WEAKNESSES to address:

Key SKILL: Writing in a *discursive* style: guiding the reader through different points of view

Current CONFIDENCE:

STRENGTHS to draw on, based on ability and experience:

Potential WEAKNESSES to address:

Key SKILL: Writing to explore *synthesis*: to see if several elements under consideration can be combined to produce new possibilities

Current CONFIDENCE:

STRENGTHS to draw on, based on ability and experience:

Potential WEAKNESSES to address:

> **Key SKILL: Writing about decisions you've reached on the subject matter in question, and the processes you followed to get there**
>
> Current CONFIDENCE:
>
> STRENGTHS to draw on, based on ability and experience:
>
> Potential WEAKNESSES to address:

This activity should prove that you've got some very strong foundations to build on, however unfamiliar some of the new work may seem. As you find out more about how academic writing works, and especially as you start *doing* it within your course, use your reflections here to help shape your approach. Maximize the skills you feel confident with already, and look for ways to strengthen the weaker ones. Keep referring back to your previous experiences – so that you develop your higher-level skills from the strong position you've already reached.

2 Get to grips with higher-level writing

To write well at this level you need to be very clear about what academic writing does, and how it does it.

In our 'real' lives we write for many reasons, often intertwined in the same piece of work: to record, reflect, explain, describe, engage, persuade ... The emphasis changes, the balance shifts. The motives are not always spelled out. Our words can work on different levels: what we *say* may not be what we *mean*. Our readers are often required to decide for themselves how to read our work, and to make their own judgements about what it means for them. Responses are complex and personal and can vary wildly.

In academic writing, all the reasons above are still relevant – but they're very much out in the open, often written about directly. Readers are still presented with information to evaluate, but they're provided with everything they need to do it to agreed standards and established rules. They should be able to explain their responses clearly, based firmly on the content of the writing, the way it's delivered, and the working methods it reveals.

Readers of academic writing know what to expect, and the writing helps them to decide if they've got it or not. The style may be impersonal, but the judgements made are very much about the *writer* – about ...

- their capacity to carry out useful research
- their understanding of the information
- their ability to present a convincing argument.

So, these are the key things you'll be judged on now. You'll need to focus on some guiding principles, which will be visible in both *what* you write and *how* you write it – particularly:

- focus
- precision
- clarity
- accuracy.

All these are reflected in the rules you need to follow – when you're acknowledging your sources, for example, or presenting your finished work. If you can meet those standards, show off strong research methods and careful content choices – and do it all in a writing style that matches the principles above – readers who are interested in your subject matter will be engaged by your words. They'll know how to read what you've given them, and they'll want to. Whatever their own judgements, they'll see the benefits in reading it, for themselves and their own work.

 ## Ask yourself

→ What are the benefits of academic writing for you?

You've got a lot to gain here (however risky writing can feel at times). Your success will depend a great deal on your commitment and motivation. So, think about the value you place on:

- increasing your knowledge, by researching and writing about a particular topic
- deepening your understanding as you evaluate evidence and organize your thinking
- achieving positive feedback and succeeding in assessment tasks
- playing a role in your academic community, using your writing to inspire debate and contribute to the development of your subject
- learning ways to cope with emotionally testing projects
- building your literacy skills to help with other writing in the future
- developing highly transferable thinking skills, including analysis, synthesis and accurate self-reflection.

> **Go to: Chapter 6** *to see whether you need to update the benefits table as a result.*

All these rewards and more are on offer when you stretch your writing skills through study. Try to remember them when the going gets tough.

Good study involves getting the most out of a wide range of writing challenges. Each type of task has its own specific purposes and particular rules, but they're all based on the core principles that give academic writing its power.

Some assignments have a very **practical** purpose, often connected to the practice of your discipline or to relevant professional work – such as technical reports, problem analyses or work placement diaries. They're likely to have a particularly tight format, to focus on details, and to emphasize the things *you* observed, experienced or worked out, rather than information and ideas gathered from elsewhere. Some language rules can be relaxed, and there may be no need for referencing, but the core standards of academic writing still have to be met: the creation of precise, accurate, clear and useful work that's aware of its own purpose and can be evaluated against agreed criteria.

Other assignments are more **conceptual**, exploring information to make an argument about what it means – with more general implications. In essays, research reports, seminar papers, exam answers and long projects such as dissertations and theses, you use writing to strengthen your own thinking by analysing existing viewpoints, perhaps adding evidence of your own, and offering your readers new ways of understanding and applying it.

Here are some of the powerful things you can *do* with academic writing – depending on the subject you're studying and the task in question:

Personal reflection

If this is appropriate for your work, you'll need to think carefully about how *relevant* your experiences are, to what extent they're *typical,* and whether there are useful *generalizations* to be made. You'll have to consider what quality of evidence they provide – in conjunction with any existing research or your own findings – and be open to different interpretations, aware of the complexities of using personal experience.

Description

This takes many forms in higher-level work, and plays a part in most writing tasks. It could involve describing:

- a scientific or technical method
- a situation, highlighting important background details
- the way something works, either physically or theoretically
- the ideas behind a particular point of view
- your own processes of thinking or working.

Relevance is vital: knowing what's important to include, and what's unnecessary, confusing or even misleading.

Argument-based analysis

This is all about precision, analysing the details behind events, processes and ideas, by testing the evidence. It's highlighted in work that presents a clear case for something (the word 'essay' actually comes from the Latin word for a legal case, *exagium*). But it also represents a way of thinking and writing that strongly influences higher-level study in general. There's a confidence to the tone that comes from analysing a range of evidence, examining possible counter-arguments, acknowledging complexities and risks – but still staking out a clear position, in a way that can be judged by others.

Evaluative analysis

As well as confidence, *balance* is a key idea in academic writing. Even when you're not asked to do so explicitly, in a variety of tasks you'll be making evaluative judgements based on comparing and contrasting, on weighing things up. You'll need to measure the strength of ideas and evidence against general academic standards and the particular demands of your chosen subject. It's this kind of thinking that makes *synthesis* possible – the opportunity to take the most successful or useful elements from different places and combine them into something new: a new interpretation maybe, a new product or a new way of doing things.

Studying successfully at this stage involves a high level of awareness about which of these elements you're using, in isolation and in combination, and why. Academic writing is purposeful and controlled, and so much of your development relies on your ability to use language as a very powerful tool, energizing and challenging your own thinking and then communicating your ideas in the strongest possible ways – always with *focus*, *precision*, *clarity* and *accuracy* firmly in mind.

The style of your writing has to be **formal** (almost always; assume it's formal unless you're told otherwise), using standard English as accurately as you can:

- Avoid contractions like 'There's' and 'didn't'.
- Avoid conversational turns of phrase: 'a round-about sort of way', 'first things first'.
- Commonly abbreviated words are usually written in full: 'especially', not 'esp.'; 'for example' rather than 'e.g.'; 'a quotation' instead of 'a quote'.
- Acronyms (like NASA) and initialisms (like BBC) need to be explained in full before they can be reused later as abbreviations: ' ... evidence from the Central Intelligence Agency (CIA). However, even the CIA could not prove ...'
- If things happened in the past, write them in the past tense – not drifting into the present tense in the way you might do in conversation: 'After that the equipment suddenly stops'; 'So the judge decides to rule in their favour'.

The tone of academic writing is **objective** and **neutral**, leaning towards formality even in reflective work:

- Use 'I obtained' instead of 'I got'; 'All the other participants' rather than 'We all'.
- In most cases, 'I', 'me' and 'my' (and 'you' and 'your') are rejected altogether in favour of an impersonal style and the passive voice.
- 'I included this point' becomes 'This point has been included'; 'You have to consider the opposite position too ... ' is rewritten as 'The opposite position must also be considered'.

Your language needs to be **precise**, particularly when you're dealing with abstract ideas.

- Be careful with your use of vocabulary. Words such as 'big' and 'beautiful' are open to interpretation, and there are so many more specific terms to choose from.
- Avoid value judgements. What do you mean that something is 'better'? Who is an 'expert'?
- Take care with pronouns. When you write 'it' or 'he' or 'they', is the person or thing you're referring to absolutely clear?

Aim for **clarity** and **definition** in the way you organize your words, creating sharply structured sentences and paragraphs to explain what you mean exactly.

- Academic writing makes powerful use of 'signposting' words and phrases at the start of paragraphs: 'In a similar way', 'Conversely', 'Following that'.
- Your reader is also guided by key words within sentences: 'Although this is statistically significant, there are *also* reasons to ...'; 'Despite first aligning himself with the King, he *later* ...'.

Be **concise**. Remove unnecessary words and phrases.

- 'Gave the explanation' can be shortened to 'explained'; 'the year 1972' can be just '1972'.

You're writing for an audience that's acutely aware of the power of language – to record accurately, evaluate information, deepen understanding, inspire debate, construct meaning; *and*, if it's not done well, to confuse, mislead, falsify … Your readers are highly alert to anything that threatens clarity, accuracy and usefulness, but they're also ready to be engaged with your ideas and gripped by the dynamism and intellectual spark of your writing.

> ### Student Tip
>
> 'Some of the best advice I ever got from a tutor was to write some short sentences once in a while. I think I'd got so caught up in being formal, signposting my reasoning and backing up everything I wrote, that I hadn't noticed how hard my writing was to read. A short sentence is often the best way to emphasize a key point or to direct the flow of the argument (especially when you're trying to work it out yourself). I often get comments now about how clear my ideas are.' **Jenny, university undergraduate**

 ❯ *Go to: Chapter 6 to check/update the sections on **general literacy** and **meeting academic standards** in your Core Development Plan.*

3 Prepare to write

A lot goes into constructing high-quality written work. The success of your finished, public document relies on a development process that no one else is likely to see.

Here's an outline of the key preparation steps:

Define the task

What sort of work are you being asked to do?

- Look carefully at the exact wording of essay questions or presentation briefs. Are you being told specifically to 'reflect on', 'describe', 'analyse', 'compare', 'evaluate', 'argue' …? Or maybe the approach to take is left to you to decipher: 'To what extent …?'; 'Find evidence of …'; 'Do you agree …?'
- It's a good idea to circle or underline key words and phrases in the instructions, which will help you to understand and remember the different types of work you'll need to do for the task.

Clarify the scope

Where are the limits to what you look at, and how you do it?

- Start with the overall topic (the Second World War, for example), and then look for instructions that narrow the focus (the Normandy Landings). And then: are you being directed to particular dates (just 6 June 1944 perhaps, or maybe all the months of planning, too) or certain places, people, perspectives ...?
- What are you told about your working methods? Should you restrict yourself to a particular viewpoint, even a single source, or are you expected to explore the evidence more widely? In some subjects there are many different ways to research, and you'll need to know what you are and aren't required to do – to get full value from the task, and to fulfil the assessment criteria.

Academic Advice

'It can be useful to distinguish between "inductive tasks" (where you're trying to put some order into information you've collected) and "deductive" ones (where you have a theory and need to find evidence to support or disprove it). I talk to students about defining their role in the task, so that they see where to direct their energy.' **Glenn, university History tutor**

Manage the project

How are you going to get everything done, and done well?

When you have a clear sense of the job you've been given – and after checking the deadline carefully – you can create a *task plan* for getting it done.

❯ *Go to: Chapter 8 to see how this kind of specific plan fits into your overall time-management approach.*

Here's an example planning format. It's up to you to write in:

- instructions you've been given, with the key words (and what you understand them to mean) made absolutely clear
- timings to show how long you want to spend on each stage of the production process
- other useful details, like where you'll work, who you're working *with*, and any materials or resources you'll need.

Be careful to allow enough time for each aspect of the task, but also mark out the points when you'll have to move on to be sure of getting everything done by the deadline.

Coordinate this plan with what's already in your diary, and bear in mind your other commitments and priorities.

ASSIGNMENT: STAGES IN THE WRITING PROCESS	TIMINGS/WORKING NOTES
Generating initial ideas	
Gathering information	
Planning	
Doing extra research	
Writing the first draft	
Thinking and reflecting	
Reviewing and rewriting	
Editing and presenting	

Start thinking

What do you already know, and where might your writing take you from here?

Make some rough notes about your initial ideas. Sketch out any existing knowledge you'll be able to draw on, and think about the directions you'll want your research to take. Within the detail and scope of the task, what creative ideas do you have for lines of enquiry or methods of investigation? What interests you here? What's likely to be the most challenging part to answer – and what kind of approach would benefit you and your studies the most?

Gather your information

What can you learn from research?

With a clear idea about the kinds of information you need to explore, you can now use your **researching**, **reading** and **recording** skills to the full.

> *Go to: Chapter 10 for a full guide to this crucial information-gathering stage.*

At this higher level, you're working on your writing *as* you gather your research materials, developing the understanding and original thinking that will eventually take shape on the page.

Plan your writing

What kind of map will you need?

Academic writing relies on clear planning. Your ideas can still be refined as you communicate them, but the majority of your researching and thinking needs to have been done before the actual writing stage begins.

If you get the note-making phase right, your writing plan should emerge naturally. What it looks like depends on the sort of task you're doing, and choosing an appropriate style (or styles) is vital because your planning helps to shape your thinking as you prepare to write.

- A simple **list** style might be the most useful way to plan writing designed to collect personal reflections.
- For writing that needs to be structured chronologically, in time order, the **list, flow-chart** or **timeline** approaches would probably be the most useful formats.
- If your work involves classifying information, the **concept map** style could be useful, reflecting the way a larger set can be divided into specific smaller groups.
- The same style should work well if you're writing about a single main theme as it applies to various examples or situations – or you might find it easier to organize your thoughts with a **grid** or a set of **mini lists**.
- Some writing plans need to be divided into clear stages – for example, work describing the short-, medium- and long-term effects of something – and a **timeline** or **flow-chart** approach to planning might be most appropriate here.
- Others would work better if they were based on the **creative** model, allowing you to draw out themes and interconnections (which you could also number, to show the order in which you wanted to tackle them in your writing).
- In analytic work, **grid-style** planning is well matched to writing about comparisons and contrasts; **flow-charts** are often used to structure written arguments; and the more **creative** styles can be helpful when you're planning work designed to be discursive, mapping a 'guided-tour' of the material.

Student Tip

'You definitely need to plan your writing. It's tempting not to, sometimes, especially if the deadline's approaching and you haven't started drafting yet. But writing without a proper plan is horrible – you're trying to plan and write at the same time, and it just doesn't work in my experience. With a good plan, the writing stage can actually be quite enjoyable. It's certainly a lot quicker.' **Aliyah, Psychology undergraduate**

Add to your research

What else will you need to write well?

Planning your writing often highlights gaps that need filling, or sketchy areas that could do with colouring in a bit more before you get to the drafting stage. If you allow a little time for this in your project schedule, you can do some targeted research, get help with anything that's turned out to be problematic, and fine-tune your plan. You can also use any teaching during this time to gather extra information and insights.

 # Ask yourself

→ How can you make your writing plan efficient and effective?

Think about the simplest ways for you to record details in your planning – like page numbers for quotations, diagrams to refer to, or links with other documents. Colour-coding might help. Abbreviations will save space on paper, and let you link to information you've stored elsewhere, so that you don't have to cram your plan with duplicated details. You'll need it to show you what to write and when, but it certainly doesn't need to hold all the content itself.

4 Write – and rewrite

However well you've planned it, getting started on your writing can still be a hurdle to overcome. It's tempting to just *keep* researching and planning, to put off the dreaded moment when you have to find out what you really know as you try to write it down.

But trust that your plan will guide you through this next stage. Remember that you've been 'doing' key aspects of the writing ever since you were first given the task – and then all the way through your researching, reading and note-making. Now you just need to bring it all together.

> **Go to: Chapter 9** *for advice on getting started on a task, then working well until it's done.*

Write the first draft

Don't worry about tidiness, conciseness, fine details ... Just write, using your plan to guide you, following the map to know what goes where.

If you can't find exactly the right words for something, just write *anything* that shows what you're trying to say.

If you realize you're missing a detail, put a line of dots and fill it in later. Focus on getting down everything that's in your plan, even if you feel you're 'overwriting' or duplicating points that could be made in a much simpler way.

Everything will be refined at the editing stage. Writing and editing are different processes. If you try to do them both at once, it's likely to take you a *very* long time to complete a draft, and you'll find it hard to get your thinking and writing to flow.

Ask yourself

→ Should you go digital or not?

Think carefully about whether drafting a particular task, or part of it, would work better on paper or on a computer. See which approach best supports the flow of your thinking and writing.

For most pieces of work, your draft will include:

The introduction: this outlines the task and what you understand it to involve. You'll probably say how you're going to tackle it, point out any significant factors affecting your choices of content or working methods, and alert your audience to any complexities they'll need to be aware of.

The main body of the text: this goes into more detail about the context, sets up lines of analysis and reasoning, and then follows them, outlining the information, evidence and ideas you've collected, and explaining the analysis you've done. Depending on the approach you're taking, you'll present your reflections, descriptions, analyses and evaluations in a clear and organized way. You'll show that your work is useful because you've considered everything you should, dealing with any potential issues beforehand or along the way.

The conclusion: this usually involves looping back to the original question to remind your reader what you set out to do; then a brief summary of what you did; and, finally, a statement of your views now.

> ## Student Tip
>
> 'I physically tick off each point on my plan as I go – which helps me to know I'm getting somewhere, and lets me check I'm using all the material I've got, at least in the first draft. I might take it out after that, but I know that the first draft is a full picture of what I've done – I just have to streamline it then for other people to read.' **Abi, English Literature undergraduate**

Get some distance

Try to create some space in the writing process when you can pause, think and see what your work looks like when you step back from it a little.

It's another reason why good time-management is so important. If you can finish your first draft a few days before the deadline, you've got time to see what other ideas occur to you before you do the final version. Valuable information can come from teaching, further reading (including in different subjects) and conversations with friends. Your subconscious mind will be mulling over any points that aren't quite secure.

And when you come back to your writing, you'll be able to approach it much more like a reader than the person who put it all together, setting you up perfectly to …

Review and rewrite

This is where your 'sense of audience' is really put to the test. You need to check that what you've written so far has the right tone, takes an appropriate approach, and uses language in the way your readers expect. Make sure that the progression of ideas is clear and that you're getting your points across concisely and with precision.

There are different ways of turning your initial draft into a piece of high-quality finished work. See what feels right for you: whether you now start again, using your first draft as a very detailed guide for the finished version; or whether you work *on* it, to shape it into its final form. A lot depends on whether you've drafted on paper or done it digitally. However, even if you've used a computer from the start, you might still find that writing the whole thing again gets you the best results.

Spend some time looking back at the title and instructions to remind yourself exactly what you set out to do. Check that your introduction reflects that – and then work through the rest of your writing, holding it up to all the academic principles you've explored in this part of the book.

Edit and present

This final step can make a great deal of difference to the assessment feedback or grade you receive, and to the value of the whole process for you.

- Fine-tune the structure, paying particular attention to the signposting words within sentences and between paragraphs. Reading your work aloud can help you hear any breaks in the logic or uncomfortable shifts between ideas.
- Check and correct any issues with spellings or grammar. If you're working on screen, as well as using the built-in editing tools, you might find that printing your writing and checking it on paper helps you to spot more corrections and improvements. Be aware of the limitations of checking software – especially when a word is spelled correctly, but is the wrong word for the sentence you're writing.
- Fine-tune any specific academic features you need to include, like quotations, references and citations, and put together a bibliography if necessary.

> ❯ **Go to: Chapter 16** *to see why and how these need to be included in different types of written work.*

- Ensure that the presentation of your work matches any requirements set. If you're not told about them specifically, find out yourself. Do you need a title page? What administrative information do you have to include? What's the right font, size, spacing ...?

> ❯ **Go to: Chapter 16** *to learn more about how to present your finished work – particularly larger-scale assignments and projects.*

It can seem pedantic and overly time-consuming, but this focus on detail is integral to your study.

- Learning how to work like this is vital for developing precision *thinking*.
- It ensures the accuracy and reliability of the knowledge you construct, so that the effort you put in delivers all the developmental benefits it should.

- It allows you to present credible material to your learning community, so that they can judge it, help you to keep improving, and include you and your work in the wider academic conversation.

 ❭ *Go to: Chapter 6 to check/update the **writing** section of your Core Development Plan.*

⑩ Ten-point summary

1. Academic writing is an intense personal challenge with a very public purpose.

2. Writing at this level helps you to test and develop your understanding, working with other people's ideas as you establish your own.

3. Assessing your previous experience and current confidence levels helps you to understand the personal skills development required.

4. The guiding principles of academic writing are focus, precision, clarity and accuracy.

5. Some writing tasks are practically or professionally oriented, and others require a more complex mix of academic approaches.

6. The key themes in academic writing are reflection, description, analysis, argument and evaluation.

7. Higher-level writing is usually formal, objective and impersonal in tone, using standard English accurately, and communicating as concisely and clearly as possible.

8. Preparation is essential, involving understanding the purpose and scope of the task, carefully managing your time, and carrying out all the thinking, researching and planning required.

9. Good note-making and planning techniques help your thought processes to flow into the writing stage.

10. Drafting, reflecting, redrafting and careful editing allow you to present written work of high quality and value – for yourself and your readers.

▷ Where to next?

Chapter 12 will get you ready for all the assessments you're likely to face as you move forward in your studies.

Testing times

Building memory and learning strategies into your study helps you to do better in assessments, and strengthens key academic and personal skills.

 ## What?

Assessment is a vital element of learning at this level – not just to get the grades you need, but to focus your efforts, enrich your thinking, and accelerate all aspects of your development.

From the very start of your course you need to be ready with a new approach to testing: still training yourself to show off what you can do, but now integrating your preparations into your study as a whole. The sort of learning that matters has to be woven into the work you're doing every day, not just left to the weeks or days (or night) before an exam.

Some of the assessments you face will be very clear – exams, practicals, graded assignments, coursework projects. But some are less explicit – because you're being assessed all the time, by everyone who sees your work – when they evaluate your ability to participate in classes or group tasks, or when they judge the quality of the written work you hand in. And even if those observations don't lead to specific feedback, scores or grades, they can still affect you in other ways: in the impact they have on your feelings; the way other students and staff respond to you afterwards; or the academic opportunities you receive (or don't) as a result.

This chapter is about working *with* assessments throughout your course. Treat them in the right way and they'll help you to see what's important in your subject, and push you to develop all the right skills – including the confidence to do *anything* well under pressure.

 ## When?

If you get to grips with these techniques early, you can weave them into every aspect of your studies. The lectures you attend, books you read, notes you make, essays you write ... they can all be done with assessment in mind. You'll *do* them better at the time, and be well prepared to be tested on them when *that* time comes.

 ## Who?

Preparing to be tested should be anything but a solitary experience, however you've done it in the past. Yes, it comes down to a test of you, and there are times when you'll be doing intense individual work to get ready. But at this stage a great deal of the work has to happen among everything else you're doing, integrated into the teaching and learning activities you do every day – in collaboration with all the other students and staff. Your family and friends are important too, to help with learning and practising, and for extra practical support when the pressure is on.

 # Why?

With a strong approach you can use assessments to sharpen your thinking and working practices and to help you develop robust knowledge, understanding and skill. Incorporating **memory strategies** into everything you do you makes your learning richer, reduces the stress when specific assessments come around, and develops skills that benefit you in every area of your life. You enjoy your course more, do better when you're tested, and your studies set you up for successful lifelong learning.

 # How?

Start by seeing why assessment needs to be different at this stage of education – and how some of your attitudes to study might have to change as a result. Analysing your current approach will highlight key areas to work on during your course.

Learn strategies for remembering the information you **read**. Make your **notes** more memorable – and more useful. Use all the **writing** you do to strengthen your knowledge and sharpen your recall.

Then see how to organize all the work you do into a **learning map**, helping you to remember it, and to use it efficiently and creatively.

By rethinking revision, you'll discover how to keep your memory strong throughout your course, not just in the run-up to exams.

Finally, learn how to use your learning journal to get better at being assessed, and see why **reflecting** is such a powerful way to boost **remembering**.

 # Steps to success

1 Maximize memory

Don't be fooled by what some books say: memory is *really* important in higher-level study.

The demands on your memory maybe aren't as obvious as they were in the past. You're unlikely to be asked to recall specific pieces of information now, and exams are more dependent on how you choose to respond to questions, rather than whether or not you can remember particular facts. The emphasis is on understanding and application.

But that means you need stronger abilities to learn and remember than ever. Your success depends on being able to retrieve stored information quickly and accurately, then using it flexibly and effectively, even under pressure. Last-minute revision just won't work any more. Learning needs to be so good now that it has to be built up throughout your course, incorporated into everything you do – so that you go into exams with deep knowledge and well-practised understanding, and real confidence in your memory to let you show off your abilities to the full.

You'll still need to prepare for exams. Just don't think about it as 'revision'. That suggests such a weak, repetitive, 'looking again' approach that doesn't even come close to what's necessary, and what's possible.

❯ *Go to: Chapter 5 to see how assessment changes when you step up to higher-level learning.*

Academic Advice

'Memory retrieval becomes particularly important at university. Undergraduates tend to focus on memorizing information for exams, because that's what's emphasized at school and college level. But here, if you're studying well, everything you do is storing the material. What you need to practise is retrieving it and using it well; to show your understanding – and apply it. Exams put you under pressure to test out whether you can do it quickly and independently. You'll have plenty of memories by the time you get there. But can you get to the right ones, and use them accurately and creatively? That's the real test.' **Ray, PhD student and tutor**

2 Analyse your approach

How well do your strategies for learning and remembering prepare you to be tested? By this point in your education you should have plenty of examples to refer to, even though it can be painful sometimes to go back over experiences of tests and exams. But it's particularly important here to use the past to help you do things better in the future.

❯ *Go to: Chapter 4 to see what you can learn from the assessments you've faced so far.*

Here are 13 of the most important steps to developing – and demonstrating – robust subject strength and flexible thinking and learning skills. Consider each one in turn, using ticks, crosses and question marks to reflect your current levels of experience, confidence and success.

Using strategies to help you remember what you've read

Experienced? ☐ Confident? ☐ Successful? ☐

Designing your notes so that they're easier to remember

Experienced? ☐ Confident? ☐ Successful? ☐

Doing something purposeful with your notes to boost long-term memory

Experienced? ☐ Confident? ☐ Successful? ☐

Rereading notes to keep them fresh in your mind

Experienced? ☐ Confident? ☐ Successful? ☐

Creating summary versions of complex notes

Experienced? ☐ Confident? ☐ Successful? ☐

Exploring extra parts of a topic, even if you don't end up writing about them

Experienced? ☐ Confident? ☐ Successful? ☐

Strengthening your recall throughout your studies (rather than just for assessments)

Experienced? ☐ Confident? ☐ Successful? ☐

Employing different memory strategies when preparing for different types of assessment

Experienced? ☐ Confident? ☐ Successful? ☐

Remembering which aspects of your studies an exam question is referring to

Experienced? ☐ Confident? ☐ Successful? ☐

Having techniques for accessing your understanding about a subject during an exam

Experienced? ☐ Confident? ☐ Successful? ☐

Knowing how to recall specific details during tests

Experienced? ☐ Confident? ☐ Successful? ☐

Constructing answers by exploring your stored knowledge creatively

Experienced? ☐ Confident? ☐ Successful? ☐

Integrating the learning required for assessments into your ongoing study

Experienced? ☐ Confident? ☐ Successful? ☐

You don't have to change anything that's working well for you. Many of the learning techniques you've developed over the years will be highly effective in your new course, and others can easily be adapted to suit next-level thinking and working. But it also makes no sense sticking with strategies that haven't even paid off in the exams you've done so far, when higher-level learning demands so much more.

Your new course is a valuable opportunity to develop the way you *think* about assessments and to build a new kind of confidence in how you learn, remember and demonstrate your abilities. Each of the 13 points you've just considered can be built into your practice as you work within your course, helping you to get the most out of assessments when they come, but also improving the quality of every bit of study you do.

It's no coincidence that exam dreams (usually nightmares) are a universal phenomenon. So much of how you feel about yourself comes down to how well you can face up to tests of knowledge, understanding, memory and self-management *under pressure.* Life throws those sorts of tests at us all the time. Some people learn to cope with them much better than others. It's one of the main reasons why higher-level studying can be transformational, if you use it to build your confidence for every kind of challenge you face.

Higher-level assessments don't just check that you've got to a particular level of development. They also help you get there.

 Note To Self

Every module in your course is likely to have a set of learning outcomes: what you need to know and be able to do by the end. They may even be explained under different headings, like 'Knowledge and Understanding' and 'Practical Skills'. As soon as you can, take a very close look at the ones that apply to the next part of your course.

Any assessment tasks you're set will be focused squarely on these outcomes, so use them to guide your study. As well as highlighting the specific information to cover and the key skills to learn, they're also likely to give you plenty of clues about the sort of approach you'll need to take. Look out for words like 'understand', 'perform', 'calculate' and 'describe', and consider what they tell you about *how* you'll be developing your abilities in this part of the course.

> *Go to: Chapter 7 for ideas about adapting your **environment** and **behaviour** to improve your memory.*

3 Remember what you read

Reflecting on the first question above, about reading and remembering, did any particular strategies come to mind?

Reading is likely to be the main way you access information during your course. Its effectiveness will depend a lot on how well you make notes, and then use them in your learning (which is explored in Step 4 below). But the quality of the reading that comes before that is just as important, allowing you to find and extract interesting and relevant material to learn.

> *Go to: Chapter 10 to learn about **active reading** in detail.*

Ask yourself

→ What goes on in your head when you're reading?

Think about it now, as you read. What's happening in your brain to turn the marks on the page into something useful – even after you've closed the book?

Lots of different memory processes are at play when you read. While you're operating all the complex meaning-making processes of the language you've learned, including accessing a vast vocabulary store, new ideas are being turned into words for you to add to your knowledge. Your brain searches for ways to connect the emerging information to things you already know, which often requires ideas to be just 'held' until something appears to explain them. At this higher level, texts are rich and complex, stretching your ability to process language and grasp the ideas that emerge.

Consider a sentence like this:

Complementarity is a term from psychology that describes the relation between two opposite states or principles that together exhaust the possibilities.

The first word is the most difficult – you might need to split it into syllables to pronounce it. And then you have to hold on to it throughout the rest of the sentence (which isn't even that long, compared with many you'll read, including *this* one), recalling what each of the other technical words mean, but also constructing the meaning here from the way they're used together, and not letting any of them slip out of your grasp until you've got to the end. Your brain will be looking for hooks into existing knowledge, and trying to find the best way to understand this new concept from the way it's explained, in order to remember it. It's a lot to handle at once.

'Working' memory is very important in reading. It's the shortest of short-term memory systems, responsible for holding on to the information you receive through your senses for long enough for something else to happen. And if that allows them to be transferred to longer-term storage, they've got a chance of being remembered in future. If it doesn't, they're probably gone for ever. They won't even make it into your notes.

It's easy to overload working memory. Distractions can be disastrous, and other processes need to be working well to change fast-fading information into a more lasting form.

You've got a *lot* to read now. Good study relies on absorbing information as you read it, rather than constantly rereading in order to take it in. Sometimes you won't even have that luxury, for example when you're reading new information in seminars or classes and having to respond to it straight away. And when you do get to write something down, the best notes you can make record what you understand and remember, summarized in your own words. It's just not good enough any more to read without remembering the main points.

Focus. Read with a purpose. Before you start, and when you stop, think about where this set of information fits into your previous learning and current studies. Focus on particular points that connect with ideas you're interested in or know more about.

Pace yourself. Each new text requires you to work out the most effective reading speed to use, based on:

- the complexity of the language
- the difficulty of the ideas
- your existing understanding
- the importance of the information.

With your purpose clear, read the first few lines very quickly, then again very slowly, and then again at the speed that feels right for your comprehension and memory. Start reading the rest of the material like this, but be ready to change pace at any time if you're not getting what you need.

Talk to yourself. Pause regularly and silently summarize what you've just read. It could be at the end of a section, a complex paragraph, or even a single sentence if you need a moment to digest its content. You check that you've taken in the information, and *understand* it (or need to look again), and you also strengthen the memory through the process of remembering it.

You've even got this reflective moment to trigger your recall, which is a crucial part of how memory works – remembering the last time you remembered something. Learning is about so much more than repetition, but repetition is still a key driver of memory.

React and respond. Keep asking yourself what you think and feel about the things you're reading. Humans seem to be hard-wired to remember emotions, which doesn't always do us favours in life – but it can definitely be turned to your advantage when you're studying. Look out for things that surprise you, reassure you, make you anxious, make you smile ... Accentuate these feelings as you read. You can use them later to re-engage your memory with the information. Meanwhile, being sensitive to the impact of the ideas on you also helps you to spot the important bits.

 ❭ *Go to: Chapter 6 to check/update the* **reading** *section in your Core Development Plan.*

4 Make memorable notes

Whatever style of notes you've chosen to match the work you're doing, they need to be memorable. It's one of the most powerful ways to make everything you do prepare you for assessments. It also boosts your understanding and makes the learning so much more efficient, creative and worthwhile.

 *Lists* **already help you to remember by ...**

- encouraging you to be clear and concise
- letting you prioritize pieces of information.

They're even *more* memorable when you ...

- highlight key points
- add personal reactions to the information.

 *Grids* **already help you to remember by ...**

- organizing and categorizing ideas
- arranging information spatially.

They're even *more* memorable when you ...

- add images to label each space
- use colours to emphasize the categories.

 *Timelines* **already help you to remember by ...**

- presenting the information visually
- ordering ideas in a meaningful way.

They're even *more* memorable when you ...

- use images as well as words
- highlight particularly important points.

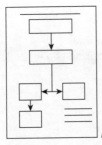 *Flow-charts* **already help you to remember by ...**

- showing you how the information works
- using a clear and interesting visual layout.

They're even *more* memorable when you ...

- use symbols to highlight key parts of the diagram
- add notes to emphasize *why* it fits together like this.

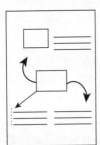 *Concept maps* **already help you to remember by ...**

- improving your understanding
- using the visual layout to emphasize the meaning.

They're even *more* memorable when you ...

- emphasize the most important aspects of the information
- back up written notes with images.

 *Creative notes* **already help you to remember by ...**

- giving you freedom to create a design that matches the information
- encouraging you to show what you think and feel about the ideas.

They're even *more* memorable when you ...

- represent key details in multiple ways
- add features based on how *your* memory works best.

When you've made a set of notes, *do* something with them. It immediately takes the learning process up a notch.

Immediately ... choose a short task that forces you to use the information you've collected in some way.

You could:

- write a set of quiz questions based on them
- record yourself reading them aloud
- make an entry in your learning journal about what you got out of this activity
- see how much of the information you can retell in one minute.

After a while ... think about how you're going to store your notes to make them easily accessible.

That could be as simple as putting them in the right folder for now, either on paper or in a computer file, where you'll be able to find them quickly. But you might decide to create another version of them to store away, too – a strategy that can be hugely valuable when you've got a large amount of information to manage.

Once again, you choose the most appropriate style for your notes (which might or might not be the same as you used the first time around) and you create a simplified version that maps out the key points. It's like a guide to the more detailed document: less information, clearer structure, easier to understand and remember.

If you look at this new version, it should remind you of details in the version 'behind' it – and the process of making it boosts your understanding and memory, too.

Your simplified note-sheet becomes a valuable part of the overall 'map' of your learning – and this is explained in Step 6 below.

And later ... take another look.

In the past you might have made notes, used them, and then not come back to them until the exams came around, if at all. Now, it's very important to keep refreshing your memory as you develop rich, layered knowledge of your subject. Step 7 will show you a strategic way of returning to these notes and continually strengthening your memory.

 ❯ *Go to: Chapter 6 to update the **note-taking/making** section of your Core Development Plan.*

5 Write to remember

Learning at this level is all about integrating different aspects of study, so that everything benefits everything else. You want all of it to pay off in your assessments, and all of it to contribute to the long-term value of your work.

But it can be tempting to forget that, when you've finished a piece of written work and you're very happy to put it behind you and move on. However, some simple strategies can help you make the most of the effort you've put in, giving you continuing access to the knowledge you've gained.

Make the finished piece of writing part of your ever-growing collection of knowledge:

- You could make a quick summary version of the main points, laying them out visually in a way that would jog your memory later.
- Or simply highlight them in the text itself, using colours, arrows, pictures ... whatever helps to make the key information clear and memorable.
- Point out where your killer points appeared. Where was the most positive news? Which bits took the longest to grapple with when you were writing?

It's time well spent. This quick activity helps to embed the learning in your memory, and you're also producing a version that's more usable in the rest of your work (and very helpful when you come to refresh your recall before an exam).

If you get a choice of question to answer for an assignment, spend a few minutes thinking about the options you *didn't* go for. Do your real work first, but then write a quick plan for some or all of the other titles. Construct them in a clear, memorable, eye-catching form, like all the other materials you create, to enrich and strengthen your learning.

 > *Go to: **Chapter 6** to check/update the* **writing** *section of your Core Development Plan.*

6 Map your learning

Step by step you build up strong, long-lasting learning. When you need to pull it all together – and pull it *out* in assessments – you have a rich and interconnected information structure that refreshes your memory, and just *is* more memorable because of the way you've made it.

Visual representations can be extremely useful for learning. Just as you shape your notes to help you understand and remember them, it's also important to structure your overall knowledge base in a way that you can 'see' and navigate.

Once you're into your course, start creating a map of your learning. Make it on paper and keep it in sight – which will mean that you also get used to it as a virtual map, available in your head wherever you are.

Your learning map will:

- provide context for each new set of information
- emphasize the purpose of your work
- focus any extra preparation you do before assessments
- keep your motivation strong, showing you how much you know.

At any point you can use the structure to help you work back to specific pieces of information – which is obviously particularly important when you're sitting in an exam.

The map reflects your study in practice, showing how your learning has been developed and strengthened, layer by layer.

Layer 1 is made up of the books, journals, websites and other materials you've used to access information. These are all still available somewhere if you need to check them or do extra research. Many of them will be referenced in your work, and you may want to refer to them when your writing or speaking is being assessed.

Layer 2 is the notes you made as a direct result of your research. Some of these documents will be very detailed; others will be looser collections of information and ideas. You'll have used a variety of styles to make these notes, depending on the work you were doing at the time, and some will be much more engaging and memorable than others. Also in here are any essays, reports and other assignments, annotated to emphasize the aspects of their content and structure that will be most useful for you to know.

Layer 2a includes any summary notes you've made based on Layer 2 documents. They're an accessible, simplified guide to what's in the full, detailed version.

Layer 3 is made up of the mini maps you've created, showing all the documents and resources relating to a particular topic or part of your course. You can use colours, numbers or notes to remind you where all this information is physically stored – directing you to a ring-binder or computer folder.

Layer 4 is the top-level plan, clearly showing how all the Layer 3 materials combine to represent your learning as a whole.

The structure takes shape as you go through your course.

A Layer 3 map will help you prepare for a topic assessment.

When you come to final exams, you'll have a Layer 4 document that shows you how everything fits together.

In the exam itself, you have a clear mental trail to follow, to support all the other ways you learned your stuff. When you read a question, you can visualize your way back to the appropriate topic(s), then back to all the documents you created to show the information you gathered, and how you understood it. And, from that, back to the original documents themselves.

You're supported to access information in a very logical way, but also to be creative about which bits of this structured knowledge you tap into to construct your answer.

This map is also an important guide as you continually strengthen all your learning – and especially when you come to the final push before an exam.

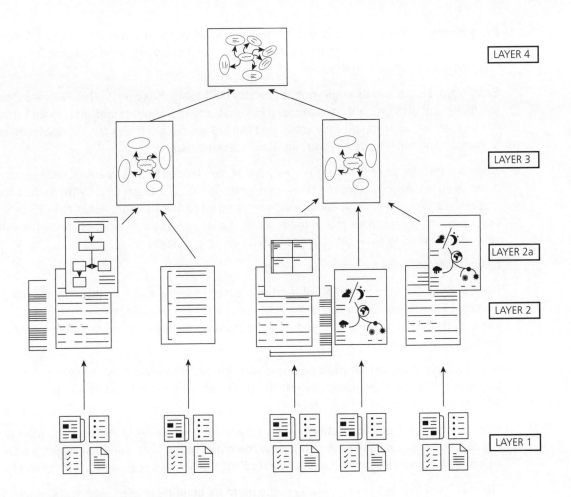

7 Strengthen your memories

Don't wait until assessments are near before you go back to your notes. Get into an ongoing cycle of returning to the materials you've created – and to some of the original research texts – to refresh and strengthen your memory.

At the end of every week, spend a few minutes reading through all the summary notes you've made during those seven days – the ones that make up Layers 2 and 2a of your learning map.

- Think about the more detailed information behind them, and check that the way they're organized still makes sense.
- Then … *do* something with some of the notes. Pick a document (or a theme in several) that's particularly important, or difficult, or likely to come up in an exam, or one you haven't thought about for a while … and do something with the information. You could list the ten most important words and their definitions on flashcards; make a set of quiz cards; turn the big ideas into a poster; think of a question to raise on a student forum. Doing something is a powerful way to embed the learning, giving your brain another way to retrieve it when required.

Every month, do the same thing with the materials you've made during that period. When you've done the reading and thinking, pick one part of it to engage with in a practical learning activity of your choice.

Every term, all the way through your course, do it all again. Keep using the new resources you make, but also go right back to the original source materials sometimes, to do extra reading, enrich what you already know, and remind yourself of the depth of knowledge and understanding represented by your personal learning map.

When a particular assessment is on the horizon, you'll need to do some focused sessions to make sure that you've got the relevant information at your fingertips. By then you'll have mapped out where it all is in document form, helping to find the right notes to work with – plus some extra resources you've made along the way – and you'll be ready to do the extra studying required to show off what you can do under pressure.

> *Go to: Chapter 19* *for a full exam preparation guide.*

However, you can also get great value from focused learning sessions throughout your course, even when there's no assessment anytime soon. You increase your subject knowledge, deepen your understanding and rehearse the key strategies you'll need when the big exams do come around.

Below is a planning format you could use, setting out the key features of a really effective assessment-focused session in the left-hand column, with room to plan timings and record what happens in the column on the right.

After recording the **session details** – the date and time you're planning to study, and the key areas you're aiming to cover – do some **memory testing** in one of those areas. Focus on a part of your course that you've recently studied in detail, to see how much of it has stuck.

The results of that will lead naturally to the **memory building** phase – when, staying with the same material, you improve your understanding and recall, going back over your notes, adding new features, and using a range of active memory techniques.

> *Go to: Chapter 14* *to see how memory systems and strategies can enrich your learning.*

Next comes a **new learning** phase – probably focused not on *completely* new information, but on something that hasn't been covered recently or learned well enough to be tested yet. You might choose to carry on with more material from the area you've just been working on, or switch to another part of your course altogether. Your wider study planning will guide you, but it's also important to be flexible and respond to the way things are going within the session itself. If your memory testing was difficult, it might be best to stick with that material for this main part of the session, and use all the powerful study techniques you've developed – reading, thinking, visualizing, practising, testing – to fix it in your memory, richly and robustly.

Do a brief learning map review after that, to remind yourself how this new learning fits into the bigger picture of your course, and to see which of your documents or resources might help you to strengthen it further.

Then spend a few minutes making a new resource to go with it. Add a note about it to the relevant *Layer 3* map.

After that, make some **next session notes** – about the aspects of this session that you'll want to test yourself on next time, and what you think the new learning should be.

Finally, spend a few moments reflecting on the whole session and noting down a few things you'd like to *keep* thinking about: **food for thought** in spare moments (maybe a question that caught you out today, an aspect of your new learning that needs more research, or a strategy you've set up for remembering something particularly hard).

Together, these elements form a very powerful learning activity – perfect for building up to an assessment. But there are also plenty of ideas here that can be used individually, whenever you return to some previous learning and want to spend a bit of time making it shine even more brightly in your memory.

Focused learning session plan	
Session details	
Memory testing	
Memory building	
New learning	
Learning map review	
Make a resource	
Next session notes	
Food for thought	

Sessions like these will drive your preparations for specific assessments, but there are some other important things to do before you put yourself to the test – to help you get even more out of all the learning you've done.

> **Go to: Chapter 19** *for more exam-preparation techniques.*

> **Student Tip**
>
> 'I'm always amazed how many students don't realize that the university actually sets the exams. The staff know what's coming up. They obviously want you to cover everything on the syllabus, but it's also in their interest for you to do well, and they're bound to plan their own teaching around the content of the exams whenever they can. So it just makes sense to listen when they tell you which bits to focus on, and let their teaching guide you when you're working out what to prioritize.' **Chris, final-year Biology undergraduate**

❯ *Go to: Chapter 6 to check/update the* **memory** *section of your Core Development Plan.*

8 Reflect to remember

Your learning journal is another powerful memory tool.

❯ *Go to: Chapter 6 to see how to record and reflect on key aspects of your studies.*

- As well as writing about what you did and how well it went, include details about how it *felt*. Use your emotions to create even richer memories of learning sessions and the information involved.
- When you're returning to previous learning, your journal can help you re-engage with it quickly by reminding you of your reactions the first time around.
- When you're preparing for assessments, reflect on the strategies you're using and their impact. How are you spacing out your learning and relearning? Where do you do this kind of study best? Which activities are most helpful for embedding memories? Use your reflective notes to help you make assessment preparation a strong skill-set in itself.
- Treat the assessments themselves as learning activities, and record your reflections on them like any other aspect of study. Write about your retrieval techniques and the different thinking strategies you tried, plus how well you managed your time and coped with the pressure. Use your emotions to help you remember what to do even better in future.

❯ *Go to: Chapter 6 to check/update the* **exam preparation** *section of your Core Development Plan*

⑩ Ten-point summary

1. Handled in the right way, assessments play a key role in developing all the skills involved in studying well.

2. A good memory is vital for building and demonstrating your abilities, even though it's not such an obvious focus in higher-level tests and exams.

3. 'Working' memory is an important part of the reading process, and you can learn to use yours better, to retain more of the information you read.

4. Use a range of techniques to make your notes even more memorable.

5. When you've made notes, doing something with them makes a big difference to how well you remember them.

6. Annotating pieces of written work helps you to keep accessing their content and structure from memory.

7. Mapping your learning shows you how it all contributes to your subject strength and helps you to navigate it in your mind.

8. Reread and reuse your notes regularly, strengthening your memory.

9. Include focused learning sessions in your study schedule, refreshing understanding, improving recall and building new knowledge.

10. Use your learning journal to strengthen your knowledge, develop better study strategies, and prepare yourself to perform well under pressure.

 # Where to next?

Chapter 13 will show you how to maximize all the different types of learning involved in higher-level study.

Part 4

Thinking skills

Thinking about thinking – to boost engagement, achievement and enjoyment

Chapter 13 explores the core processes and practices that drive higher-level study, laying the foundations for **conscious, unconscious** and **experiential learning**.

Chapter 14 focuses on the **active learning** that's vital at this stage, allowing you to engage in advanced **critical analysis** and to use **memory techniques** to support all aspects of your study.

In the zone

Exploring how learning works helps you to use all aspects of study to enrich your knowledge and understanding – in the process developing a range of highly valuable thinking skills.

 ## What?

Higher-level study gets you **thinking** for yourself. Grappling with complex ideas pushes you to develop your own understanding, and it lets you start contributing to progress in your chosen field. But it also teaches you about yourself: about the thought processes that lead to better understanding of *anything*, and how you can make them work to your advantage in everything you do.

You've done plenty of learning before, but now you're **learning how to learn**. This chapter and the next focus on the key parts of that process, helping you to engage fully with all the opportunities on offer., You'll see how to get the most out of studying on a particular university course, so that you come away from it knowing what you've gained personally, confident that you can keep getting better from here.

 ## When?

As you learn how to study the subject you've chosen, all the strategies in this chapter will be invaluable. You'll make them your own by incorporating them into all the different aspects of learning that make up your course. But there's also useful groundwork to be done, and you can go into your studies (or particular parts of them) with a significant head-start, building **key skills** early and getting into the right **attitudes** and **habits**.

The thought processes exercised here will also be important for the way you tackle student life in general – and they'll be greatly strengthened if you can weave them into everything you do from now on.

 ## Who?

These are personal thinking skills that are built up within a community of learners. This chapter sets you up to benefit from everything that academic staff and fellow students have to offer, showing you how to get the most out of **shared learning** – including involving other people in the development of your core learning skills.

Why?

The training here is vital for meeting the higher-level challenge you've taken on. These strategies will help you to get stuck into the struggle for understanding – of your subject, and of yourself as a learner. They'll give you access to ways of thinking and working that will help you operate with confidence – on your course, and in your professional life beyond.

 # How?

Start by exploring what learning involves at this stage of education. Consider how well your previous experiences have prepared you to do it well.

Then look at that learning in practice, to see both the challenges and the opportunities presented by different academic activities: **reading**, **writing**, **speaking**, **listening** and **doing**.

Significant amounts of learning are subconscious, happening without you doing anything actively to drive the process – but you'll still need to be ready, to make the most of the rich environment you're in, and to learn through all your **experiences**.

Put yourself in the right frame of mind, sharpen your senses, and step into the zone where the best learning happens and some of the most important thinking skills are gained.

 # Steps to success

1 See the thinking behind the learning

When you're 'in the zone' as a student you're in the best place to learn, whatever sort of learning you happen to be doing. You're ready to strengthen your existing abilities, and to add new layers to what you know and can do. Prepared for each activity, equipped to take a very active approach, you're also curious and open to whatever happens next – including how you'll add this experience to everything else you're learning, and how you'll use it to keep on getting better.

You've seen that good study involves *gathering* information, *recording* it so that you can work with it, then *organizing* it as you explore what it means.

The first half of this model lines up well with the practical steps of studying:

Researching includes accessing information in libraries and online as well as from teaching, group projects and placements.

Recording involves getting copies of the material to keep, and making notes from what you read, watch and listen to, particularly in lectures, classes, seminars and presentations.

Organizing starts with storing your physical records intelligently, but it's also about the way you organize the *ideas* so that they make sense to you, helping you to remember, use and communicate them – for example, discussing them in groups, planning and writing essays and talks, and continually reflecting on what they mean.

From there, different types of *analysing* deepen your understanding as you locate the elements that are important for you, and use and develop them in various ways. Testing and sharing your thinking also makes you better at *remembering* what you're doing, which in turn helps you to keep *applying* it, continually strengthening and extending the learning.

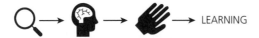

And it's in the second half of this model where higher-level learning really takes off.

The information you gather is now subjected to much more intense scrutiny and new kinds of analysis. Deeper understanding stretches your ability to remember. Applying it involves some very public tests of your ability, as well as constantly grappling with the information in your own head as you shape and reshape your ideas.

As you specialize in your subject, *using* information is integral to *learning* it. You work with your emerging ideas and skills to keep challenging your own thought-processes and those of everyone else in your field.

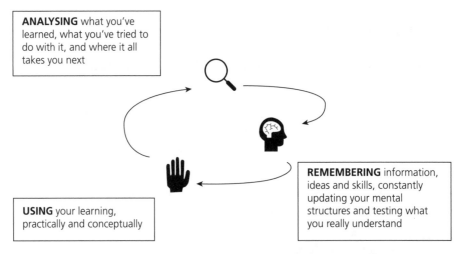

This is the kind of learning that allows ideas to be combined, **synthesizing** new ways forward. And central to it all is **evaluating**: the constant questioning of how useful your learning really is, and how well you're doing it.

Being 'in the zone' means being geared up to learn in this rich, dynamic environment, entering whole-heartedly into the struggle with shifting knowledge, changing ideas, and intense academic and personal growth.

2 Start from here

This kind of studying involves developing advanced thinking skills, and it's important to know where you're starting from.

> **Go to: Chapter 2** *to assess your feelings about five important thinking styles, and to consider how you see yourself as a learner.*

> **Go to: Chapter 4** *to see how your past experiences might affect your confidence now.*

> **Go to: Chapter 5** *to explore some of the new challenges of thinking and learning well at this level.*

> **Go to: Chapter 6** *whenever you need to check or update the relevant sections of your Core Development Plan – particularly* **organization**, **analysis** *and* **evaluation**.

As you learn more about what's involved in *any* challenge, your confidence can go up and down. So, when you're taking part in the activities here – and as you start putting the skills into practice within your course – allow your feelings to guide your development. This will help you to move forward in ways that are appropriate, realistic and as useful to you as possible.

3 See the pros and cons

Higher-level students need to be keenly aware of both the opportunities and the challenges in any learning activity, ready to adapt their approach accordingly.

Reading to learn	
Advantages	**Disadvantages**
If you can borrow, buy, copy or download a text, it's yours to explore whenever and wherever you want.	There's a lot of irrelevant material to avoid, even within texts that are useful overall.
You can make notes directly on to the text (or a copy of it), on paper or on screen, or just return to the document itself to learn more from it or to use it in your work.	High levels of concentration and engagement are required to explore texts on various levels.
You can read at your own pace, in whatever order you want, missing out some parts and rereading others as you choose.	You need to be able to focus on individual details, but also to follow big themes as they emerge – and often to make sense of the document as a whole.
Language has been used carefully to convey a precise meaning, and you have time to unpick it.	The writer has had time to construct detailed, dense text, including precise vocabulary which may be unfamiliar, demanding high levels of engagement and stamina from the reader, and possibly additional research or support.
The way a text is organized and presented helps you to understand and use the information it contains.	
Many texts come with built-in assistance: perhaps a glossary, index, FAQs or links to other documents.	If documents lack distinguishing visual features, their standardized style can make them hard to separate from other things you've read.

> **Go to: Chapter 12** *for a guide to using reading to gather and engage with the information that fuels your learning.*

Writing to learn	
Advantages	**Disadvantages**
The planning process guides you to gather a range of information and to think carefully about its value.	Difficulties with writing can reduce the quality of the *thinking* involved.
Writing allows you to use information and try out ideas in order to develop and present your own understanding, pushing you to be clear and precise in your thinking.	The emotions involved in writing can get in the way of learning.
As well as communicating your subject knowledge, and outlining your ideas about it, writing shows the thought processes that have gone into developing your understanding.	Your confidence can be shaken when your learning is exposed to detailed criticism.
High-quality finished work becomes a useful resource for your future learning.	
Detailed feedback can be considered carefully and returned to over time.	

> ❯ *Go to: Chapter 12 for more ideas about using writing to accelerate your learning.*

Speaking to learn	
Advantages	**Disadvantages**
Speaking about something reveals how much of it you really understand – and can remember.	The emotions involved can hamper thinking and learning.
Discussions can be dynamic ways to test out your learning, using other people's ideas to strengthen or reshape your own.	It's harder to be precise, so your thought processes may become less rigorous.
Preparing a presentation clarifies your thinking, and delivering it lets you test your understanding and boost your memory.	There's often no lasting record of what was said.
You can get instant feedback – and respond, to ask questions, challenge the points raised or test out new versions of your ideas.	

> ❯ *Go to: Chapter 17 to see how collaborating and communicating are vital aspects of learning at this level.*

Listening to learn	
Advantages	**Disadvantages**
Speakers can use a range of communication techniques to get their message across clearly and memorably.	Aspects of the speaker's language use and presentation style can get in the way of communication and disrupt learning.
You can learn from visual materials while you're listening to spoken words.	Learning depends on high levels of concentration and stamina, in order for the listener to take in the information and make sense of it.
Note-taking can happen at the same time as listening.	Competing information can cause cognitive overload.

You can practise physical skills while listening to instructions and guidance.	You may have no control over the pace of learning, and only one chance to listen.
You may be able to interact with the speaker to ask for clarification, test out your own thinking or even challenge the things you've heard.	It can be hard to see the overall shape of the information and to judge the value of individual ideas.

❭ *Go to: Chapter 15 for advice about getting the most out of all the teaching on offer.*

Doing to learn	
Advantages	**Disadvantages**
Doing something helps to build up physical familiarity and 'muscle memory'.	Appropriate learning activities can be complicated and costly to set up.
The feelings involved in a practical task – both positive and negative – help you to remember it.	It may not be easy to take risks, and time-consuming or expensive to make mistakes.
Abstract ideas can be much easier to understand when they're seen in practice.	Wrongly practised actions can quickly become habitual.
Well-rehearsed routines become frameworks for new learning.	It may be difficult to record what happened to help with future learning, particularly the thinking processes involved.
Showing what you do and don't know helps other people to give you specific advice and support.	

❭ *Go to: Chapter 15 for advice about using feedback to improve your skills.*

There are plenty of challenges to negotiate, whatever sort of learning you're doing – especially as the content is likely to be complex and highly demanding in itself. Your course moves quickly, student life comes with plenty of additional pressures, and the learning required at this level *has* to be ambitious and intense.

To help you rise to the challenge, go back to each of the tables above and highlight one of the *advantages,* and one of the *disadvantages* – the ones that you think will be most important for you to recognize, and *respond to,* from now on.

4 Switch on to learning

It's important to be ready to learn from everything you do while you're a student. Some things you can prepare for specifically and then engage with very actively. Other things are less predictable, more *experience* than active study, unconscious rather than conscious learning. But they all contribute to your development, and you need to set yourself up to make the most of all the learning on offer.

So, to prepare yourself to learn unconsciously as well as consciously ...

Be organized

Use your time-management skills to get you *to* all the learning opportunities: to one-off talks, specialist demonstrations, relevant exhibitions and any other special events – as well as all the core activities that make up your course.

 Note To Self

Put at least one thing on your week plan that's not active study, and not total relaxation – something in between, like a film that has a slight link with your subject, or a journey that takes you past somewhere connected with your work. It should remind you to be ready for learning that emerges *anywhere*, and get you used to the idea that higher-level study is still being developed even when you're not actively studying.

Be alert

It's hard to do your best thinking and learning if you're not feeling well. Be proactive about looking after your physical, mental and emotional health, trying as hard as you can to eat a balanced diet, take exercise, find time to relax, and get enough sleep.

 Note To Self

Use your learning journal to monitor your alertness over a week. When did you feel sharpest, most ready to learn from everything you experienced – and when did your mental energy dip? What could you do to look after yourself better? Are there any ways of reorganizing your life so that your most alert periods coincide with the most valuable learning opportunities?

Be observant

You get used to focusing on details when you're reading, writing and listening – particularly the exact words used, and the precise techniques chosen to explore and present ideas. But you can also pick up important details from the world around you, if you're ready to notice them and include them in your learning.

Some of the ideas that have changed the world have come from people simply *spotting* things and realizing they could be significant – often in nature, like the way spiders' webs are constructed, or how grass seeds stick to animal fur. You'll get more insights into your subject if you're observant about relevant details – within product labels, ingredient lists, movie soundtracks, athletes' warm-up routines ... But there's also plenty of useful evidence in life in general, and being open to it prepares you well for detail-focused academic work.

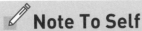 **Note To Self**

Find some spare moments this week to work on your senses. When you're waiting for something (a bus, a friend, a slice of toast) take a little time to isolate one sense and notice everything it has to offer. At the bus stop, how many different colours can you see around you? What two things are exactly the same shade? Can you spot any patterned materials – and how would you describe their style of design? Sitting in the café, you might reflect on the different layers of sound. In your kitchen, what else can you smell apart from the grilling toast?

Be interested

Curiosity is a key theme in this part of the book: questioning exactly what's going on, and why, how you can understand more about it, and where the ideas might lead.

 Note To Self

The next time you see a baby or toddler at play – maybe in the park, on the beach or at a family event – notice how their interest in the world reveals itself, and what they do to pursue it.

Learning about our environment is a very basic impulse, and the youngest members of the species do it through a range of senses: touching, smelling and tasting things close by as well as looking and listening. Children often turn things over or pull them apart, looking for evidence of how they work, interested in what they can get out … which are exactly the habits you need to get into again as a student.

Be ready …

… with a notebook, phone camera or recording app, for whenever important material appears. The more you immerse yourself in the rich learning opportunities of student life, feeling alert, using all your senses and being interested in what happens, the more valuable information will emerge – for you to record and involve in your studies.

 Note To Self

Check you have a way of recording your observations and ideas wherever you are, even if it's just a cheap notebook that's always in your bag, or a tab in the 'reminders' function on your phone. Higher-level learning stretches you to think originally and make new connections and combinations, and that's often easiest when you're doing something that's not the 'official' focus of your studies at the time. And, whatever you're doing, your subconscious is likely to be working away at issues connected with your learning, and it may offer solutions when you're least expecting them.

6 Learn from experience

Experiential learning is: *learning* by *reflecting* on *doing* … and then doing better as a result. In many ways it's academic study at its very best.

You create the right external and internal conditions for learning.

For example, you sit in a good seat in the lecture theatre, are aware of what the speaker's going to be talking about, are motivated to learn, and are equipped with everything you need to make notes.

You combine new information with previous knowledge, carefully deciding how to do something useful with it.

You notice connections with things you've already learned and mention them in your notes, questioning the information as you listen, and thinking about ways you'll be able to use some of it in your next essay.

You analyse this activity, using it to show you where to go from here. The learning you've achieved here provides some firm foundations for whatever comes next.

Later, shaping up your notes and storing them away carefully, you write down some interesting new lines of enquiry, and you spend a few minutes reading more about a particularly interesting issue that came up.

You also focus on the learning process itself. If you evaluate it accurately, there's something to take out of every activity to help you improve your approach and get even more value from your study next time.

In your learning journal, you write a short analysis of your experiences:

- *Did it turn out to be useful to prepare for the lecture?*
- *How well did you engage with the ideas being discussed?*
- *Were you able to see the thinking that went into constructing the argument?*
- *What new insights have you got from re-reading your notes?*
- *Have you recorded your ideas in a memorable way?*
- *What impact has this activity had on your preparations for your essay?*

All the time you're alert to what went well, and what could be improved next time.

Use the table below to come up with some questions that you could ask yourself after a learning activity – whether it's **reading**, **writing**, **speaking**, **listening** or **doing.** Think carefully about the most useful information to collect (and the types of thinking that might help you collect it) and use the examples to get you started.

Leave some space in each box. You'll be coming back here at the end of the next chapter, after exploring analytic thinking in more depth. But you can put your ideas to work in your study straight away, so that focused self-reflection becomes another powerful weapon in your armoury.

Learning journal lines of enquiry	
Learning activity	Possible questions
Reading	Were you aware of the writer's overall position on this subject? How easy was it to find the most important parts of the material to focus on?
Writing	How well did you guide your reader through your evidence and reasoning? Did you have any problems getting started with your work?
Speaking	Did your learning benefit from dialogue – having to argue your point of view? Did the emotional aspects of speaking in public impact on how much you learned?
Listening	Did the speaker's presentation style or body language affect the way you evaluated their words? Were you able to make effective notes as you listened?
Doing	Did you benefit from feedback or advice during the activity? How well did your memory work – retrieving what you already knew, and learning new elements to add here?

❯ *Go to: Chapter 6 to check/update the self-reflection section of your Core Development Plan.*

❯ *Go to: Chapter 4 to see whether any of your feelings about higher-level thinking and learning have changed.*

⑩ Ten-point summary

1. Higher-level learning pushes you to analyse and evaluate complex information and ideas.

2. Your analytic thinking needs to extend to your own learning, so that you're continually improving the way you study.

3. With the right approach, you develop your abilities within your subject at the same time as growing in confidence to think and learn beyond it.

4. It's important to understand the challenges and opportunities of different activities, to create the best conditions for thinking and learning.

5. Student life includes conscious learning – prepared and active – and unconscious learning – receptive and open.

6. Improving your organization helps you to access valuable learning opportunities.

7. Looking after your physical, mental and emotional wellbeing keeps you energized and alert.

8. Train your senses to boost your powers of observation.

9. Being interested in learning lets you tap into advanced thinking skills.

10. Experiential learning combines what you *do* as a student with how you *think* about it.

 # Where to next?

Chapter 14 will boost your confidence to think, learn and remember well at this new level of education.

Taking control

As a higher-level student you need to control each element of the learning process, so that you can solve complex problems, turn memory to your advantage, and use your thinking skills to support your academic and personal growth.

What?

At this level, being an **active** student means, above all, *thinking* actively – using a range of techniques to process information effectively.

It feeds into what you *do* in your study – how you organize your time, handle your materials, tackle each activity, prepare for exams – and there's a very powerful learning effect when *doing* and *thinking* are combined. But it's all driven by your **thinking skills**, and they need to be the best they've ever been.

This chapter shows you how to enter into an exciting struggle with complicated information, big ideas and specialist skills, and come out smiling.

When?

Active learning is valuable before, during and after everything you do as a student. It's important to be able to combine different **modes of thinking**, rather than seeing them as a sequence, especially when you're tackling complex problems. And timing is particularly important when you're using the **memory techniques** explained towards the end of this chapter, to make sure that the testing and reviewing phases embed robust, long-term learning.

Who?

It's time to learn to think for yourself. Studying well is about having the confidence to go it alone, doing independent research, examining the evidence closely, and reaching your own conclusions about what it all means.

But you also need to convince other people about your ideas – ideas which themselves come from analysing other people's work. You're developing a highly personal approach to learning, but you're doing it in the dynamic spaces created within a crowded academic community.

 **Why?**

The academic world demands action, because all information needs to be tested, all arguments probed for weaknesses, all ideas held up to the light. That's how knowledge is advanced – and, in the process, how some of the most important thinking and learning skills are forged.

This is a community that values academic competition as well as collaboration. It relies on learning happening quickly. It challenges you to seize opportunities, to reach out and grab everything you need to do well. An active approach is absolutely vital to survive and thrive.

 How?

Start by exploring the seven principles that power **active study**, combining *thinking* and *doing* to energize learning.

Curiosity is a key driving force at this level. Question everything, even your own previous ideas, but stay open to the new possibilities that emerge.

Coordinating a range of thinking skills allows you to develop a highly active approach to **problem-solving**.

And you need a repertoire of **memory skills**, so that you keep adding extra layers to your learning, ready to use, share and test it all – and yourself – with confidence and flair.

 Steps to success

1 Go into action

The seven key principles of active study are:

Preparation. Collecting background information and all the materials and resources required. Getting your attitude right for the task at hand. Setting up all the best conditions for learning.

Interrogation. Questioning the purpose of the activity, the value of information, the best ways to deal with it, the opportunities it opens up.

Organization. Storing physical and digital material so that you can access information, and explore patterns and connections within it. Shaping it to help you remember and use it well.

Modification. Being ready to change your ideas and reshape your understanding. Engaging in debate, on paper and in person. Drafting and redrafting pieces of work, improving the quality of both your thinking and your communication.

Connection. Seeing how new information relates to existing knowledge and understanding. Finding ways to synthesize separate elements to create new possibilities.

Evaluation: Having criteria for testing the quality of information, ideas, processes and products.

Discussion: Outlining conclusions that can be tested by others. Building your ability to communicate and collaborate. Using feedback to refine your skills and extend your learning.

On one level, these concepts provide a series of steps to help you operate well in any activity or aspect of study – from preparing to do it, to discussing the outcomes and deciding on ways forward. But you can get even more out of them than that. You can weave them together and draw strength from all of them, all the way through a piece of work.

In one piece of writing, for example, you might be:

- **preparing** ... by remembering useful information to help you shape the next section of your writing, and by using self-management techniques to stay positive
- **interrogating** ... your existing knowledge to see how much you could use here, while asking questions about the best ways to analyse the evidence
- **organizing** ... the different stages of the writing process – and the ideas you were structuring into an argument
- **modifying** ... your approach to the task, and your views about the subject matter
- **connecting** ... ideas here with information you'd read recently, combining several key themes to suggest a new way to interpret your research
- **evaluating** ... the evidence you'd collected, and the methods used to collect it
- **discussing** ... your ideas on paper, while debating different ways of expressing them in your head.

 ❯ *Go to: **Chapter 6** whenever you want to add any thoughts to your Core Development Plan, particularly about **creativity, problem-solving, analysis, evaluation** and **memory**.*

2 Be curious

There's an element of curiosity in all seven of the principles listed above. Presumably there's at least a glimmer of curiosity in your decision to go further with your studies, beyond the point where you have to do it. Now, it's about *wanting* to do it – to find out more about your subject, your world and yourself.

At this level, questions are more important than ever. In the past, you've probably been on the receiving end a lot of the time, but now you're the one doing most of the asking.

Here are some of the key question types you'll need to get used to, whatever subject you're studying: questions about ...

... the quality and usefulness of the information in front of you:

- What kind of information is it – objective or subjective?
- How will you know how reliable it is?
- Are there ways to measure its value?
- How can you tell if it's relevant to the work you're doing?

... the theories and arguments you're presented with:

- Does the logic hold up to scrutiny?
- Is anything unclear, inaccurate or misleading?
- What's missing from the evidence?
- Do these ideas have wider implications?

... how separate elements being studied compare with each other:

- What are the similarities between products, processes, points of view?
- Is there value in seeing where things overlap?
- Where do the key differences lie?
- What can you learn when there's no common ground at all?

... how different parts of the whole are related:

- What different sorts of connections are there?
- How is the structure formed?
- What's significant about the way things are organized?
- Which parts fall outside the patterns?

 ## Ask yourself

→ **Which are the most important questions for you?**

Based on everything you know about your subject, which of these question types are you most likely to be using? Think about some of the learning tasks you'll be doing, and the subject matter you'll be examining. Is there one question that's going to be particularly significant? Do any of them not apply at all?

❯ *Go to: Chapter 7 to think about how your analytic thinking can be affected by your **environment** and your **behaviour**.*

3 Look for problems

Questioning is vital for developing one of the key aspects of higher-level study: the ability to find flaws in arguments.

It sounds negative – and it is, in the sense that it's about probing for problems and asking why something doesn't work (or is going to break before long). It's a highly critical approach – it takes nothing at face value, subjecting everything to rigorous examination, and is unafraid to say when issues arise.

But it's based on the high standards that everyone working at this level needs to understand and sign up to. It's aiming to drive positive learning and meaningful progress by avoiding paths that don't go in the right direction.

The important questions to ask include:

What exactly is the argument?

Look for clues about the author's overall point of view to help you engage with their ideas here. Let signposting words and phrases lead you to the important points and guide you through the reasoning – so that you can test it.

Is the reasoning flawed?

It might be, if it includes:

- details that confuse the issue

Iceland was a founder member of NATO, despite having one of the lowest average temperatures in the world.

- irrelevant themes

To understand coastal erosion, consider the emotional difficulties faced by someone who loses their home.

- bias about sources

We need to listen to this writer because they won awards in some other areas of research.

- opinions presented as facts

People were obviously happier before the internet.

- emotional triggers

Are we really willing to take this risk with babies' lives?

- false dilemmas

Either we ban live animal exports, or let famers do anything they want.

- inappropriate analogies

The homelessness crisis is like an atomic bomb about to be dropped on the country.

- forced answers

If climate change isn't the direct cause, what else could it possibly be?

- assumptions about cause and effect

The more plastics we consume, the faster global temperatures rise.

- illogical conclusions

Top runners eat more pasta than the average person – so we know that pasta makes you run faster.

Is data used effectively?

Statistics can add clarity, precision and convincing evidence to strengthen an argument. But they can also be unclear, confusing or even misleading. Be particularly alert to:

- sample size

Is it significant that 75 per cent of people agreed, if only 12 people were asked?

- generalizations (again)

Just how representative are these figures about children's health, since all these children live in South-East England?

- collection conditions

Does it matter that the data about footwear was collected in a sports shop?

- calculation methods

How have the totals been rounded up/down? Which type of average has been used?

- presentation techniques

Why has this form of data handling been used? Could be scale chosen for the graph be misleading?

Are generalizations justified?

It's certainly possible to make wide-ranging points that show how an idea applies in a range of situations, or even everywhere. But it has to be based on very convincing evidence, explained clearly so that it can be evaluated accurately. Be alert to any generalizations that don't meet these standards.

- Can you be sure that this material will always behave in this way?
- How can you know whether the pattern will continue?
- Does everyone agree on what this concept means?

In some subjects the burden of proof is particularly clear. But it's *every* student's responsibility to spot any attempted steps forward that aren't as safe as they might first appear.

Academic Advice

'A key marker of students' development at this level is their confidence to suggest problems with the thinking and working practices they examine – their own and other people's – and their ability to use evidence to back up their opinions and recommendations.' **Russ, university lecturer**

❯ *Go to: Chapter 6* *to check/update the section on* **meeting academic standards** *in your Core Development Plan.*

4 Be open to the possibilities

On the other side of the problems ... are the possibilities.

If a line of reasoning holds up to testing, and maybe even gets stronger as you deal with problems and make changes in response, where might it lead? It may well have to be modified again in the future, because that's how learning works; and it might even be overturned altogether. But what insights does it give you for the time being? And where does it suggest you take your learning next?

It's not as simple as calling this the positive approach. Your discoveries may contain bad news or raise difficult issues, and you're unlikely to be able to say you've 'solved' the problem. But you are contributing to the development of understanding. You're going a little further into parts of the landscape, as some paths are shown to be dead-ends, but others look to be worth a try.

You need flexible, open-minded thinking, and the ability to see issues from different angles.

To put yourself in the right place for this kind of learning ...

- **Practise seeing both sides of an argument.** Pick a real issue, consider your personal views on it, and then experiment with the opposite standpoint. How many different reasons can you think of why this opposing view might be valid?
- **Remember times when you got things wrong.** Self-confidence is important, but it's not helpful to assume that you're always right, or that new evidence won't change your opinions. So, think back to times when something you were pretty sure about proved to be wrong – or had to be adapted significantly in the face of evidence or experience.
- **Challenge your own habitual behaviours to keep your thinking elastic.** Take different routes. Order new things in restaurants. Find people who don't always agree with your viewpoint. Keep evaluating everything, see whether you can combine approaches, stick with any habits that serve you well. But also practise experimenting – and maybe even *changing*, if the new way of doing things turns out to be better.

5 Relish the challenge

The thinking skills developed in this chapter all help you to tackle problems. Questions you've been set within your particular subject. Issues you want to grapple with yourself. Also, the problem of learning itself: *how* you're going to learn, so that you can arrive at a verdict that you can share and test, and maybe even use to take your subject a step further on.

So, whether you're tackling a specific question, investigating an argument, formulating a theory, or pausing mid-race to work out where you are and what direction you need to go in next ... here are some strategies to help. They'll become real when you start using them in your work, but it's important to see this ten-part framework now because it draws directly on all the thinking strategies outlined in this part of the book.

Once again, this isn't a series of steps to follow. You'll need to use different strategies at different times, combine techniques as you choose, and interweave them with the multi-layered thinking skills you're trying to use all the time.

Define the issue. The key words are *clarity* and *precision* again. What exactly are you trying to achieve?

Describe the answer. This should be based on the question: what *sort* of answer are you looking for? Is it a definitive solution, a suggested argument, a range of ideas, a new process, a finished product ...?

Put the problem into words. You've seen how writing tests your understanding and forces you to be exact in your thinking – so get the benefit of that now.

Investigate its shape. See whether a map, diagram or other visual representation gives you more insights into the problem and how to tackle it.

Simplify the situation. Strip away everything that's not essential to the core question. You can add it back later but, in the meantime, what's the fundamental issue?

Compare it to something familiar. An important aspect of learning is drawing on experience, seeing a new challenge in the light of something similar you've faced before. Think about anything like this that you've done previously – in the same subject, another area of education, or a different part of life altogether – and see whether there's any aspect of it that might be helpful here.

Make it real. Abstract aspects of the problem (or the way you're trying to tackle it) might be better understood through real-world metaphors. Does this philosophical idea make more sense when you compare it to a process in nature? Perhaps you're trying to construct an argument the same way you build flat-pack furniture.

Consider various approaches. Use your flexible thinking skills to consider a variety of options. Be open to a range of ideas, and leave them on the table long enough to evaluate them properly.

Follow logic. Take it step by step, considering whether one idea naturally leads on to the next. Signposting words and phrases like 'also', 'therefore', 'however' and 'in contrast' can help you to explore logical routes of thought, and to communicate them to others.

Combine options. Stay alert to potential problems ... be open to possibilities ... and see whether elements from some of the different approaches you've tried could be combined to move you on further. A highly logical argument might be enriched by a thought-provoking metaphor. After mapping a conceptual process on paper, would it help to compare it with an example from the real world? Sometimes, *attempting* to tie together possible solutions, and failing, makes the most appropriate approach absolutely clear.

Case Study: Tom

Tom was the first person in his family to go to university, and for a while he wondered whether he'd made the right decision. 'For most of my first two terms I was completely at sea. It just didn't feel like the sort of thinking I could do. I would go through other people's ideas and try to put them together into essays, but the feedback I got wasn't great, and I didn't really think I was learning anything. I'd never been afraid of working hard – I just didn't know what to work *on*.'

A breakthrough came when Tom's tutor talked to him about using a learning journal.

'I think the penny dropped then. I wasn't just at university to learn about a subject. I had to learn *how* to do it. I wasn't expected to know that already – which was a revelation.'

Tom's learning journal helped him to focus less on getting things 'right', and more on making each task useful. 'I stopped being so concerned with just explaining what other people thought, and started focusing on what happened when I tried things out myself. Suddenly there was a lot more point in me being there. My tutor was great. He kept asking me about my journal, and he got me into the habit of using it to plan my strategy for something, and then give myself some feedback afterwards. And I've stuck with it ever since. It keeps me focused on my "job" – getting better at learning.'

❯ *Go to: Chapter 1 and reflect on the impact of emotions on study.*

❯ *Go to: Chapter 13 to consider how self-analysis can boost learning – and to see whether this chapter has given you any new ideas.*

6 Learn to remember

Sometimes it's necessary to combine active learning with active *memorizing* – when you need to take ownership of particularly difficult or important information. Specialized memory techniques help you to retrieve and apply what you know with speed and accuracy, giving you the confidence to push yourself further in academic activities – including exams.

They're all based on four guiding principles.

Think in pictures

Imagery has a powerful role to play in activating memories, so add pictures when they're not there – sometimes by including memorable images into your notes, but more often by *visualizing* key pieces of information.

When you meet an important idea in your field of study, think how it might be represented visually – to check that you understand it, and to create a picture clue to trigger your memory. It's a good way to explore the precise meaning of abstract terms, and to see what they mean by comparing them with things you already know. If you can't illustrate something easily as it is, be creative and play with the way the word itself looks or sounds to help you come up with image ideas.

In science, *ductility* might suggest a plastic *duck*, which you could stretch in your imagination until it started to tear apart (reminding you about the property of materials that ductility measures).

In geography, a *bight* could be visualized as a river with a huge *bite* taken out of it where it bends, with water seeping in to the hole to form a bay (the real meaning of the word).

For the *Enlightenment* you might use a light bulb – and exaggerate its size and brightness to make it even more memorable. You could stamp it as an 18-watt bulb, to remind you of the eighteenth century, and even imagine writing key words about this period of history on to the curved glass of the bulb: *reason*, *progress*, *tolerance* ... This process might lead to thoughts about *why* the Enlightenment got its name; to possible connections (maybe with the *Illuminati* from around the same time); and new questions (such as whether there is any connection with *illuminated* manuscripts).

Picture clues can also be linked into imaginary stories to help you learn them as a list. It's a great way of learning key points to include in exam essays or presentations. It's also very useful for holding instructions in your head while you practise something, helping you to become fluent with a new skill.

Make each picture clear and striking in some way, and create stories that are unusual, interesting, funny, emotional ... all those qualities that make information more memorable. Set up a clear chain of events that brings each picture to mind in turn. A few well-chosen images carefully stored in your mind can underpin complex structures of knowledge, helping you to understand what it means and how it fits together as well as letting you navigate it all from memory.

Structure your learning

It's easier to remember information when it's organized – because you can understand it and engage with it on a meaningful level. You also spot where it connects with your existing knowledge, helping it to take root. And you can picture its structure, using your powerful visual memory to boost your learning.

Experiment with different ways of making your notes memorable. Find out whether imagery, colour or particular design features such as bullet-point lists and boxed sections help you to 'see' a page of information in your mind's eye and get back into the content from memory.

Creating memory 'journeys' around familiar structures is a way that many students hold on to the information they're working with. We seem to be hard-wired to remember our environment and how to navigate it, and you can use this natural skill to improve your ability to retain key information, explore it creatively, and then retrieve and apply it whenever you want. Try the following technique:

1. You pick a route you know well – a walk through the rooms of your house, for example, or the journey from home to the local shops – and choose memorable stopping points along the way (rooms in the house, and probably shops, road junctions and other landmarks on a neighbourhood journey).

2. You practise travelling this route in your imagination a few times, checking you know the order of your chosen stopping points and making sure that you can picture them clearly.
3. Then, to remember a set of ideas (about anything), you visualize each item along the route, inventing picture clues to stand for any hard-to-see ideas.
4. If possible, you connect each picture in some way with the real location, which helps you to incorporate emotional reactions and strengthen the memories even more.
5. To recall the information, you simply retrace your mental steps. You don't have to work hard to remember the route, because you know that already. And now there's something unusual at each stopping point, reminding you about an important idea for your work. You can quickly reel off the whole list in exactly the right order, or go straight to particular details within the set.

If you took an imaginary walk around your home and found a *priest* sitting on your doorstep, a crowd of *noblemen* in your hallway, and a *peasant* sitting in your kitchen sink, your memory would be jogged about *church, nobility* and *peasantry* – outdated institutions that supported the monarchy before it was overturned in the Russian Revolution.

On the way to the shops, broken *plates* on the pavement, *socks* filling up the post box and dirty *marks* all over a big advertising hoarding would remind you about the philosophers you wanted to include in a group discussion: Plato, Socrates and Marx.

Test yourself – at the right time

Use memory-testing for memory-*building*.

After studying some information that you want to be able to recall well in future, it's fine to test yourself straight away – but that only really shows that you've accessed the information, and that it's sitting in your short-term memory.

The really crucial testing stage occurs a while later, at a point when you think you'll remember most of what you learned, but you know it'll be a struggle. That's the sweet spot you're aiming for – because remembering something when it's an effort is a very powerful way of embedding it even more firmly in your brain.

When you've done your best to recall it all, check your success, correct any mistakes, create extra reminders ...

Repeat and refresh

... and then *keep* coming back to it, to test yourself again, to add more memory clues, to make links with other things you've learned in the meantime – and to stay familiar with it all through regular repeat visits.

> **Go to: Chapter 19** *for more ways to maximize your memory.*

The more you practise active memorizing, the more you'll know how to get the most out of it in your studies, with a growing awareness of how memory works – so that you can keep using it to your advantage, for anything.

Ten-point summary

1. This stage of education demands a very active approach to study.

2. Energetic thinking skills allow detailed analysis, helping you to explore your chosen subject and to get better at learning in general.

3. Higher-level learning is driven by curiosity and constant questioning.

4. It's important to be open-minded, able to see different points of view, and ready to adapt your ideas as new evidence emerges.

5. Academic problem-solving relies on understanding the task at hand, and being able to test out a number of different approaches.

6. Specific memory techniques can help you to store important material, as well as making it more understandable and easier to use.

7. Create visual prompts to jog your memory about key details, particularly abstract ideas.

8. Arranging image-clues around familiar structures helps you to remember lists – such as key points for an exam answer, or instructions for practical skills.

9. Challenging your recall at the right time can play a significant part in strengthening your memory.

10. Refreshing your knowledge regularly, and combining it with new information, improves learning in the long term.

Where to next?

Chapter 15 will let you see the sorts of teaching you can expect now, and what you'll need to do to make them work for you.

Part 5

Study in action

Getting full value from all the activities involved in higher-level study

Chapter 15 shows you how to utilize all the teaching on offer, including **lectures, tutorials** and **lab/studio work**.

Chapter 16 outlines strategies for meeting the challenges of independent study, turning thinking into writing – particularly **essays, reflective accounts** and **reports**.

Chapter 17 reveals how to work well with others, engaging in **academic dialogue**, making the most of **shared learning**, and using **presentations** to enrich your study and stretch your skills.

Chapter 18 tackles large-scale writing tasks: **research projects, extended essays, dissertations**.

Chapter 19 explains the steps to success in exams: **preparation, practice** and **performance**.

Instructions included

Teaching works differently at this stage of education, so you need to understand how each activity operates – including the active role you have to play – to get the full benefit for your study.

 ## What?

As well as challenging you to work independently, providing you with resources, and surrounding you with fellow students to help generate good learning, higher-level courses connect you with the people best equipped to **teach** you how to study well. Their teaching accounts for a large portion of your course fees, and what they have to offer is extremely valuable, as long as you know how to make the most of it.

Once again, so much of it is down to you. Teaching is delivered in a number of different ways: **lectures**, **tutorials**, **seminars**, **classes**, **workshops**, **fieldwork**, **online guides** ... The quality of it will vary – it has to, because you're taught by human beings with their own strengths and weaknesses, fellow members of a complex and challenging community. It's your responsibility to make the very best of what's available.

Higher-level study relies on the energetic interplay of ideas. There's real dynamism to be found within teaching activities here – chances to pit your wits against leaders in their field, to collaborate with them in the struggle for understanding, and sometimes to get very specific guidance and personal support.

You can't do much about the teachers you get, but you can improve the learning you do with them. This chapter outlines the main teaching activities you'll encounter, explores how strong **academic relationships** are built, and explains some very practical things you can do to make teaching work for you.

 ## When?

Learn how to make the most of teaching as soon as possible, because university courses move quickly, and each of these key learning opportunities will come around only once. You may have some important things to consider before your course even starts to make sure that you can engage fully with the teaching on offer.

There are *definitely* things to do before each taught activity. While they're happening, your thinking and learning will need to be as active as ever. And even afterwards there are some key things to do, to ensure that it supports your work in the short term, fits into your subject learning as a whole, and boosts your development long term.

 # Who?

Your academic success will depend very much on how well you can work with the staff in your university, including tutors, lecturers, and graduate students with teaching responsibilities. Much of the teaching will happen within your subject department and the school it sits in, but there may be opportunities to work with staff beyond that, and to gain expert guidance and support from people in the community, specialist networks, other organizations, and online. You'll also need to know how to learn from other students, and in some activities, some of the teaching may even be done by you.

 # Why?

An organized, active approach helps to keep teaching interesting and enjoyable, as well as letting you take out everything you need to do well. There's also an opportunity here to develop essential skills for the world of work (and life in general), so that you keep benefiting from the experience, knowledge and skills of others, and make every bit of teaching on offer a valuable chance to *learn*.

 # How?

Start with an overview of teaching at university level. It's important to see which activities you're already familiar with, and which might take some getting used to. Think about how they do, and don't, match the key conditions for learning, and what that might mean for the way you approach them.

Next, consider everything you now know about yourself as a student, to spot the challenges and the opportunities you're likely to face when you're being taught.

Then explore how to be an active **participant**, in large-scale lectures, small-scale tutorials, and everything in between: classes, workshops, seminars and laboratory/studio work.

Learn how to cope with different sorts of **teacher**, so that you can benefit from the unique things they have to offer while still judging the quality of their information and ideas.

Finally, prepare to enter into **dialogue** with the people who teach you, so that you're collaborating in the learning process, and coming away from every interaction with very clear ways to move forward.

Steps to success

1 See how you're taught

To study well you'll need to get to grips with some new forms of teaching – and realize that even the familiar-looking ones have moved up a gear.

It's important to consider your particular learning needs, to help you shape the approach that's right for you.

You'll also have to get used to adapting to the way different teachers operate, and to the events within each individual session as they unfold.

> **Go to: Chapter 5** to check how you're feeling about six important aspects of university study, all with a link to teaching.

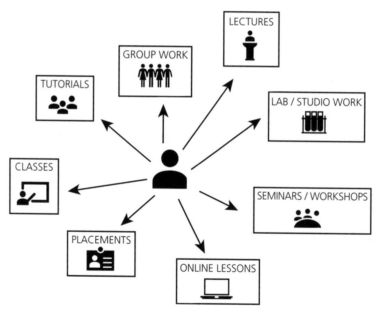

The main methods of teaching at this level are:

Lectures. A lecture usually involves a large group of people listening to one person speak, typically for around an hour at a time. It can include additional audio/visual elements, and there may be opportunities to discuss ideas with peers.

Classes. Depending on the subject being studied, these involve a teacher presenting information to a fairly large group, with opportunities for discussion and practical activities.

Seminars/workshops. They can be led by a teacher, or by nominated students. They focus on particular research work or process development, allowing participants to contribute and test their own ideas and abilities.

Lab/studio work. This is teaching through practical work, with staff facilitating activities and giving instruction, advice and feedback as appropriate to the subject.

Group work. This can involve students playing the role of teacher as they present their work to the group. Group projects may involve students directing and supporting one another to complete separate parts of the task.

Tutorials. These are small group sessions led by a teacher, involving students in close conversation about a chosen topic. They usually focus on writing or research done beforehand by the students, who then present it for others to analyse and discuss.

Placements. In some courses, students spend periods of time learning in the workplace or another specialist location, instructed there by resident staff – often also supervised by a tutor from their university.

Online lessons. These can be official recordings and streamed events from your own university, or instructional videos from elsewhere online.

For any of these forms of teaching to be truly effective, the conditions for learning have to be right.

> *Go to: Chapter 2 for details of some of the main factors influencing how well you learn.*

And then fill in the table below to help you prepare to get the best out of every type of teaching. Which of these teaching activities are well matched to good learning, and which could make it difficult? The more alert you are to the challenges, the readier you'll be to deal with them.

Write a number in each box, from 0 (not matching the learning condition in question at all) to 5 (strongly supporting it).								
How well will you be able to …	LECTURES	CLASSES	SEMINARS/ WORKSHOPS	LAB/STUDIO WORK	GROUP WORK	TUTORIALS	PLACEMENTS	ONLINE LESSONS
… stay motivated throughout?								
… work at the right pace?								
… make the work relevant to you?								
… pursue your own interests?								
… access expert teaching?								
… set up a good learning environment?								
… get actively involved?								

2 Know how you learn

How much you benefit from the teaching available to you will depend a lot on how well you understand yourself as a learner, and the choices you make as a result.

> **Go to: Chapter 2** *to consider your learning habits, styles and preferences, and how you get on with some of the key thinking skills.*

Bear in mind everything else you've learned about yourself as you've worked through this book, and use the following activity to prepare you to put your self-awareness into action.

For each kind of teaching, what are the ...

- personal strengths you'll be able to draw on?
- current weaknesses you'll need to address?
- best opportunities here for your development?
- most significant challenges you'll face?

Leave the final space blank for now. You'll be coming back to it at the end of the chapter, by which time you'll have explored a variety of possible ways to respond.

TYPE OF TEACHING: Lectures	
PERSONAL STRENGTHS:	OPPORTUNITIES AVAILABLE:
CURRENT WEAKNESSES:	CHALLENGES TO OVERCOME:
KEY PERSONAL STRATEGIES FOR SUCCESS:	

TYPE OF TEACHING: Classes

PERSONAL STRENGTHS:	OPPORTUNITIES AVAILABLE:
CURRENT WEAKNESSES:	CHALLENGES TO OVERCOME:

KEY PERSONAL STRATEGIES FOR SUCCESS:

TYPE OF TEACHING: Seminars/workshops

PERSONAL STRENGTHS:	OPPORTUNITIES AVAILABLE:
CURRENT WEAKNESSES:	CHALLENGES TO OVERCOME:

KEY PERSONAL STRATEGIES FOR SUCCESS:

TYPE OF TEACHING: Lab/studio work

PERSONAL STRENGTHS:	OPPORTUNITIES AVAILABLE:
CURRENT WEAKNESSES:	CHALLENGES TO OVERCOME:

KEY PERSONAL STRATEGIES FOR SUCCESS:

TYPE OF TEACHING: Group work

PERSONAL STRENGTHS:	OPPORTUNITIES AVAILABLE:
CURRENT WEAKNESSES:	CHALLENGES TO OVERCOME:

KEY PERSONAL STRATEGIES FOR SUCCESS:

TYPE OF TEACHING: Tutorials

PERSONAL STRENGTHS:	OPPORTUNITIES AVAILABLE:
CURRENT WEAKNESSES:	CHALLENGES TO OVERCOME:

KEY PERSONAL STRATEGIES FOR SUCCESS:

TYPE OF TEACHING: Placements

PERSONAL STRENGTHS:	OPPORTUNITIES AVAILABLE:
CURRENT WEAKNESSES:	CHALLENGES TO OVERCOME:

KEY PERSONAL STRATEGIES FOR SUCCESS:

TYPE OF TEACHING: Online lessons	
PERSONAL STRENGTHS:	OPPORTUNITIES AVAILABLE:
CURRENT WEAKNESSES:	CHALLENGES TO OVERCOME:
KEY PERSONAL STRATEGIES FOR SUCCESS:	

Note To Self

Make sure that you've let your course staff know about any special needs they can help you with. When you meet the main members of your teaching team in person, check that they've received the message, and let them know whether any special measures put in place have helped – or whether you'll need more support to engage fully with the teaching on offer.

3 Play your part

For teaching to work it has to help you to carry out all the *thinking* processes that are important at this level.

As always, to learn well you'll need to be able to **access**, **record** and **organize** information well, so that you can **analyse**, **use** and **remember** it.

And to achieve higher-level understanding and long-term learning – and to keep moving yourself forward as a learner – the seven key principles outlined in Part 5 will be more important than ever: **preparation**, **interrogation**, **organization**, **modification**, **connection**, **evaluation**, **discussion**.

Here are some of the most useful things you can do (and the main types of thinking behind them) in the typical teacher-led activities you'll encounter. (Collaborative, student-led sessions are explored in Chapter 15.)

'At-a-distance' learning: lectures, online lessons

Before ...

- Find out what the lecture is about, who's giving it, and what their purpose and perspective is likely to be. Do some research about the topic, so that you can see where it fits into your course as a whole and how it's going to help your learning. Having a foundation of understanding will help you to take in new information, and you can also use it to build up some curiosity and plan some questions. [*preparation, interrogation*]
- Get together any materials you'll need to make notes. [*preparation*]

During ...

- Ensure that you can see and hear well, and that you'll be able to ask questions or interact with the teaching in other ways if necessary. [*preparation, interrogation*]
- Label your notes with the date, session title and the lecturer's name. [*organization*]
- Choose a note-making style that suits you and the topic and type of learning taking place. (**Go to: Chapter 10** for a guide to some of the main note-making formats and techniques.) Even if your university offers 'lecture capture', in audio or visual form, it's no substitute for attending in person and making notes during the live event. Use abbreviations, condense your writing and make sure that it helps you engage with what's being said rather than stopping you listening and thinking. If the speaker says things that seem particularly important, write down phrases or sentences in those exact words – but do this very sparingly. [*interrogation, organization*]
- Do your best to focus on the different parts of information presented, as well as seeing how larger themes or arguments are being developed – which you can sketch with a simple diagram or map as you listen. [*organization, connection*]
- Use a range of analytic techniques to question everything you hear, and look for any problems in the evidence or reasoning (**Go to: Chapter 14** for some essential questions to ask, and for a guide to what you *might* find). [*interrogation, evaluation*]
- Include personal reactions to the teaching in your notes, to help you develop your own verdicts and to remember the information you've heard. [*interrogation, connection*]
- If there's a chance to interact with other people, or even the speaker, do your best to be supportive to others, but make it as useful – and as manageable – as possible for you. [*interrogation, connection, discussion*]
- Make sure that you collect any handouts and keep them with the notes you've made. [*organization*]
- Keep a record of any areas you'd like to research further yourself. [*interrogation*]

After ...

- Spend some time tidying up your notes while it's all still fresh in your memory. [*preparation, organization, modification*]
- Look at any handouts and think carefully about what's worth keeping. [*organization, evaluation*]

- Carry out any extra research you've given yourself, adding more notes into the mix. [*interrogation, connection, evaluation*]
- *Do* something with the information you've collected. Discuss it with a friend, use it to start planning an essay, or make a resource to help you remember it later on. [*preparation, interrogation, organization, connection, discussion*]
- Sometimes, write a short reflection about the session in your learning journal, including thoughts on getting even more out of this sort of activity in future. [*preparation, interrogation, evaluation, discussion*]
- Store your notes and other materials carefully, adding information about them to the relevant parts of your developing 'learning map'. (**Go to: Chapter 12** to see how this important study strategy works.) [*organization, connection*]

Academic Advice

'Consider the pros and cons of taking notes on a computer. Its efficiency depends a lot on your typing speed, but you also need to think about the impact it has on your engagement, understanding and memory. Some students find note-taking on a laptop keeps them focused and helps them to recall what they've heard, but I know others who've discovered that they think better and remember more when they return to writing notes by hand.' **Amina, university tutor**

Student Tip:

'It's tempting to miss lectures sometimes, if you think you can get away with it, especially if they look like they're covering stuff you've done before. In my first year there were quite a few lectures that seemed to go through things I'd only just done at college. But you quickly realize that every lecture is important, and that they get you to look at things in new ways. It's actually very useful if you've done something before because it helps you to see what's different at university level.' **Heidi, third-year Biology undergraduate**

Close-up learning: tutorials, lab/studio work, placements

Before ...

- Read any instructions carefully and do all the preparatory writing, practising or thinking required. [*preparation*]
- Prepare some discussion ideas about the work you've done. Which aspects of it would be most useful to talk about? Can you predict how other people are likely to challenge you (and have some answers ready)? Are there elements of the thinking and working processes you've gone through that you'd like to explore? [*interrogation*]
- Use notes about the previous session, or reflections in your learning journal, to see whether there's anything important to follow up this time. [*preparation, evaluation*]

During ...

- Embrace the opportunity to test out your knowledge, understanding and skill. [*interrogation*]
- Make the most of dialogue and feedback. Listen carefully to everyone present, not just the teacher, but analyse all the ideas raised and be active in deciding which ones you're happy to adopt. [*interrogation, modification, evaluation, discussion*]
- Make some simple notes if necessary, but also use memory techniques to record ideas and processes (which you can then write down in full later on). **Go to: Chapter 14** and **Chapter 19** for some practical memory strategies. [*organization, preparation*]

After ...

- Think carefully about what happened in the session – and your reactions to it – and make notes about any detailed information you want to retain, to store carefully with all your other learning materials. [*organization, evaluation, discussion*]
- Do something as a result of the activity: maybe redrafting an essay, practising a skill or discussing some of the issues raised in an online chat. [*modification, discussion*]
- Reflect on it in your learning journal. What have you learned about the subject you explored – and, even more importantly, about *learning*? Where do you go next in your work as a result? [*preparation, evaluation, interrogation, discussion*]

> **Go to: Chapter 7** *for ideas on adapting your* **environment** *and your* **behaviour** *to help you to learn by* **using** *what you know.*

4 Know your teachers

What connects all these different activities is ... someone teaching. It's no surprise that 'quality of teaching' ranks so highly when education providers are being judged, and it's definitely something to look at when you're choosing your course.

However, it's also important to realize that your development will involve *collaboration* between you and your teachers. The quality of your learning will depend on you both – what you can achieve together.

You'll have to adapt to the different approaches of the people who teach you, to draw on their strengths and cope with any weaknesses.

Recognizing someone's teaching techniques will help you to evaluate the information they're presenting. It will also give you a way into the thinking they're doing – especially the ways they're constructing meaning from the evidence they've got to work with.

But you'll also have to see past the person in front of you – past the way they look, how they talk, what they've done in their life so far – to engage with what they've got to teach you, all of which needs to be analysed rigorously on its own merits.

Ask yourself

→ What's *useful* to see, and what you should try to see through?

The things to consider about the person teaching you include their ...

- ... **reputation.** Does knowing what they've done in their career help you to get more out of their teaching, or stop you properly analysing what they have to say?
- ... **confidence.** How does their fluency – or lack of it – match the quality of their thinking? Does it make you too trusting of their ideas, or miss valuable information?
- ... **humour.** What's their purpose in being funny? How does it impact on your learning?
- ... **emotion.** Does their passion (or the opposite) for their subject help you to recognize its significance, or make it harder to examine it properly?

5 Develop dialogue

Together, higher-level teaching and learning are designed to create a *dynamic*, where there's great potential to accelerate your development in your chosen field, and as a learner all round.

The way you work with other people in general will be significant here.

> *Go to: Chapter 17* for a detailed guide to studying well with others.

But there are also some specific things to consider in relation to the key teaching and learning activities.

In lectures and online sessions

Coming prepared, with foundation knowledge and interesting questions, and then engaging with the ideas as they're presented, analysing the arguments and forming your own views, all helps you to enter into a kind of conversation with the lecturer, even if you never actually speak to them.

You're already questioning them by being curious before they've even started, so that when they do speak, you can judge whether their answers satisfy you or need to be challenged.

If you get a chance to ask questions out loud, you'll have some detailed points to address – but you can also involve others in the dialogue by discussing the lecture with friends.

In classes, seminars and workshops

There's usually much more chance to interact directly with the person up front. Find the level of interaction that suits you best.

As always, it's about being aware of what you're doing, its impact on your study, and adapting your approach accordingly. Some people like to plan at least one contribution in advance, rather than worrying that they'll have nothing to say. Others write down questions as they occur to them during the activity, so that they can be precise when they ask them.

You might relish the chance to challenge other people's ideas, or be most interested in clarifying details of your own work while there's an expert on hand.

It's easy to sit back and not get involved at all (or, for some students, to offer too *many* questions and ideas). Afterwards, use your learning journal to think about how useful your involvement in the dialogue was, for others as well as yourself, and whether there are any changes you'd make next time.

In laboratory/studio work and placements

There's often plenty of functional dialogue, involving instructions about what to do and guidance on how to do it. But there's also an important opportunity here to discuss the thinking involved in practical tasks.

Good teachers will sometimes open up their own internal dialogue, revealing what's going on in an expert's mind as they work through a process.

And the more alert you are to your own thoughts and inner voice – and prepared to share them – the more help you can get with your thinking as well as your practical skills.

In tutorials

Dialogue is absolutely key. You prepare yourself through research, reflection and written work.

Then, in the tutorial itself, you find out how well all of that holds up to scrutiny, during inquisitive and challenging discussions between you, your teacher and any other students involved.

Like higher-level study itself, dialogue isn't meant to be easy (and for students from some cultural backgrounds, critical discussion can be a particularly daunting concept). You'll benefit from it fully only if you're confident enough to test your ideas and skills on people who might have different opinions about what's right.

Preparation is essential. You can boost your confidence by checking that your ideas are reasonable, and by practising key skills in advance. Feedback from teaching staff will help to move you on rather than sending you back to square one.

Your mindset matters. Constructive criticism is highly valued in the academic community. You're paying to get it, and the people teaching you want to help you think and work and learn. Be open to their advice, and as positive as you can about using it to improve.

Put it in perspective. Try to recognize the major and minor points in the responses you receive, so that you know how to prioritize your efforts from here. It guards you against getting disheartened (or complacent). Consider the overall message in the feedback, be led by that, but also recognize the smaller points and respond to them appropriately.

Get clarification. As much as you can, ask for more details about any comments you're not sure about. The conversation that follows might well be the most valuable dialogue of all.

Support the process. Dialogue is, by definition, a joint activity, and it can be challenging for everyone involved. Try to make it as easy as possible for people to give you useful feedback by welcoming it, acting on it, and demonstrating what's changed as a result. Even if you never say a word to a teacher, but act respectfully in their session, engage with the arguments they present, and use some of their ideas as you move forward in your study, you've been in it together, and both of you have done your job.

Note To Self

Return to the activity in Step 2 to plan how you're going to put all of this advice into action.

- Think about the specific types of teaching prioritized in your course.

- Bear in mind how you've coped in similar situations in the past.

- Consider everything you know about your learning, and yourself …

… and then answer the final question in each table, preparing yourself to face up to each of these scenarios for real.

 ❯ *Go to: Chapter 6 to check/update the section on **learning from teaching** in your Core Development Plan.*

⑩ Ten-point summary

1. The principles and practices of teaching change when you get to higher-level education.

2. At this stage, teaching only works well if it's a collaborative activity.

3. Recognize the challenges as well as the opportunities involved in different teaching activities, and adapt the conditions to suit how *you* learn best.

4. Teaching is most effective when it lets your thinking skills flourish.

5. Preparation is important to get the most out of any teaching session.

6. You need to be actively engaged while you're being taught, aware of the sorts of thinking and working that will accelerate your learning.

7. After each session, reflecting on what went on helps you to embed the learning and improve your approach next time.

8. Analysing someone's teaching techniques can help you understand how they're thinking.

9. It's vital to see past someone's reputation, presentation skills and personal style to be able to judge the true value of the information they're offering.

10. Use the different forms of dialogue opened up by teaching to support and strengthen all aspects of your study.

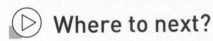 # Where to next?

Chapter 16 will explain everything that goes into producing high-quality independent work.

Going it alone

Higher-level study involves a variety of independent assignments, challenging you to turn your research and reflection into writing that demonstrates your intellectual, academic and personal strength.

What?

For many students, how they feel at any given moment is directly linked to when their next essay's due. **Independent assignments**, particularly pieces of **written work**, are an integral part of learning, and they present a significant challenge on every front. This chapter is about understanding why these tasks are so important here, and what you have to do to complete them well – and use the experience to the full.

Some courses are more practically-based than others, and not all assignments involve writing. But it's extremely hard to do well without the ability to channel what you're reading, doing and thinking about into high-quality written work. The processes involved are intricately linked with the intellectual, academic and personal skills you need to learn – and demonstrate – to achieve success in this phase of your studies.

When?

Written assignments feature throughout almost every university-level course, and the advice here will be important every time they appear. You'll need to remind yourself of the key strategies and processes before you start each one, but also keep checking that you're on track along the way. There's some key self-management advice to keep you going, especially when things get tough.

Who?

The core challenge of these tasks is the personal responsibility involved – to do the **research**, **practical work** and **thinking** in the first place, and then to shape it all into a product that will hold up against some demanding criteria. You'll have to manage your work and your emotions well, but there are some very powerful development opportunities on offer if you can.

You've also got your readers to consider. You'll need to be acutely aware of your audience, your assessors and your whole academic community, since this work needs to meet their exacting standards. But if you can understand how to do that, you're getting to the absolute heart of higher-level study.

Why?

These assignments need to be done, and done well enough, to keep you on your course and contribute to your results and final qualifications. If they're done *really* well, they'll drive forward your development like nothing else.

Writing tasks push you to focus on the things that are valuable in your field. You engage with them closely as you gather evidence, do your own research, analyse and evaluate. And the writing process helps you to do your very best thinking. You end up with work that's worth other people reading. And because they can judge it accurately, the **feedback** they give you is priceless.

Writing is integral to learning at this stage. The documents you produce now will become part of your growing knowledge base, and each one sets you up for the work that comes next.

But you also discover so much about learning – including how to manage yourself through any complex task; how to bring all your skills to bear on any kind of problem; and how to communicate what you're doing with clarity, accuracy and impact.

How?

Start by exploring the main types of written assignment, to help you identify the specific ways they're used in your subject. Think about why you're set these challenges, and which **thinking skills** are being tested and stretched.

You'll need to be focused and **strategic**. There are some useful techniques for working out exactly what you're being asked to do, and deciding the best ways to do it.

It's vital to be **organized** in your thinking and working throughout, so that you produce writing that fulfils the requirements and communicates your understanding well. You can sharpen all the key skills you need to shape your ideas, and mapping out your work visually can help to make both your thinking and your writing strong and clear.

Learn how to manage your **emotions**: to get started, cope with difficulties along with way, and get all the way through a lengthy and testing process in one piece.

Finally, see why it's important to show how you've made use of other people's work to create your own, and to present your finished work to match the **standards** of your new community.

Steps to success

1 Understand the challenge

It's essential to see your assignments in the context of your chosen course, since they're integral to the way learning is developed there. They need to reflect its interests, values, and also the practical ways it gets things done. A great deal of your overall understanding of your subject will be developed through writing about it.

> **Go to: Chapter 5** *for questions to help you explore the theories of learning in your field of study.*

> **Go to: Chapter 4** *to consider what your personal challenges here are likely to be.*

Three of the main assignment-types to look out for are **essays**, **reflective accounts** and **reports**.

Essays

An essay is a tightly structured piece of writing that focuses on a very specific question and explores it in detail, in formal, academic language, using a number of technical features to help readers evaluate its accuracy and usefulness. Writing essays helps you to examine the evidence you've collected and develop your understanding by communicating it clearly and precisely, leading your reader through your analysis to reach a conclusion you can stand by.

> **Go to: Chapter 11** *to see how different types of essay are based on different styles of thinking – depending on the needs of the subject, topic and task.*

Reflective accounts

These combine aspects of essays (above) and reports (below). Still very much based on established academic principles, and relying on the clarity and precision of academic writing skills, they help you to connect theory and practice.

- Sometimes you'll begin with a particular theory to test, and you'll find an appropriate way to put it into practice.
- At other times, an issue or problem will be the starting point, leading you to research possible ways to address it – and then test those.

Reports

Even though reports are widely used in higher-level education, they're based more in the professional than the academic world, focusing on real-world problems and solutions.

- The way you've created the report is explained in the writing.
- Your findings (from your own research) are outlined in detail.
- Conclusions are reached and recommendations given – including discussing how this work itself could be improved, and suggesting possible next steps.
- The report's structure – with headed sections, numbered points, diagrams and other subject-specific features – guides the reader through the text, rather than the flow of information being controlled by the writer's use of language.

Different subjects treat all of these types of assignment in different ways, and it's important to know what you'll be required to do as early as possible. The sooner you see some good examples of real, subject-specific examples, the sooner you'll see why certain preparation tasks are being set, and why lectures, tutorials and other activities are run in a particular way.

Everything you do should be guiding you to produce written work that intensifies the kinds of thinking valued by your subject. All your writing should be clearly linked to the development of knowledge, understanding, academic ability – and, in many courses, specific practical and professional skills.

Some pieces of work – particularly the longer projects explained in Chapter 18 – will draw on more than one of these approaches. There are plenty of other kinds of written work you could be asked to do for your course, but they'll all include at least some elements of the models described above.

Bear in mind the following variables when you're working out exactly what's involved:

- how research is collected
- what counts as useable evidence – particularly how measurable it needs to be
- to what extent different theories have to be taken into account
- how descriptive writing is used, if at all
- whether personal experience is valuable
- how much your own processes need to be evaluated
- what sort of recommendations, if any, can be made.

But all assignments at this level also have some important things in common, directly related to the values of higher-level study overall:

- high standards of literacy
- personal evaluation
- established methods of presentation
- clear referencing of evidence.

They're all designed with clarity, precision, accuracy and useful application in mind. Everything's geared to helping you show exactly what you understand, and how you've come to your conclusions – in ways that your readers can judge with confidence.

2 Be strategic

Whatever kind of task you're taking on, you need to know:

Exactly what you're being asked to do

A good way to practise this is to find some essay titles or exam questions from the course you're taking (ones you might actually be doing at some point, or from essays that other students have written in the past) and pick out the key 'instruction' words. Think about how explicit they are. Spot when more than one approach needs to be coordinated. And consider which themes seem to have the highest priority in your subject:

- **reflecting** on your experiences or observations
- **describing** situations, systems, processes, perspectives
- **analysing** the evidence to argue a case
- **judging** between several possibilities.

If you can do this early on in your studies, you'll be well prepared for the kinds of writing you're likely to face. You'll know the importance of starting each one with a clear idea of the thinking involved.

It's also important to know the scope of the task. Look closely at the title for anything that *limits* you – in what you explore, and also how you do it – because you'll *need* some clear boundaries to be able to produce focused, rich, high-quality work.

> ❯ *Go to: Chapter 11* for more advice about unpicking assignment questions and understanding the best way to approach the specific task you've been set.

The steps you'll need to carry out in order to produce your assignment

This is vital if you're going to plan and use your time well. There may be a number of practical arrangements to sort out, as well as important decisions to make about when and how to do all the research, thinking and writing required.

Here's how it might look for the most common independent tasks:

Essays

- Explore the question.
- Carry out research.
- Reflect – on research, existing knowledge and emerging ideas.
- Carry out additional research.
- Plan the essay.
- Write the first draft.
- Allow time for further reflection and research.
- Write the second draft.
- Write the references and possibly a bibliography.
- Do any final editing, proofread the text and polish the presentation.

Things to think about:

- *How much research will I need to do?*
- *What's the best way to plan my writing?*
- *What will I need to help me check the quality of my work?*

Reflective accounts

- Understand the question/decide on the issue.
- Research relevant theories.
- Put the theories into practice, recording what happens.
- Reflect on your experiences, comparing theory and practice.

- Analyse the strengths and weaknesses of your approach, to reach conclusions and recommendations.
- Plan the writing.
- Write the first draft.
- Leave time for further reflection and research.
- Write the second draft.
- Write the references and possibly a bibliography and appendices.
- Do any final editing, proofread the text and polish the presentation.

Things to think about:

- *What would be a useful theory to investigate?*
- *Are there any practical arrangements to make?*
- *How will I record what happens, so that I can use it in my writing?*

Reports

- Explore the question set, or design your own.
- Carry out any necessary background research.
- Do your own research, including practical work.
- Analyse your findings, referring to other research if necessary.
- Reflect on the effectiveness of your methodology.
- Evaluate your work to draw conclusions and make recommendations.
- Plan the writing.
- Write the first draft.
- Leave time for further reflection and research.
- Write the second draft.
- Compile all additional materials, including appendices and glossary.
- Write an 'abstract' or summary of the report, which will appear at the start.
- Do any final editing, proofread the text and polish the presentation.

Things to think about:

- *Exactly what sort of report am I writing: factual, instructional, persuasive …?*
- *Are there any skills I'll need to develop beforehand?*
- *Do I have to contact anyone to organize permission, access or expert advice?*

With practice you'll get used to all these different parts of the process. You'll learn how long each one is likely to take, and you'll be able to create effective, task-specific plans as part of your overall time-management system.

> ❯ *Go to: Chapter 11 to see how to set yourself up with a strategic and informed plan for getting every element of the work done, and done well.*

What your writing has to contain, and how it should be communicated

Your job is to learn exactly what's required in your subject, and each task will have to be approached on its own terms. But it's still valuable to see the *main elements* within the most common assignments you'll be given, along with the *key features* you'll need to reflect in your thinking and writing.

ASSIGNMENT TYPE
Essay
MAIN ELEMENTS
Title
Introduction
Development of argument/reasoning
Conclusion
References; possibly also bibliography
KEY FEATURES
Control of language: carefully constructed paragraphs guide readers through the arguments
Objectivity of tone: explaining, comparing and contrasting
Analysis of information and perspectives
Synthesis of elements from different thinkers or schools of thoughts
Evaluation of the evidence to provide an answer to the question set

ASSIGNMENT TYPE
Reflective account
MAIN ELEMENTS
Title
Introduction
Research/explanation of theory
Description of practice
Reflections, referring to theory
Evaluation of learning – including methodology
Conclusion and recommendations
References; possibly also bibliography and appendices

KEY FEATURES

Comparisons between theories and real-world experiences

Descriptions of practical work

Analysis of practice – and of the quality and usefulness of the testing carried out

Balance between advancing general understanding and improving personal outcomes

Confidentiality strictly observed

ASSIGNMENT TYPE

Report

MAIN ELEMENTS

Title; possibly a separate title page

Abstract/summary (written towards the end of the process)

Introduction

Research/literature review

Methodology

Findings

Discussion of findings

Conclusions

Recommendations

References; possibly also appendices and glossary

KEY FEATURES

Knowledge of the context: established practices and the theories behind them

Awareness of the methodology chosen – and how effective it turns out to be

Balance between general academic standards and specific real-world applications

Confidence in the delivery of findings/recommendations, backed by a high level of detail

Structure, using a situation-specific format

Academic Advice

'Think of your introduction as a guide for you as you write. Keep checking it as you're working. At the end, read back through your introduction in detail. Make sure that you've included all the information you wanted to, but also see whether you've completed all the processes you said you'd be doing. If you set out to identify, or describe, or compare, or calculate, or recommend or whatever else ... have you actually done it?' **Jackie, university tutor**

❯ *Go to: **Chapter 1** and consider the questions there now – in the light of everything you've learned about independent writing tasks.*

How to present your finished piece of work

The precision and control of your thinking needs to be reflected in the presentation of your writing. It shows that you can follow instructions, and that you respect academic standards. It helps your readers to understand and evaluate your work.

There's a detailed list of things to consider later in the chapter, most of which can be sorted out easily towards the end of the process. But it's good to get as much information as you can from the start, because some aspects of presentation also affect the work that has to go in.

For example:

Are you required to present a full bibliography? If you are, this will need to be taken into account when you're planning your time (and it might also tell you something about the amount of research you're expected to do).

Can some data be presented as an appendix? This might free up valuable space in the main body of the writing.

Do some aspects of your work need to be presented confidentially? If they do, this will require care, and extra time, at various points in the process.

 > *Go to: Chapter 6 to check/update the* **writing** *section of your Core Development Plan.*

3 Get organized

To produce clear, well-thought-out, convincing writing, your working practices will need to be extremely organized throughout.

> *Go to: Chapter 10 to see how to gather information effectively and efficiently.*

> *Go to: Chapter 12 for a guide to mapping your learning, helping you to remember it well, and to find your way back when you need something for your work.*

 ## Academic Advice

'I tell my students to think – really think – what it would be like if they lost all the work they'd stored digitally: research work, notes, plans, schedules, programming, projects in progress ... Many of them have probably never stored anything before that they couldn't do without. But you've got to think about the worst-case scenarios, to make sure they can't happen. Back up to a separate hard drive. Email stuff to yourself or upload it to the Cloud. It's just not worth the risk.' **Rick, university course leader**

The way you make notes from your research will be particularly important here, affecting both your thinking and your writing. Choose the most appropriate strategy for each piece of writing you do. Will it help you reflect, describe, analyse, argue, evaluate?

> *Go to: Chapter 10 to see some of the options open to you.*

Your planning will flow from your note-making.

> **Go to: Chapter 11** *for various ideas about this.*

In some assignments, the way the writing needs to be structured is already very clear from the purpose of the work – maybe with a specific format to follow.

But in more explorative essays, reflective writing, and even in some highly analytic and practical reports; the best way to see how to compare, contrast, evaluate and present the different elements is to map your work *visually*.

As part of planning an essay, visual-mapping might involve:

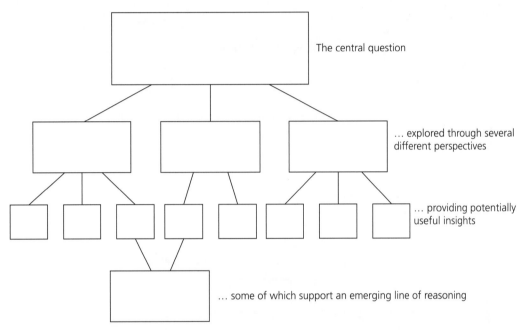

The central question

... explored through several different perspectives

... providing potentially useful insights

... some of which support an emerging line of reasoning

It can help to clarify your thinking and provide a very clear way to explain your analysis:

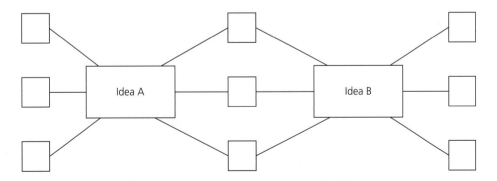

... connected by the aspects they have in common

Writing a reflective account, your planning might include:

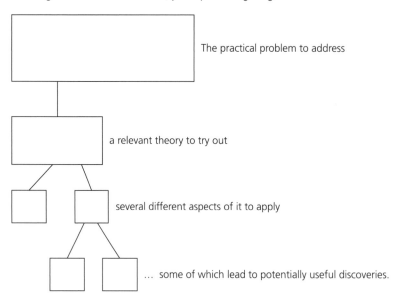

The practical problem to address

a relevant theory to try out

several different aspects of it to apply

... some of which lead to potentially useful discoveries.

Preparing a report, it might be helpful to map:

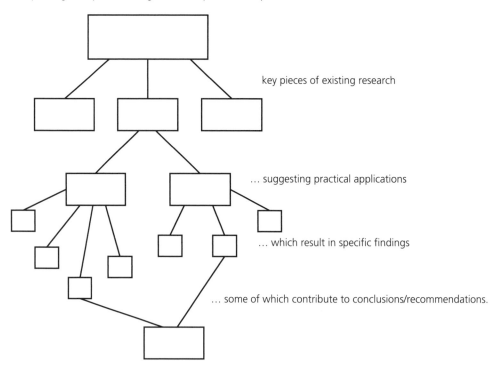

key pieces of existing research

... suggesting practical applications

... which result in specific findings

... some of which contribute to conclusions/recommendations.

❯ **Go to: Chapter 6** *to check/update the* **organization** *section of your Core Development Plan.*

4 Stretch your thinking

Written assignments train you to use a wide range of thinking styles:

- when you're developing your ideas, putting theories into practice or carrying out investigative tests
- when you're communicating the results of this work (and how you reached your conclusions)
- when you're reflecting on it all afterwards, to help you do it even better next time.

You can also benefit from consciously training some key mental skills, ready to use them confidently in your study.

Improve problem-solving

Look around the room you're in and invent a problem based on something you can see. For example:

- How could you be more efficient with the way you use your dishwasher?
- Why are you not using your bike very often?
- What would help you know how much spice to put in your cooking?
- Which is the most important book on the shelf?

Give yourself a few minutes to find some solutions, practising using as many of the problem-solving techniques as you can. The more confident you are with them, the more you'll be able to incorporate them into the specific problem set by an assignment, as well as all the different problems involved in completing the work well.

Improve *logic*

Your reader needs to be guided along a clear line of reasoning, however creatively it's being developed. Logical thinking is vital for spotting when there are problems in the arguments you're exploring or developing yourself. You need it to see what's required to back up the points you're making, and it's also essential for structuring a tight, effective, finished document.

❯ **Go to: Chapter 14** *to see some of the typical flaws in logic you need to look out for.*

Pick a solution to a problem you've set for yourself (about dishwashers, bikes or whatever else). What's the most logical way you could persuade someone it was the answer? And if you had to limit yourself to the fewest words possible, what would those words be?

Improve *creativity*

This will feed into the way you search for information, find patterns and themes, and develop new ways of thinking about your subject. You can still be accurate, disciplined and rooted in the evidence, but creative thinking will help you to go beyond what's been done so far, especially when you're making recommendations based on your findings, for yourself or others.

Practise by picking an object and challenging yourself to think of as many different uses as you can. Set your target high to push yourself to be as creative as possible. Can you think of 50 uses for a paperclip, a windscreen wiper blade, a cotton bud? Or pick two things at random – two objects, people, places, ideas – and see how many similarities you can find between them. Or choose an action and a random abstract idea and see whether you can link them. How is parachute-jumping like marriage? Why is cooking like faith?

Improve *synthesis*

Higher-level writing provides many opportunities to synthesize information and ideas in order to make improvements and move understanding on. In essays you'll often take elements from different schools of thought to suggest a viewpoint that's made stronger by drawing on them all. Reflective accounts let you try out several approaches to see how they work in combination. The recommendations in reports are often constructed from several ideas or techniques.

Pick a real-life problem someone might have. Then pick two people you know at random – famous people as well as friends and family. If you could pick one key attribute from each of them to help you solve the problem, what would it be? Or choose three objects from your surroundings and decide how they could be combined most beautifully; then most usefully; and then most inventively, to achieve something that no one has even thought of before.

Improve *analysis*

This is a key theme in all independent writing tasks, whether you're analysing existing evidence and ideas, reflecting on your own practice in the light of particular theories, or carrying out rigorous practical or conceptual tests. You need to be confident to analyse the things that matter in your subject, exploring how to take them apart and understanding how they fit together – and always ready to analyse your own approach.

Pick articles at random from newspapers and magazines. Think about the purpose of the writing. What information can you use to analyse its accuracy? Is there anything getting in the way of you judging it accurately? Use one colour to highlight facts, and another for opinions. Focus on quotations. Have any of the words or phrases been chosen to have a particular impact? Do they help you be more or less precise in your understanding? What overall impression have you been left with at the end? How sure are you that it's justified to feel like this?

> *Go to: **Chapter 6** to check/update your Core Development Plan, particularly the sections on **creativity**, **problem-solving**, **analysis** and **evaluation**.*

5 Manage your emotions

As well as putting your intellectual and academic skills to the test, independent assignments can present a significant emotional challenge:

There's a high level of uncertainty. You don't know exactly what you think until you've worked it all out on paper or screen. There are infinite ways to put your writing together. It's unpredictable what other people's response is going to be. You can't know how you'll cope with the demands of a task until you're in the middle of it.

You take a risk when you present your work for scrutiny. You're revealing your ability, and (in theory) you've had enough time to make this an accurate reflection of what you can do. Just like hearing your spoken voice on a recording, it can be extremely unsettling to see your words in print.

Feedback can be a difficult process (on both sides). It breaks lots of the conventions of adult behaviour, since we don't normally pick apart other people's thinking or criticize their work in such depth. To be of any value, feedback needs to show you how to do certain things better – but that can also be extremely demoralizing, especially if you feel you've already done the best you can.

So, bear in mind that writing academic assignments is hard, and don't be too tough on yourself if your confidence and commitment waver sometimes. But do make sure that you have some tactics up your sleeve to help.

See the value. You'll be rewarded by the grades you get, the extra knowledge and understanding you gain, but also the long-lasting skills you develop in the process.

Remember you're a learner. We don't usually see writing by people who aren't completely confident. We only get to read their stuff when they've learned how to do it really well. But you're still learning, so treat each piece of work as training – as good as it can be at this stage, but also just another point on the learning curve.

Manage your time. Start early, plan to finish before the deadline, and carefully allocate the time in between to get everything done well, among everything else you need to do. Stay flexible to cope with the unpredictable, but also be as strict as you can about moving on through the different stages of your work.

Start gently. Try writing the easiest sentence first, the point you're most confident about – wherever it happens to appear. Then, whether your pages are on paper or screen, get used to moving sections of text around as you go, using the writing process to enrich your thinking, and working in whatever sequence feels right. Your confidence will grow as the writing builds up in front of you. When you get to the toughest parts, you'll already have a good proportion of the work done, and a clearer idea about what to write next.

> **Student Tip:**
>
> 'I've always found it really hard to start writing. I hate seeing that blank computer screen staring at me. What I usually do is type the title straight away and put my name in the header, so there's something on the page. Then I write headings for the different parts of the essay (which I'll get rid of later) because I like having a structure that I can type into. I usually go for the bit that I'm clearest about first, then work outwards from there.' **Jodie, English Literature and Language undergraduate**

Set yourself free. If you get 'writer's block' and feel completely stuck for ideas, try 'free writing'. Give yourself five minutes to write *anything*, without stopping – about the question you're trying to answer if you can, but not worrying if you drift off into other thoughts, or even write about not knowing what to write about ... The important thing is to free yourself from trying to find the 'right' thing to say, and to remember what it feels like when your thoughts flow into written words. At the end of the five minutes you may have some useful ideas, or a page of nonsense. It doesn't matter: you'll have loosened up your thinking, ready to re-engage with the real writing process.

Don't be perfect. Be alert to over-analysing your work and worrying about the details, especially early on. There's no one, perfect way of doing it, and it's easy to lose the all-important flow of ideas if you go too slowly. You'll definitely need to polish your writing later, to check it reflects high-quality thinking and meets academic standards, but you can't expect to do that as you write. Allow yourself to get something down that's *reasonably* accurate for now, knowing you'll get a chance to sharpen it all later on (which will be so much easier when you've got a full draft of the writing to work on).

> ❯ **Go to: Chapter 3** *to review the personal resources you can draw on throughout your studies – particularly when things get rough.*

6 Acknowledge your sources

When you write at this level you get to try out other people's ideas and use them to shape your own. Acknowledging their work is about more than just showing them respect, and it's certainly more significant than just following administrative rules (however much it looks like that in some books).

It helps you to work precisely. It pushes you to go off and find the very strongest materials, and then to think carefully about how to use them to produce the highest-quality work. It lets your readers check your sources, and use them, too. Crucially, it deepens your understanding of how knowledge is constructed in your subject. Referencing techniques can become powerful tools to support the way you think and learn.

You confidently highlight what you're using, where it's come from, and what you're doing with it, including:

- work that's inspired the direction of your thinking in general
- existing theories and viewpoints you're considering or trying out
- research other people have done (because, in an academic community, it's there for people like you to use)
- materials that have given you suggestions to try out and helped you form your understanding
- specific quotations from published work (and again, the authors expect to have their ideas tested – and want it to be done accurately).

When it's finished, an accurately referenced piece of writing:

- shows that you can follow guidelines and understand established academic procedures
- lets your readers make better judgements about your arguments, because they can test the value of the evidence you've based them on
- helps you to see where you agree with other people, and where you might have found original possibilities
- allows the people assessing your work to see what they're most interested in: the processes you've applied, and your developing academic skills
- becomes a valuable, condensed collection of detailed information
- points you where to go for more research on this topic – and suggests other, related areas of interest that might also be worth investigating.

 Note To Self

As soon as possible, find out the agreed format for referencing in your course. There are various approaches, and if you try to compare and contrast them, they can look confusingly similar (and pointlessly pedantic). So, don't do that: just get a clear guide to the way the staff on your course want you to do it, ideally with an example for each rule, and get into the habit of doing it that one way.

A few ground rules

The key information you'll need to record somewhere in your work is:

- the author's surname and initials (and there may be several authors)
- the full title
- the year the work was published
- the publishing company and its location
- the edition number – unless this is the first edition.

Depending on which format you're asked to use, the full reference for a **book** you've referred to might look like this:

Burman, E. (1994). *Deconstructing Developmental Psychology*. London: Routledge.

That's E. Burman's book *Deconstructing Developmental Psychology*, published in London in 1994 by the publishing house Routledge.

For **journal articles** you need to be particularly precise:

Gray, L. (2018). Exploring how and why young people use social networking sites. *Educational Psychology in Practice*. 34(2), 175–94.

That means you've used L. Gray's article 'Exploring how and why young people use social networking sites', published in 2018 in the journal *Educational Psychology in Practice*, volume 34, issue 2, between pages 175 and 194.

If it's an online article, the full web address and the date you viewed it are both important and need to be added after the rest of the information above (or as much of it as you can find):

... Retrieved 28 October 2018, from https://www.bbc.co.uk/news

And for any websites you've referred to, give the full address and, once again, the date you visited – because information can change quickly online.

https://www.britishmuseum.org. 27 April 2019

Most of this will be contained in a list of references at the end of the assignment: full details of everything you've pointed to in your writing. You might also have to include a complete bibliography, showing this information for everything you've read as part of your work.

Within the main text itself, you just need to label each source clearly – a citation – so that your reader can carry on reading but still have an idea about what sort of information this is and how it's being used. The full reference details are there for them at the end of the document, allowing them to evaluate your work in the light of the sources you've used.

They'll judge the sources just like you've done, based on the qualifications/experience/ views of the author; how recently the work was done; the academic standing of the publisher; the peer-reviewing it may or may not have undergone. You give them an easy route to plenty of that in your full reference list or bibliography.

Different subjects have different requirements for citations. The humanities tend to use footnotes/endnotes, with either full or shortened bibliographic references. In science – or science-based – subjects, you're likely to be asked to include the name(s) of the author(s) within the text itself, plus the date of the work in question (since most authors have written lots of different things) and possibly the page number.

> *According to Burman (1994), the reason why ...*

> *Social media use is one of the most popular pastimes for young people (Gray 2018: 16).*

Find out and follow the rules in your subject, make your citations clear, but try not to let them disrupt the flow of your words.

> ✎ **Note To Self**
>
> As soon as you can, look at some high-quality written work from within your own course. Make sure that it matches the rules you've been given exactly, and look at how the writer uses citations to highlight sources, reference evidence and acknowledge other people working in the field, while still producing a confident piece of work that arrives at conclusions of its own.

Plagiarism

Accurate referencing matches so many of the core principles of academic thinking and working – just as its opposite, *plagiarism*, represents a major threat to learning, and is treated as such.

You plagiarize when you use someone else's work without acknowledging it. That could be:

- claiming their ideas as your own
- paraphrasing their words without explaining where this content has come from
- including sections of someone else's writing word for word and allowing your reader to believe they're your own work.

Plagiarism defeats the whole point of higher-level study. It stops you developing the valuable skills that come from putting in the right amount of thought, research, care and time. You're very likely to be found out, and the consequence can be serious.

Academics know their subject well and are very familiar with the research that's been done already. It's not hard for them to spot ideas that haven't been properly acknowledged. Most universities also use anti-plagiarism software which compares your work forensically with a vast range of published material, in print and online, and quickly alerts staff when it finds potential issues of concerns. Universities are also very aware of the companies offering paid-for assignments, and have ways to detect them, too.

If the staff on your course are convinced you've plagiarized, you can lose your place there. It's just not worth it, on any level.

7 Perfect your presentation

It's vital to leave time to check your work before you submit it. You're not expected to 'have' perfect grammar, punctuation and spelling, but you are expected to do your best to *use* perfect grammar, punctuation and spelling in your work – by getting software, dictionaries and other people to help.

❯ *Go to: Chapter 11 for more guidance about the final quality-control stage of any writing task.*

Check that any supporting information – such as figures or diagrams within the text, or appendices attached – are labelled accurately. Make sure that the document you submit has been 'cleaned' of anything you might have used to help you write it – like colour-coding, temporary headings or 'add evidence here'-style notes.

Student Tip:

'Once I managed to submit the wrong version of my work entirely. I'd gone through several stages of drafting and redrafting and I'd created a new file each time. When it came to printing the one to hand in, it was late and I was rushing – and somehow I printed off one that was about three versions out of date. I think it even had some of my working notes still in it. Never again.' **William, Politics undergraduate**

As well as perfecting the content, you also need to get the presentation spot on. Use your course handbook or other resources to see the official requirements, but be prepared to be flexible. Individual staff can have their own preferences, and some pieces of work come with their own rules.

Academic Advice

'Get hold of the presentation rules, and then you can make things easier for yourself by creating template files on your computer for particular types of work. Instead of having to adjust to the right font, character size and line spacing every time, make a blank file, with all the settings correct. You can write things like "Title" and "Section Heading" and "Opening sentence" so you just need to type over them when you're writing for real. Make sure that you "save as" to keep the template unchanged for next time.' *Chris, university English tutor*

You'll need to consider:

The preferred font and size of type. Different heading levels may need to be different sizes, and in some assignments you'll have a degree of flexibility. But consistency is key so that your structure – and your meaning within it – are clear.

Line spacing and page layout. Find out whether you're expected to indent paragraphs or leave a clear line between them. Some courses may want you to leave a certain amount of space in the margins, or use 1.5 or even double spacing between lines, for annotations and feedback.

Page labelling. Do you need to number your pages, or add any details (like your name, or a simple form of the title) in the header or footer?

The front page. Do you need a separate cover page? If so, what goes on it? You might be supplied with a template to fill in, possibly including a declaration to sign about it being your own work.

Anonymity. Some courses ask you to hand in assignments anonymously. More commonly, it's the content (or parts of it) that needs to be kept confidential – particularly when it's about particular people or organizations. Think very carefully about whether anyone could trace the exact sources of any sensitive information from the way you've described it (including by joining up the dots between details in different parts of your work).

Submitting your work. Find out whether you can submit your work digitally, by uploading it or sending it as an email attachment, or whether it has to be a hard copy. If you do have to print it, leave plenty of time (and if you're using your own printer, check that you've got enough ink and paper before you start). Print on one side only and find out how you're expected to fasten your pages together.

 ❯ *Go to: Chapter 6 to check/update your Core Development Plan, particularly the sections on **completing academic work** and **meeting academic standards**.*

 Ten-point summary

1. Independent assignments help you to develop a wide range of personal and academic skills.

2. It's important to understand how writing is used in the context of your own subject.

3. Typical higher-level tasks include essays, reflective accounts and reports.

4. A strategic approach helps you to see what's required at each stage of the writing process.

5. Your research needs to be organized and efficient to support high-quality written work.

6. Academic writing involves a variety of thinking skills, including problem-solving, logic, creativity, analysis and synthesis.

7. Writing tasks challenge your emotions, so it's important to know which self-management strategies work for you.

8. By acknowledging your sources you can learn more about how your subject works, and make your writing more useful to others.

9. If you plagiarize other people's work, you gain none of the rewards of study – and risk being removed from your course.

10. The quality of your thinking needs to be matched by the presentation of your finished work.

▷ Where to next?

Chapter 17 will show you how to communicate and collaborate successfully during this next phase of your learning.

All together now

Learning to work well with others in the academic community can be a challenge, but it's one that can enrich all aspects of your studies, and help you to develop a range of valuable personal skills.

 ## What?

Higher-level education involves joining lots of new groups, large and small. How well you operate within them will go a long way to deciding the success of your study overall.

As well as being part of the overall **academic community**, you're a student at a particular university and a member of a school, of a department and of a specific course within that. You're living and working among a very complex collection of people, all with their own needs and goals, but with some important shared ambitions, too. Yes, this phase of education is very much about you as an individual, responsible for leading your own learning, developing your own ideas, and achieving qualifications with your name on them. But you simply won't be able to do it on your own.

This chapter explores why **collaboration** and **communication** are valued so highly at this stage. It's not easy (what in higher-level education is?) and you'll need a range of strategies to survive and thrive. But there are exciting opportunities here to become a truly independent thinker, through extremely *inter*dependent activities.

 ## When?

Working well with others has to start from day one. As well as adapting to the values and standards at each layer of the academic world, you'll need to find your place within various different forms of **group learning**. You'll be quickly involved in **classes**, **tutorials**, **workshops** and other shared activities, and they'll all help to stretch your interpersonal skills as you use them to energize your studying. There'll be times of extra challenge too, particularly when you're involved in **group projects**, if you have to lead **seminars**, and whenever you're called on to **present** or **perform**.

 ## Who?

You're likely to be studying with people from many social and geographical backgrounds, at different stages of life, with extremely varied attitudes and attributes. While you're learning how to get on well with them, you'll also be collaborating with academic staff, professionals you meet on placements, even members of the public involved in your research. They've all got lots to offer to your studies, and you have plenty to give in return.

Why?

There are rich opportunities here to deepen your understanding of your subject, strengthen a wide range of higher-level skills, play a part in contributing to progress in your chosen field – and come away well prepared for the world of work or future study. There's great pleasure to be taken from contributing to the wider life of the university, as well as the chance to build some of the most valuable personal abilities of all.

How?

Learning with others can be far from easy, especially if you're the sort of person who's always managed very well on your own. But it's a big part of life at this level: so, start by exploring the things you've got to gain from engaging with some new kinds of collaboration.

Next, reflect on your personality and previous experiences to help you choose the best ways forward. You'll need to step out of your comfort zone, but it doesn't have to be traumatic. Build on your strengths and you can start using your people skills to improve core elements of higher-level study.

When you understand the principles of successful **group work**, you'll see how to play a variety of roles, always supporting others, and always accelerating your own learning. Discover the secrets of successful group projects, and prepare yourself to make the most of feedback – giving as well as receiving.

Finally, face up to the challenge of **presentations**, which can be perfect opportunities to put yourself and your learning to the test. Find out how to plan, practise and present with confidence, so that you add to your own understanding, discover more about how new knowledge is built, and gain some of the most valuable personal skills that higher-level study has to offer.

Steps to success

1 Understand the benefits

Universities, colleges, conservatoires and all other providers of higher-level courses are run as communities of thinkers and learners. They have major responsibilities to promote cutting-edge research, and one of the main ways they do that is to get people working together, to learn from each other, challenge each other, and take each other's research off in new directions. Key values such as respect, honesty and fairness are all based on promoting healthy cooperation.

And you can benefit from all of that, and more, if you know how to join in, getting invaluable support for your learning – and the chance to contribute to the wider academic mission.

Information and ideas. When you step up to this level you get access to a wide range of existing research, through lectures, classes, tutorials, libraries, online resources. You're also introduced to different perspectives on it, as academic staff present their own positions as well as guiding you through a range of other points of view. The tasks you're set encourage you to explore your subject widely and make the most of the important work done by everyone else.

Teaching and learning. As members of a teaching organization, the staff you work with know that people learn in different ways (they're also here to learn themselves) and they run the learning activities that way, too, giving you multiple ways to take in information and experiment with ideas. Working closely with other students should also reveal things to try out in your own study.

Lifetime skills. One of the most important benefits of all will come later. If you can learn to work productively with others now, cope with all their different attitudes, behaviours and needs, achieve things together – and also get out what *you* need – then you're training yourself extremely well for life beyond education. These are absolutely key professional skills, as well as being very important routes to confidence and continued personal growth as you step into the adult world.

Meanwhile, while you're still very much in education, it's possible to pick out immediate and ongoing benefits of working closely with others – without which it would be quite hard to see the purpose of higher-level study at all. You don't even have to be physically present: everything on the following list is also available if you're learning at a distance, or only meeting fellow students occasionally – as long as you have a variety of ways to communicate with them and opportunities to work together, one way or another.

- **Encouragement:** other students boosting your self-belief and helping you to stay committed
- **Feedback:** getting advice from peers about how to improve, and benefiting yourself from analysing and commenting on their work
- **Discussion:** hearing different perspectives, testing out your own, and learning how knowledge can be developed dynamically
- **Comparison:** looking at other people's work, and the feedback it got, to help you do things differently next time
- **Collaboration:** taking part in joint projects, sharing ideas and developing your work on the foundations other people have laid
- **Challenge:** gaining from having your knowledge, ideas, abilities, and particularly your memory tested by other people, and from getting opportunities to test *them*.

Student Tip:

'Listening is a really important skill at university. When I started my course, the way people talked in lectures and seminars seemed very different from what I was used to. But a few years down the line, I can now recognize that same sort of language in my own essays. You just pick it up along the way – from hearing it first, then starting to talk like that yourself, and eventually I suppose it shapes the way you think.' **Tariq, final-year History undergraduate**

2 Decide your priorities

Chapter 3 examined five key aspects of collaborative learning:

1 contributing in groups
2 giving presentations
3 engaging in academic dialogue
4 collaborating on tasks
5 working supportively.

〉 *Go to:* **Chapter 3** *to explore your previous experiences of studying with others, highlighting strengths you can use now as well as areas for improvement.*

As you think more and more about what good study is going to mean for you, in your subject, it's important to explore these skills in relation to the particular challenges you'll face now. All these skill-sets have plenty to offer at this stage of learning, but there are also some pitfalls in them to avoid. You'll need to consider your own needs, and your own character, to develop the best approach for you.

The following activity focuses on five big themes in this book, and in all university-level courses:

- organization
- information gathering
- benefiting from teaching
- academic writing
- assessments.

Which 'people skills' could – maybe with a bit of practice – help you grow in each of these influential areas of study? Be specific. Some forms of working-with-others might feel like exactly the *wrong* thing for you.

Which of the five numbered skill-sets above could help you to ...	*(Write numbers from the list.)*
... be organized?	
... gather information?	
... benefit from teaching?	
... do academic writing?	
... do well in assessments?	

When you've done that, go back and circle any numbers in the grid that represent areas you want to focus on now. It could be because they're already strong and you can capitalize on them, or you know they're in need of some work.

Use your responses to direct the way you use the rest of this chapter – particularly when you're deciding which bits of advice to start trying out for real.

3 Join the group

Good study demands that you know how groups work – the potential threats as well as the opportunities. There a lot that's unpredictable here, and that makes it more important than ever to be aware of what to look for, to know what you can do, and to be ready to act.

Here are some of the most important factors affecting the quality of group work, for all involved, along with ways for you to respond – in everyone's best interests.

Key factors in group work	Strategies to help you study well with others
Atmosphere Does it feel like a supportive learning community, where everyone is welcome and hopes of success are high? Are people motivated to turn up and take part? Can energy be maintained for long-term tasks? Do the dynamics within the group help energetic, creative, ambitious learning to take place?	Do everything you can to be friendly and helpful. You can get on with people and learn well with them even if you don't *like* them. Are everyone's physical needs being met? Think about temperature, lighting, comfort, refreshment … If there's a problem but no one does anything, nothing will change. (**Go to: Chapter 7** for a list of environmental factors to consider, in any learning space.) Check that the appropriate levels of communication are in place. When you're together, can everyone see, hear and get involved? Make sure that you speak clearly and inclusively. When you're not together, are you in touch via email, learning platform or group chat? Sort out your own communication links and do your best to get everyone else connected. Think about your language – what you say out loud, and what your body language says, too. Are you showing that you're interested and engaged? Do you seem open to ideas? Can you disagree with someone without them getting upset? The way you communicate will affect the whole group, but it also has a big impact on how you think while you're in it. Keep to clear boundaries for supporting others in the group. Together, you should be helping each other to do the best work possible, and there may be times when particular people need to be given extra time or assistance. But be aware of people draining the group's resources, and signpost them to the help available from academic staff or official support services.

Key factors in group work	Strategies to help you study well with others
Behaviour Do people know the rules of engagement: how to be challenging and driven without making anyone feel threatened or anxious? Is it safe to explore disagreements – about working practices as well as ideas? Is everyone aware that behaviour needs to match university standards? Do they feel able to draw on help from beyond the group if required?	Ensure that the group sets some ground rules. At this level it should be fine to do it verbally, but if you need to, write them down, circulate them or even display them every time you meet. Some people may need them more than others. If behaviour problems aren't easily fixed within the group, get help from academic staff. You've invested time and energy in this, and your success depends on it, so you should expect support to resolve any serious issues – including moving people out of groups if necessary. Model good behaviour yourself, in your attendance, punctuality and preparedness. Show people that you can challenge ideas precisely and respectfully, offering evidence about your own viewpoint – but also building on theirs as much as possible. Use the way you talk about, plan and shape group projects to demonstrate strong academic behaviour: high standards of accuracy, honesty in the way you gather evidence and ideas, and robust thinking in your reasoning. Everything is worth testing, and everything can lead to new understanding – so no one's views should be dismissed out of hand.
Purpose Is everyone clear about what you're trying to achieve, why you're working on it together, and how you're going to get it done? Is there a long-term plan for the group? Does each session have its own agenda, either formally or informally, to keep everything on track? Is everyone part of the purpose and being helped to contribute, and benefit, to the full?	Help the group to draw up a long-term plan. Discuss how to allocate time intelligently, maintain momentum and get everything done, but also allow room for manoeuvre along the way. Let everyone have a say in this, so that they can highlight any issues – or offer useful solutions – early on. Remember to incorporate group work into your overall time-management systems. (**Go to: Chapter 8** to see where project plans fit in to the bigger picture.) Only agree to contributions that you can achieve within the time allowed, using your diary, to-do list and other plans to see what's possible – and then to do it as promised. Consider whether the group needs a leader – for the whole project, parts of it, or a different one each time you meet. In some groups, it's hard to make the best use of time without one person being allowed to make some decisions and keep things moving forward, but you'll need to see what's best for yours. It may be possible to agree an agenda for each session. If not, create your own personal one, which you can refer to (in your head) to help you focus the group on the tasks at hand. Be alert to people not contributing. There may be easy ways you can help them – through eye contact, bringing them into the conversation or offering them a particular role – or you may need to minimize their negative impact and be wary of giving them jobs that affect your success.

Make sure that you know what the main purpose is, as well as the underlying benefits. All group sessions can help you improve your people skills and enrich your understanding of learning, but maybe this one is also part of developing a particular project, or set up to provide a specific experience or form of mutual support.

Self-awareness

Are people able to reflect on how things are going and make changes if required?

Does everyone have ways of knowing if the work is progressing well?

Are people given helpful feedback about their own contributions?

Is the group set up to help its members learn about *learning*?

Check that your group's planning (and any personal planning you do) has some checkpoints built in: moments to reflect on how things are going. Use your logical thinking to prepare for eventualities in advance – if *this* happens, then we'll do *this* – and your creative mind to find a variety of solutions. Leave time in the process to deal properly with any issues that arise.

Encourage people to share how they're feeling about the work, as well as what's going on with particular tasks.

Demonstrate to others how feedback – managed well – can be beneficial for the person giving it as well as the recipient. (**Go to: Chapter 17** for a best-practice guide.)

Talk about the *processes* you're using in your work, including what's going on with your *learning*, to get others talking about their own unseen experiences of study. (This is particularly important in Problem-Based Learning (PBL) scenarios, where the key learning comes from understanding the *processes* used to find a solution.)

Responsibility

Is everyone aware of their own role in the group, committed to the enterprise and able to use their own attributes and abilities to help it succeed?

Are there ways to check that everyone's playing their part?

Can people offer their most applicable skills without making the balance of effort unfair?

Is it possible for individuals to address their own needs through the work, as well as sharing in the responsibility for its overall success?

Be clear about your own role, and refer to it when necessary in discussions, to remind others that there are different jobs to do.

The more specific you are in analysing strengths and weaknesses of your work – or the group itself – the easier it will be to notice if anyone's having problems fulfilling their responsibilities, and to suggest ways to change things around.

Listening and watching attentively will often reveal people's specialist skills, including strengths in thinking and communicating as well as particular academic or practical skills. Help them, and others, to recognize how these could be used to the full, but make sure that people are also allowed to drop certain responsibilities to keep things fair.

As well as giving everything you reasonably can to the group, keep your own needs in mind, and expect everyone else to do the same. Your greatest responsibility is to yourself (and your community needs everyone to be driven by high personal standards). This work will only be truly successful if you come away with strong assessment results, improved skills and greater understanding of how to work well with others. Don't sacrifice any of that in your efforts to get a group task done.

❯ *Go to: Chapter 1 to consider some of the emotions than can affect people's attitudes to learning and their behaviour in groups.*

Student Tip:

'If you have to lead a seminar at some point in your course, think about it like any other group session, where all the usual principles apply – just more so.

'Prepare yourself well. You'll probably have to present a paper, so aim for a good balance between what you're confident writing about, and what you'd be happy to get help with. Make sure that there's enough in it that you're secure with, but include some more tentative ideas or plans, and anticipate the questions you'll get. Also think about what you'll want to ask the other students, to draw on their strengths and get some different perspectives.

'When you're leading the discussion, get everyone involved, help to point out links between what different people say, and narrate some of your own thought processes as you consider the ideas that are being discussed. Go in with a pretty clear idea of the sort of conclusions you're likely to reach, but be open to new ideas.

'Seminars can be helpful for strengthening your thinking about methodology, but also explore the meanings you might be able to draw from your work. Use the opportunity to test your reasoning and try out different ways of exploring competing points of view in your writing.

'Go about it the right way and you can make it an enjoyable and useful session for the other students, but first and foremost is has to benefit you.' **Andy, Philosophy graduate student**

Academic Advice

'If you can, as well as trying to negotiate your role in groups and engaging with everything that's going on there, try to take a step back sometimes and observe what's happening. The struggle with academic thinking is being played out in front of you, and how each group session works (or doesn't work) can be a really important learning experience. Try to spot why people have difficulties, where misunderstandings arise, why some things can't be resolved. Look at how you and the group try to take things forward – because it's a mini version of everything that's going on in learning at university.' **Mike, university course leader**

Note To Self

Use your learning journal to reflect on group tasks. As well as reminding yourself of the work you need to do before next time, there's likely to be a great deal you can learn from studying with others. Note down any useful techniques you picked up. Consider what you could do to get even more out of the experience next time. And think about ways to keep using and improving your people skills in other parts of your life.

❯ *Go to: Chapter 6 to check/update the **group work** section of your Core Development Plan.*

4 Be a critical friend

Feedback at university is much more than being told how well you've done, or even how to do things better next time. The people giving the feedback are at different stages of their academic journey, and you may or may not agree with what they have to say. But there's a great deal to gain if you can buy into feedback as *dialogue*, analysing other people's work, evaluating the comments you get, and sharpening your self-reflective skills in the process.

The advice below applies in all the different scenarios when you're called on to give or receive feedback, spoken or written, as part of your learning. Remember, people are unpredictable (you included) and you need to be ready to adapt your approach if it's not working.

Receiving feedback

- Try to assume that the other person has the best intentions and is trying to help.
- Listen – and *show* that you're listening.
- Clarify anything you're not sure about, asking for details or examples if necessary.
- Reflect on the feedback carefully, prioritize the points raised, and decide which – if any – have the potential to help.
- Try out the ideas that seem useful, and show or tell the person who gave you them what's happened as a result.

Giving feedback

- Remember that your feedback is only useful if it helps the person receiving it to improve.
- Don't make it personal: focus on the work.
- Keep it recent, be specific, and give examples to show exactly what you mean.
- Talk about effect and cause: this happened, or you had this reaction, because they did this particular thing.
- Be honest (otherwise, what's the point?) but also be selective and as balanced as possible. There are strengths and weaknesses in every piece of work, and you can mention both, whatever the overall message.
- Give realistic recommendations. Try to point people in the right direction, but let them decide how best to respond to what you say.

5 Present with confidence

Presentations are possible, even for you.

You're not expected to be able to do them perfectly straight away. Like all other aspects of your studies, the skills involved are developed through your work and in the context of your course.

You're also not required to be an expert, presenting yourself as a specialist in a particular topic. No one's going to demand you know all the answers off the top of your head; you're not going to be judged to professional broadcasting or business standards.

But you will be stretched to produce work that will stand up to scrutiny, in an unpredictable environment, through a style of communication that involves lots of risks. It's definitely a challenge, but one you can learn to relish.

There'll be some specifications for the task, and you'll be given time to do your research, sort out your thoughts, plan what you're going to say and how you're going to say it. Lots of it you'll be able to practise beforehand, although you won't really know how it's going to go down until you're doing it.

When that time comes, your job will be to show off the quality of your content *and* your abilities to communicate it to the people in front of you. Your presentation may not need to entertain your audience (although it will help if they enjoy it), but it definitely needs to engage them.

If it's an assessed activity, you'll also need to impress academic staff, who'll be looking closely at the way you match your presentation to this particular crowd. They'll want to see that you can gather relevant information, structure it to make it manageable and understandable, and present it in a way that supports learning. They'll be hoping for clear signs that you're discovering the *epistemology* of your subject: that you recognize the styles of thinking and communicating that are valued here, and you're starting to use them.

If you can do all that, you'll have used the challenge to the full. You'll have boosted your own intellectual and academic skills, enriched your subject knowledge and played an important part in collaborative learning. Perhaps most importantly of all you'll have had valuable experience of communicating under pressure, training a whole set of grown-up personal skills.

Planning

Lots of the planning process should be very familiar, as it's similar to developing any piece of academic work.

You'll have to be particularly organized about the practical requirements, such as *when* you're speaking, *where* and for *how long*. Your attention to detail will be very clear to see. The time limit will guide how about much to write in preparation. You'll be drafting notes rather than carefully constructed sentences and paragraphs, so you'll have to experiment to see how long different parts take to explain aloud.

Make sure that you know exactly what you're supposed to cover: the question you're addressing; the focus for your research and reflection. Your audience will be very sensitive to anything in your presentation that misses the mark. Like the word limit in an essay, the time limit for a presentation drives you to be precise and succinct, able to encapsulate rich information within the boundaries set. You'll have to be very clear about what your material means.

Your introduction will need to be especially strong, as you'll be giving your audience a route to follow and asking them to remember it. After that, the way your structure your speech will also reflect your personal take on it, as you draw out themes, emphasize particular parts, and follow a logical path to a memorable conclusion. The way your points flow will be a major factor in how well you take your audience with you.

Your literacy skills will also be utilized if you decide to produce visual aids or paper handouts to reinforce everything you plan to say aloud.

But when you get to the point when you've planned all the points you want to make in your presentation, organized the structure and found the best examples and strongest analogies – instead of writing it in full, you get ready to *perform*.

Case Study: Alice

Alice started her course feeling very unsure about speaking in front of a whole group. She'd tried a few times in school and always found it uncomfortable. 'It just felt embarrassing, like I was pretending. I used to think: why put me through this? I hate public speaking – so just let me write it all down! I lost all my confidence when I had to get up and talk.'

In her first term at university, Alice was asked to prepare a short presentation to give in front of her class, and told it would be assessed. 'It was exactly what I didn't want to do, just with more pressure. I could see myself standing there, out of my depth, sounding like I had no right to be telling anyone anything.'

Alice got some advice from a final-year student as part of a mentoring scheme. 'Scott, my mentor, suggested I should think about playing a role, rather than it being me up there trying to be believable. I liked that – it made me think maybe it could be like essay writing, I suppose, moving myself to the side and taking on the style of someone who was *actually* confident at giving their views. The thought of my *acting* being judged, rather than me, felt OK.'

Alice told a few people about her plan. 'They totally understood – which made up my mind that it was worth a try. And it was *so* much easier. I'm not saying I enjoyed it, but I certainly didn't feel as out of place as before. I sounded like I knew what I was talking about, at least!'

Preparation

You're not preparing a *speech*. You can't just read an essay out – that would miss the point. Part of what you're learning to do is talk *to* the particular audience gathering to listen to you. So, you'll need notes, not a script, in order to:

- engage your audience
- use eye contact and body language effectively
- emphasize key points
- seem knowledgeable and confident
- make the audience know you're talking to *them*.

You can create these notes by condensing the main ideas from your plan into a few words or phrases and writing them on file cards – manageable to hold in one hand while you talk. If you're using slides or other visuals, those will also help you to remember what you want to say – but it's always a good idea to have everything on cards, too, just in case the technology lets you down.

Each card should give you enough information to speak confidently without having to glance down at it too often. Experiment to find out what sort of prompt notes work best for you. Occasionally, you'll need to add specific details – such as statistics or quotations – that have to be precise, but mostly you'll be able to use key points to remind you of the ideas you mapped out on paper.

Memory techniques can also be useful here.

> ❯ *Go to: Chapter 14 and Chapter 19 to see how visual imagery and mental structures can help you to learn different sorts of information.*

It shouldn't be necessary to learn a whole presentation using specific memory techniques. Trying to would probably take far too much time and add pointless stress. But it might be useful to create a few trigger images to jog your memory and let you rely a little less on your cards.

If you do use display software or other visual aids, think carefully about the impact. Showing your audience detailed information and just reading it out to them doesn't really get to the point of what academic presentations are about. People's minds will wander, and they'll probably wonder why they couldn't just have read this for themselves.

They're likely to be even more confused if you show them lots of complex information and make them listen to you talk *about* it at the same time as they try to read it. You're risking cognitive overload: the brain can't do both things well at once, and it's exhausting to try.

 Note To Self

If you're using computer slides, make sure that they all appear from the same direction (imagine how tiring it would be reading a book where the pages slid in and out in random ways) and avoid any transitions, animations or other audio-visual effects that could distract your audience and detract from the quality of your content.

But appropriate illustrations, a few key points of detail, enriching quotations, headings to help structure your ideas – these can all help to keep your audience interested and alert, able to follow your argument and to remember lots of it.

Just as important are the images you create for them in your words: metaphors, models and real-life examples that make your concepts easier to grasp and retain. It can be tremendously powerful to let people into the way you see the information, sharpening your own comprehension as well as theirs.

Presentation

Practise ... your performance several times beforehand, including using any visuals or props, and you'll increase your confidence to guide the audience through your ideas. Picture the real audience sitting there, to help you think about what they need to know, and how they'll be expecting it to be communicated. Keep an eye on the clock to see how much you can talk about in the time available, so you don't end up having to speak too quickly, or sounding like you're padding it out.

Start ... in a friendly way, with a smile if you can. Nothing puts an audience at their ease more than a presenter who looks in control. Use your introduction to persuade them to pay attention to what you're going to give them, with an idea of the structure you'll be working to. Help them to realize that you've got a manageable amount of information to pass on, and that it's important stuff.

Manage ... your audience carefully if you want them to do anything, making instructions clear and non-negotiable (so also non-threatening, even appealing). Try out activities on friends beforehand. The same goes for question-and-answer sessions: rehearse some likely questions, prepare your responses – and then keep in control on the day by choosing when the Q&A begins and ends, and by restricting it to areas you've researched.

Conclude ... just like in an essay, by bringing everything back to the promises made in the introduction, recapping the main points, and showing how they all come together. In your words and your demeanour, help the audience to feel positive, confident that they've gained something they can take away and use.

> Go to: Chapter 7 *for ways to strengthen your own learning by **using** it well in activities like this.*

To be worth doing, presentations should be engaging and meaningful experiences for the presenter as well as the audience.

- Capture any particular insights you gained as you record and reflect on what happened in your journal.
- Add extra notes to your plans to highlight anything extra that came out in the presentation itself or discussions that followed.
- Keep your prompt cards as more valuable resources to add to your collection – and use again in the future to keep this learning fresh.

> **Go to: Chapter 6** *to check/update the* **giving presentations** *section of your Core Development Plan.*

(10) Ten-point summary

1. Communication and collaboration are key features of higher-level learning.

2. Working with others can be challenging, but there are significant academic as well as personal benefits on offer.

3. Effective group work requires a supportive atmosphere, high standards of behaviour, a clear sense of purpose, accurate self-awareness and shared responsibility.

4. When you're receiving feedback, be positive and open, but keep the comments you receive in perspective.

5. When you give feedback to others, be honest, selective, precise, realistic and kind.

6. Like written assignments, successful presentations allow you to engage with the construction of knowledge in your subject.

7. Plan presentations with your audience in mind, adapting your content and style to help them learn and remember.

8. Use visuals carefully so that they enhance your message rather than getting in the way.

9. Practise, so that your presentation strengthens your communication skills, and you demonstrate your growing academic confidence.

10. Public speaking improves your ability to develop clear arguments, to have your ideas challenged, and to do *anything* well under pressure.

▷ Where to next?

Chapter 18 will explore everything it takes to complete large-scale academic projects.

Major works

Longer writing projects are opportunities to enhance all your higher-level skills, as you investigate subjects that are interesting, challenging and useful to you and others in your field.

 What?

Along with essays, reports and other relatively small-scale assignments, nearly every university course now also includes at least one significantly larger writing task. It's a chance to see what happens when you get to grips with a substantial piece of work over a considerable amount of time. Every aspect of your development up to this point is on show. It's a major test of your ability to operate at this level, with some risks but also serious rewards.

Whatever it's called on your course – a **research project**, **long essay**, **thesis**, **dissertation** – there are common aspects to the challenges involved. You'll be in charge of conducting your own research, examining the evidence in depth, drawing together your findings, and shaping conclusions that you can explain clearly and convincingly. You're likely to have choices about what you explore and how you generate your evidence, and lots of the time you'll be left to your own devices. There will be extremely tight **assessment criteria** to meet, as well as long-established ways of **organizing**, **writing** and **presenting** your work.

These tasks are there to drive your studies forward and to let you demonstrate the progress you've made. There's freedom to think and explore, and a great chance to get involved in the wider work being done in your field. There are also some clear rules to follow and key academic standards to meet, and your personal strengths will also be tested at every stage.

There's a lot riding on this work, and a great deal to gain if you get it right. This chapter explains how to use these 'major works' to your advantage, putting all the elements of good study into action to advance all your skills, and to take you a big step closer to getting the final results you deserve.

 When?

Traditionally, these tasks were set in the final year of an undergraduate course, giving students time to develop the higher-level skills required. Sometimes they appeared in the second year, too, but now they're being set even earlier on some courses, with differing levels of expectation and importance.

While they remain key components of postgraduate studies, these extended assignments are playing an increasingly important part in first degrees. And since they draw together so many essential aspects of academic thinking and working, it helps to be prepared for them as soon as possible so that you're working towards them bit by bit, training for them in all the other work you do.

Who?

It's your choice of topic, your wording of the title, your methodology, your analysis, your verdict. Ideally, you get to choose a question that interests you, plays to your strengths and pushes you to go further in your thinking, and this is an opportunity to start contributing to the advancement of knowledge in your subject as a whole.

But you're not alone, and an important part of your success will be dealing with other people – including your **tutor** or **supervisor**; other **academics** who may need to give their permission; **research subjects**; other **students**, particularly if there's any joint working involved; and the **examiners** who'll read, assess and maybe even question you in person about your finished work.

Why?

As an 'apprentice' academic, these tasks are the perfect opportunity to show what you can do. You're still supervised, but you're trusted to make lots more of the key decisions for yourself, taking on a new level of responsibility for a complex project and managing yourself and others to achieve real academic results. This is how you really find out what you can do, for all to see.

It's a big test (often with very significant results attached), but it's an absolutely vital stage of your journey. It's only by going through the process of planning, producing and presenting this kind of in-depth work that you'll bring together all the essential elements of degree-level thinking and working, so that you can go further in your education or step confidently into the world of work.

You'll have to give it your all, but the long-term benefits are definitely worth the investment of time, effort, emotion and the considerable amounts of personal, intellectual and academic challenge involved.

How?

These are large and complex projects, so it's important to start with a very clear idea of what's involved, and a carefully composed plan of action.

Pay close attention to your **study environments** – internal as well as external. The physical conditions will need to be right, for you to be more organized, efficient and effective than ever. You'll also have to monitor your **motivation**, **energy levels** and **general wellbeing** throughout.

There's a lot to think about when you set your **question**, to make sure that your project is manageable as well as meaningful. You'll need to know how to work with academics to get approval for your plan, and to access all the support you need along with way.

And then every one of your best study practices will need to be incorporated into your approach, as you gather information, carry out your research, analyse the findings, and shape everything you've done into a strong piece of academic writing that shows off all aspects of your development to the full.

 # Steps to success

1 Understand the challenge

It's a challenge you build up to gradually. Every time you write something in your course, get feedback and reflect on the whole process, you grow in confidence and skill. By the time you come to take on one of these longer tasks, you have a very clear understanding of how study works in your subject, and how to use writing to strengthen your learning and communicate your discoveries. Yes, there are some new things to consider, but the important foundations are all there.

You'll need to know exactly what you're facing. Here's a checklist of the things you need to be clear about from the start:

- the deadline for completion
- the lower and upper word limits
- how much choice you have about what to explore, and how
- in projects with a set question or title, exactly what you're being asked to do
- any resources, tools or techniques you're expected to use
- how your work will be assessed
- what the rules are about presentation
- how you'll submit your finished work.

 ### Academic Advice

'Don't be tempted to regard the task requirements as "admin", or pedantic rules to make your tutor's life easier. They've been set very carefully to give you work that's clear and manageable, with enough challenge to advance your subject knowledge and stretch your academic abilities. Understanding what you're being asked to do is an essential skill in itself, so focus on unpicking the key criteria, and then planning and completing the project to match them. It's possible to produce innovative work that also satisfies all the criteria you've been set.' **Catherine, university lecturer and tutor**

✎ Note To Self

Get a printed copy of the task instructions and put it where you can see it while you work. Highlight the key practical points in one colour, like the word-count and deadline, and in another colour mark out all the other important requirements or guidelines. And then keep looking at it. You'll be doing lots of different types of work in this project, over a long time, but it all has to fulfil these rules. These are the instructions for getting good results – and for getting full personal benefit from all the effort you put in.

There are a couple of new questions to ask when you're starting projects like these:

- **Do I have a choice about my supervisor?** If you do, talk to previous students, check out supervisors' own work, and remember: you'll need someone you can work well with, who can give you appropriate support, but who also provides a healthy level of challenge.
- **What details or documents will I need to supply?** A proposal, requests for ethical/safety permissions, interim reports?

Student Tip:

'Have a look at finished projects by past students. Our tutor showed us some recent examples, and that made it a lot easier to understand the task we'd been set – including what 10,000 words actually looked like. It was helpful to see all the different sections to include, and how they wanted us to lay it all out.' **Jack, third-year Engineering student**

These tasks test how well you know how to operate within the conventions of your subject, conforming to its values and matching its standards. By the time you come to take on a major piece of work like this, you should have a very clear idea of what it's going to involve – but you'll still need to focus on exactly what's required, so that your finished work includes everything necessary to make the grade. Take time to study the assessment criteria so that all your efforts go towards fulfilling them.

Depending on your discipline, you'll discover that there are many familiar elements in the work ahead, along with a few new ones – and that they're all there for a reason:

Title. This shows clearly and succinctly *exactly* what you're exploring – often describing what you're analysing or how you're investigating something, but with a clear underlying question or problem: 'The impact of social-media use on teenagers in the UK'; 'Improving the fuel-efficiency of cars by using aerodynamic modelling'.

Abstract/summary. This provides a brief summary of the whole project, including the basis for doing it, the methodology used, the results you obtained, and the conclusions and recommendations you were able to draw (or not) as a result.

Contents. This outlines the separate sections within the work along with their page numbers.

List of illustrations. This identifies the diagrams, graphs and tables you've included and locates them in the text.

Introduction. This briefly outlines what you set out to do and why; presents the hypothesis or the main purpose that drives your research; and then summarizes what you did, what you discovered, and whether it matched what you set out to do.

Literature review. Rather than simply listing relevant research, this highlights the most significant work and shows how it has influenced your approach.

Methodology. This explains exactly how you carried out your research, and the thinking behind it, describing the context you were working in and detailing how resources, apparatus, software or people were chosen and managed.

Results. This gives a clear, succinct summary of the key findings – the things that support your hypothesis as well as those that don't.

Discussion/analysis. This presents your analysis of the results, guiding readers to see clearly what you believe to be significant in them, and why; compares them with any initial hypotheses; and points out strengths and weaknesses in your approach.

Evaluation/conclusion. This draws everything together (the theories, what happened in practice, your assessment of results and processes) and states what you believe can be learned, how well you achieved your purpose, and whether any hypotheses stood up to testing.

Recommendations. This provides detailed responses, numbered as a clear list of next steps.

References/bibliography. This acknowledges your sources and signals the quality of your background research.

Glossary. This defines the key terms, particularly specialist vocabulary.

Appendices. These provide additional information referenced in the main work, including graphs and tables, and relevant documents such as interview scripts and questionnaires.

In some subjects, these features need to be clear, headed sections on the page. In others, it's important to be clear about where and how you're including them in your writing, but your use of language will be more significant for organizing and signposting the structure of your work and guiding your reader through.

So there's a lot of information to present in your finished work, and a significant amount of work involved in getting it all done. And however daunting it may look in the beginning, it's vital to see what you're facing:

- **Organizing the project:** checking all the requirements, planning your time, scheduling meetings with key staff
- **Conducting early research:** doing some reading and thinking about possible questions to investigate, and discussing ideas with other students and staff
- **Choosing the question to answer:** depending on how much choice is available, selecting the topic to explore and designing the core question to investigate or specific hypothesis to test

- **Designing your methodology:** planning your processes in detail, based on typical methods used in your subject, and ideas gained from researching similar work

Student Tip:

'The big lesson I learned from my first project was to think about the data early on, and plan ways to get it. Think really practically. What are the methods that are most likely to give you the most useful information? Then build your methodology around them. Writing is so much harder if everything turns out to be incomplete or inconclusive, and you end up describing all the things you should have done differently.' **Jacqueline, final-year Sociology student**

- **Getting permission:** agreeing your plans by discussing them with your supervisor/tutor, or by submitting a detailed proposal or outline plan – possibly to get specific ethical permission for your research
- **Carrying out a literature review:** reading, note-making (including recording references) and evaluating the most significant and useful materials to include

Academic Advice

'As early as you can, spot the "key players" in the field you're working in. Notice the names that keep coming up and trace them through citations and references. Try to get a sense of how their influence has spread – by people agreeing with them and building on their work, or disagreeing and finding different perspectives. It helps to map out how the thinking has developed, and to see the different dynamics affecting it, so that you can start seeing how your work might fit in.' **James, PhD student and teacher**

- **Writing the literature review:** explaining how the most significant documents relate to your project, and drawing out relevant themes from the collection as a whole
- **Doing personal research:** sourcing, creating and preparing everything you need, then carrying out whatever tests are appropriate in your subject, and collecting a variety of information as a result
- **Writing about your methodology:** explaining what you planned to do, and what you actually did in practice, using notes and other records to help you describe your methods in detail
- **Analysing results:** preparing to present them clearly and accurately in your work
- **Writing the analysis/discussion:** explaining what you learned from each aspect of your research, and when you analysed your own strategies and practical approach – perhaps suggesting some improvements
- **Writing the introduction:** with everything you've done still fresh in your memory, explaining what you set out to do, why, and how far you feel you succeeded
- **Writing conclusions/recommendations:** drawing together all your research, testing and analysis, to present a confident assessment of what you were able to demonstrate – and what needs more investigation

- **Redrafting everything you've written so far:** checking all the information matches up, and that your explanation ties it all together in a clear and logical way
- **Writing the abstract/summary:** creating a brief, tight summary that would work as a stand-alone document if necessary
- **Compiling references/bibliography:** making sure that everything mentioned is referenced in full
- **Adding appendices:** checking everything here is useful and accurate, and that it's correctly signposted in the main text
- **Proofreading and checking:** using software, reference materials, and other people's help, to make sure that your use of language is correct, and that all aspects of your presentation are up to the standards set and consistent throughout.

2 Control the conditions

There's clearly a significant long-term challenge to take on here. To work at your best all the way through, you'll need to set up the right conditions from the start.

The *external* conditions

❯ **Go to: Chapter 7** *for a step-by-step guide to adapting your environment to suit your work.*

The *internal* conditions

Tackling major independent work like this can ask a lot of you emotionally – especially if things haven't gone well with similar tasks in the past.

Case Study: Jamie

Jamie felt a sense of dread about taking on his final-year project. When he'd done anything like this before, he'd always struggled to get started, usually overestimated how quickly he could work when he did, and often lost heart along the way. He came to this task with very low expectations of success – but a very high sense of its importance to his overall result.

Jamie knew that he was unlikely to get off on the right foot now unless he addressed his feelings and used his experiences to help him do things differently.

By recognizing some of the problems (usually to do with getting started), analysing exactly why they'd arisen in the past (such as his tendency to be a perfectionist), thinking what he could change this time (setting more manageable, shorter-term goals) and assessing his best sources of support (particularly the friends who were good at nudging him into action), Jamie was able to develop a much more positive approach, and his confidence grew as the project took shape.

Self-awareness is especially important in independent work. Here's a set of questions to consider before you start. Use your responses to guide your decision-making at every stage.

How confident do you feel about taking on a project like this? Be honest and try to consider everything that this particular task will involve.

What 'evidence' do you have from past experiences to suggest you'll be successful here? What can you take from those memories to help you now – practically and emotionally?

What tells you that there could be difficulties? Think about how negative experiences might still be affecting the way you think and feel and the way in which you approach important tasks like this.

Which aspects of this work play to your strengths? How can you maximize these – and draw on them, to drive the success of the project as a whole?

Which parts of the process are you likely to find most challenging? Think about how you can use this awareness to help you plan and prepare, and where your most likely sources of support will lie.

Based on past experiences, what emotional ups and downs are you likely to experience? What will you need to do differently this time to support your wellbeing and ensure high-quality working and thinking throughout? Are there warning signs to look out for, triggers to avoid, key things to put in place that could make all the difference?

3 Set your question

This is an absolutely crucial part of the process. Once you've chosen your topic, and then the specific question you're trying to answer, it's going to take up a great deal of your time and effort for weeks, maybe even months to come. There's an opportunity here to immerse yourself in a subject that really engages you, helps you in your work in the future, and enriches all aspects of your studies. You'll want to get this right.

Some courses give you a fair bit of scope to pick a topic and design your question. Others present you with a list of topics to select from, with the chance to choose your own focus. There are also courses where you have to pick from a list of specific titles. If there are any restrictions on how many people can do a particular type of work, there may even be a first-come-first-served system in place.

Whatever the state-of-play for you, the key considerations are the same:

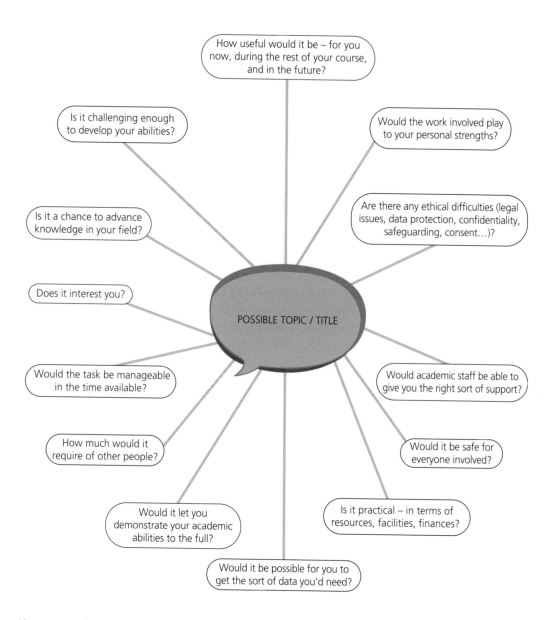

How useful would it be – for you now, during the rest of your course, and in the future?

Is it challenging enough to develop your abilities?

Would the work involved play to your personal strengths?

Is it a chance to advance knowledge in your field?

Are there any ethical difficulties (legal issues, data protection, confidentiality, safeguarding, consent…)?

Does it interest you?

POSSIBLE TOPIC / TITLE

Would academic staff be able to give you the right sort of support?

Would the task be manageable in the time available?

How much would it require of other people?

Would it be safe for everyone involved?

Would it let you demonstrate your academic abilities to the full?

Is it practical – in terms of resources, facilities, finances?

Would it be possible for you to get the sort of data you'd need?

If you can, discuss your thinking process with fellow students, family and friends, and especially with academic staff. If you have any concerns, voice them and get feedback. However much you might *want* to do something, people who know you (and who know studying) may have some important questions to raise that persuade you there are better choices to be made.

Try to find some good examples of similar work done by people who've done the course before you. Do they look like the sort of thing you could do, and do well? If you've got time, plan a few possible titles to get more of a sense of what they'd involve in practice.

And, as you keep narrowing down the possibilities, remember:

- There's no perfect one
- Every good question is challenging in its own way
- Once you've chosen yours, it's all about making it work for *you*.

 Academic Advice

'If you're on a course where there's little or no choice about the topic for your research, it usually means you get the advantage of being supported by a tutor with particular expertise in that area – so make the most of that focused, specialist help at every stage.' **Reuben, university tutor**

4 Get it approved

On some courses you need to get official approval for some of the work you do. On others it happens more informally, through dialogue with tutors and general agreement about your plans. Make sure that you know the situation for you, and then use whatever process is in place to your advantage. It's another of those academic activities that can seem like admin, but can actually be extremely valuable, because it:

- pushes you to do early research that helps you choose your focus wisely
- guides you to develop an appropriate methodology for what you're aiming to achieve
- lets you know about potential difficulties as well as opportunities, so that you can see whether there's enough challenge for you to demonstrate your abilities
- forces you to be honest about whether your ideas are practical, achievable, ethical and safe
- shows you how your time will have to be allocated, the best order to do it in, and where you're most likely to need support.

As you develop your proposal, a useful technique is to keep asking yourself whether *you* would approve it, if you were in charge.

Base your judgements on the questions the real academic staff are likely to ask:

- Does the proposal reflect an up-to-date, informed and accurate view of the topic? ☐
- Are the aims clearly focused and outlined in detail? ☐
- Is the plan realistic and achievable? ☐
- Does it match all the course requirements? ☐
- Is it sufficiently original to warrant the effort involved? ☐

- Are the methods appropriate and fully thought through? □
- Have ethical and safety considerations been fully addressed? □
- Will the work be challenging enough to develop the necessary skills? □
- Does this project allow high-quality working and thinking to be demonstrated clearly? □
- Is it likely to improve the student's abilities and help them achieve the academic standards required? □

> **Go to: Chapter 3** to add any ideas to your plans for **meeting standards** and **following protocols**.

5 Research, reflect, write

Research

You're likely to be doing a combination of reading and practical research – probably lots of both.

> **Go to: Chapter 10** for a detailed guide to the principles and best practices of academic research.

Existing research will influence your choice of question and the approach you take to answering it. You'll be looking for theories that you can test and evaluate, and evidence to compare your own results against. You'll need to be highly organized with all your source materials, so that you can use any literature review to give your work clear context and direction, and accurately reference everything you incorporate.

New research will depend heavily on the subject you're studying.

On some courses, it will still be done on a very *conceptual* level – although new types of analysis are likely to be included, maybe even injecting some quantitative research into areas were the qualitative approach is usually enough.

On others, this is where *practical* experimenting really comes into its own, including complex scientific studies, technical analyses and the real-world testing of ideas. For some students it's where they finally get the freedom to try out investigative processes they've mostly only read about so far.

Designing your methodology is a vital part of your planning. As long as you've chosen your question carefully and done appropriate research, your basic approach should be clear. But it's vital to map it all out in detail – to help you get the high-quality results you need, and to let you *analyse* your methodology as a key part of the learning.

> **Go to: Chapter 3** to reflect on your existing plans for **using equipment** and **using processes**.

As well as any specific testing processes demanded by the work you're doing, there are various other options to consider – whether your approach is qualitative, quantitative or a mixture of both.

Think carefully about what's going to deliver the most useful information about the question you're trying to answer. Be alert to methods that might confuse the issue or provide misleading data. And remember that so much will depend on *how* you use different research techniques – which you'll need to be extremely clear about, to be able to analyse that too.

Questionnaires

Think about ...

- **The questions:** make them short, easy to understand, unambiguous
- **The answers:** how precise and measurable do you need them to be?
- **The format:** what difference will it make if it's presented to people on paper or online?
- **The conditions:** make sure that you control the way the questionnaire is administered so that you know any factors that might affect the results
- **The participants:** it's important they know what they're being asked to take part in and why, and how their information will be used
- **The sample:** how have you decided who takes part, and what does that mean for the results?
- **The process:** before you use the questionnaire for real, try it out on a friend, checking everything is clear and that the form you get back gives you everything you're expecting.

Interviews

Think about ...

- **The questions:** make sure that they're clear without being *leading* (hinting at a particular answer or desired response)
- **The answers:** how will you record what people say, and will they deliver the qualitative or quantitative information you need?
- **The format:** script the questions (and possible prompts) so that they're the same for each interviewee – and that every *interviewer* knows exactly what to ask
- **The conditions:** which aspects of the interview process will you be able to keep the same (and what are the implications of anything that's different)?
- **The participants:** as well as giving full details of the project, you'll need to be very mindful of confidentiality, and about maintaining appropriate distance between interviewers and interviewees, particularly when emotionally difficult issues are being discussed
- **The sample:** think carefully about how you choose your interviewees, and how that process impacts on the results you get
- **The process:** do some practice runs with friends or family, making sure that you've thought through the whole process – from greeting them to saying goodbye – and that you'll be able to capture useful information when you do the interviews for real.

❯ *Go to: Chapter 6* *to check/update the* **research** *section in your Core Development Plan.*

Analysis

You'll need to allow plenty of time to analyse the results you get.

- Look closely and honestly at what the data reveals, and with a keen eye for what it *doesn't*.
- Be particularly careful not to confuse *correlation* with *causality*. There may well be a connection or a correlation between two or more factors, but can you be sure that one thing is *causing* another to happen?
- Focus on your original hypothesis or the question or problem driving your work. Does this data support your thinking, oppose it, do some of both ... or not really illuminate things at all? And then, crucially, why? Why was it so persuasive? Or why did it not provide you the sort of evidence you were looking for?
- Compare your results with those in the existing literature. Whether they match or not, there will be implications for you to tease out.
- If you could go back and start again, what would you do differently – and how do you think that might affect the results you got? Moving forward, are there new questions raised by this work that present interesting directions to take from here?

 ❯ *Go to: Chapter 6* *to check/update the* **numeracy** *and* **analysis** *sections of your Core Development Plan.*

Reflection

With your conclusions (and possibly recommendations) emerging, it's valuable to return to the initial work you did with the existing research.

- What can you say now, when you compare what *you've* discovered with the theories and perspectives that were the starting points for your work?
- Bear in mind your analysis of your own methodology. How confident are you about what you have and haven't been able to learn?
- What next? What could or should you or other people do as a result of this project?

These questions are at the heart of the intense reflective process that will shape your writing – so give it time, discuss it with other students, use sessions with your supervisor to test it with an expert ... and continue to strengthen and sharpen your thinking as you translate it all into a strong writing plan.

Planning

A visual approach to planning can be particularly helpful here, especially as you're likely to have so many different forms of notes, data, responses and other background information to pull together. The less structure imposed on you by the task you've been set, the more important it is to have a strong idea of how to compose your work to make it interesting, engaging and absolutely clear.

> **Go to: Chapter 16** *to see how visual planning can help you structure complex written work.*

It's natural to feel uncertain, even if this task comes towards the end of your course. You're responsible for this whole project, and the work that comes out of it will expose your abilities very clearly – to people who know a lot more than you about this subject, and are likely to have a great deal more academic experience. It can feel very uncomfortable to be claiming to have anything new to say – but you can.

If you've worked through all the stages of the process, tried to gather as much useful information as possible, been honest about what you found – and about the strengths and weaknesses of everything you did – then the work you're presenting is valid and potentially very useful to your academic community.

So, be confident to tell them about it.

 # Writing

Even though it's brief, make sure that your **introduction** reflects the level of preparation you've put into your project. Show that you've chosen your topic and question with care, and designed your approach based on a strong understanding of relevant issues and context. Prove that you can see your project as a whole, are able to summarize the journey you went through succinctly, and that you've stayed focused on your driving purpose throughout. This is also where you need to set the formal, authentically academic tone of your writing.

If you have to include an **abstract** or **summary**, that's also an excellent way to show your control of the whole project; to stress the value that comes from it being completed in full; and to establish the focused, concise style that you'll need to maintain throughout your work.

When explaining your **methodology**, make sure that you give convincing reasons for the choices you made, based on established practices as well as your own theories. Show that you were ambitious to get answers but also aware of risks and possible pitfalls.

You need to present your **results** transparently, confident that they provide useful information – even if they don't support your original idea, or reveal flaws in your methods.

Your **discussion/analysis** needs to show that you can navigate your findings and experiences in order to analyse them effectively, including looking honestly and accurately at the approach you used. As with all the work you produce during your course, the style of your writing here needs to match the way ideas are explored and presented in your chosen subject, proving that you're able to operate to the values and standards of your close academic community.

The **evaluation/conclusion** and **recommendations** are where the strength of your tone is particularly important. With evidence to back up your points, along with detailed and balanced analysis of their significance, you can say exactly what you think, and why you stand by it.

> **Go to: Chapter 6** *to check/update the* **evaluation** *section in your Core Development Plan.*

6 Stay strong

Large academic projects test you on a very personal level. Each stage has its own particular challenges, a lot of which you can't really understand until you're there and trying to cope. You have to solve problems as they arise, get help when you need it, find the resilience to bounce back from knocks, and know how to keep up your energy and enthusiasm to the very end, learning by doing it for real.

There are plenty of things you can do to boost your chances of success.

> **Go to: Chapters 8 and 9** *for advice about getting started on any writing task, and staying strong through every stage of the process.*

Some of the best ways to thrive in this kind of challenge can be found in the work itself:

• You chose this topic because it interested you, so draw on that to keep you going. Do some extra reading – even if it's not directly related to the work – to boost your energy and remind yourself that this is an area than can be engaging, intriguing, even fun to investigate.
• When the work gets tough, see that as useful, giving you valuable insights into the problem you're tackling and extra material to write about. If something hasn't worked, if there are difficulties with the data, or if your reasoning seems to be faltering, maybe that's where the absolutely *best* learning is to be found.

It's also important to make the most of all the support on offer:

• Get advice and guidance from your supervisor throughout the project. Go to meetings with a list of questions to raise. Give them samples of your work as it progresses to get feedback, then make sure that you act on it (or go back and discuss it further if you really don't think it's right).
• As well as your supervisor there may well be other staff in your department who can help – even people in other organizations, professional bodies or community groups who wouldn't mind answering a quick question via email. Use all the different dialogues you develop to turn difficulties into *content*, exploring why certain things are hard or confusing or contradictory, to develop a deeper understanding of the things you're exploring – and a clearer awareness of the processes you're using to do it.

Stay in touch with other students and keep discussing your experiences:

• Some may have specific insights from their own, similar work, but others doing completely different subjects may have an interesting take on yours.
• They're all facing the same core challenges as you, and it's worth finding out how they're coping to see whether there's anything you could do differently to help yourself.

- There may be ways to share resources, collaborate on some aspects of tasks, or even just work together sometimes on your separate projects for reassurance and mutual support. Just explaining out loud what you're trying to do can be enough to make you realize where you're going wrong – without them saying anything at all.

And your own self- and task-management strategies should come into their own during tasks like these:

- Now, more than ever, you need to be looking after your working environment, taking care of your wellbeing, and communicating with friends and family to get their support but also to protect your precious time.
- With that in mind, create a specific time-management plan for the whole project, thinking carefully about how much time you'll need for each aspect; which things can be done simultaneously; and whether any parts can be combined with other things you're working on.
- Be clear about when to move on from each stage, but also build in some flexibility as plenty of things can change – in life outside your study as well as in it – within a time-frame as long as this.
- Keep the deadline in focus but aim to finish everything well before it, as things always take longer than you think.
- Schedule in enough non-academic activities throughout the time you're working on your assignment, to keep you motivated, energized and healthily connected to life outside study.

> ❯ **Go to: Chapter 3** *to review your plans for* **project management** *and* **producing academic work**, *and add any new insights you've gained.*

> ❯ **Go to: Chapter 4** *to check how you're feeling now about some of the core aspects of higher-level study.*

⑩ Ten-point summary

1. Large-scale assignments give you new freedom to test out all your academic skills.

2. Research projects allow you to explore existing theories in your field, then contribute to constructing new knowledge by carrying out investigations of your own.

3. You need to know exactly what's required of you from start to finish, including how your final work will be assessed.

4. Take control of your study environment to support high-quality working and thinking throughout.

5. Be aware of your internal conditions, too, as this kind of work presents a significant emotional test.

6. When you choose your focus area, question and title, consider your interests and abilities, what's manageable, and how you can make the work most beneficial for you.

7. Plan research that will deliver sufficient accurate and relevant results.

8. Follow an established writing structure that fulfils all the requirements you've been set, then use it to clarify your thinking and strengthen your conclusions.

9. Manage the project carefully, to maximize your efforts at each stage and deliver a high-quality finished project on time.

10. Get regular feedback as your work progresses, and be proactive in seeking guidance and help as required.

 # Where to next?

Chapter 19 will reveal what success in exams *really* involves at this level.

Under pressure

To do well in exams you need to do the right things throughout your course, spend time in focused preparation and, finally, use all the skills you've developed to put in your best performance on the day.

What?

It can be hard to believe it sometimes, but **exams** are your friends. Or, at least they can be, if you understand how they work at this level, and you have a strong set of strategies for handling them. With the right approach all the way through your course, effective preparation in the build-up, and then a clear plan of attack on the day itself, you can use exams to get more out of all your study, then prove how much you've achieved when you're put to the test.

This chapter shows that getting good grades is important and completely possible – but only part of the reason for doing exams. If you can work with the whole assessment process, you'll have a much more meaningful time exploring your subject, and you'll come away from your course with the confidence to learn *anything* well – and to show what you can do under pressure.

When?

At this level, exams aren't memory tests as such. It's the **understanding** you build up, and the **intellectual** and **academic skills** you develop over time, that matter most. If you do everything well throughout your course, you'll be ready to make the grade.

But there's a new intensity and added pressure, and memory is still very important because you have to take everything you've learned in with you, then access and apply it well. So there's a special preparation phase in the run-up to exams, when you pull everything together, check your understanding's still strong, and do some *extra* memory work to help you cope with the particular challenge ahead.

You also need clear strategies for **performing** well on the day, to demonstrate your ownership of the subject you've studied when most of the usual resources are removed. As everything you've done on your course gets focused into that one moment, that's when you really need to shine.

Who?

Exams isolate you to see what you're made of: what you know, what you can do, how you cope on your own. But while you're getting ready for them, relationships are more important than ever.

You'll need to manage friends and family carefully so that they give you the time and space you need – but also know how to support you, practically and emotionally.

And your fellow students can play a big part in your success if you work together to strengthen each other's learning, and make the preparation process intense and effective, but also manageable – and maybe even fun.

Why?

Tackle exams well and you'll get grades that reflect all the hard work you've put in. The long-term preparation will have helped you to engage with learning, and you'll come away with a good level of knowledge and understanding to take into other things. In the process you'll have strengthened some of the most important skills in life, like focus, self-reliance, active learning, time-management and memory. And you'll have built lasting confidence to face up to any kind of pressure test and come out on top.

How?

You've already spent time thinking how you feel about assessments generally. Now, get specific. Work out what you'll need to focus on to turn the whole examination process to your advantage.

It's vital to see how everything you do in your studies is preparing you for exams, all the time. When the moment comes to step things up, you've got strong systems in place, the important skills are all very familiar, and you're ready to bring everything together in the final stages of your training.

Strategy is more important than ever now as you focus your time and effort onto a very specific test.

Learn how to gather all the knowledge you've amassed, check it still makes good sense, and parcel it up so that you can carry it with you into the exam. There are some valuable **memory techniques** to help you use all the detailed work you've done, and they'll also boost your confidence to *think* well under pressure.

Finally, see what has to happen for it all to come together in the exam itself. Take control of the moment, use the intensity of the experience to produce high-quality work, and make it easy for the examiners to give you the grades you want.

Steps to success

1 Face your fears

The emotions involved in exams mustn't be underestimated. Many people have strongly held and deeply negative beliefs about them, often based on experiences from the distant past.

> **Go to: Chapter 4** *to reflect on your feelings about exams, now that you know more about how higher-level assessment works.*

To prepare to bring all your efforts together under the intense spotlight of exams, it's important to get more specific about how you're feeling. High levels of commitment will be required, plus a good degree of active learning and energetic thinking – and any negative views will only hold you back from doing your best and make the whole process even harder.

Read the following seven statements – all real responses received from students past and present. Tick any of them that ring true for you. And consider *why* you might feel the way you do.

- 'Exams are designed to try to catch you out.' ☐
- 'Revision is boring.' ☐
- 'It's impossible to remember everything.' ☐
- 'There's never enough time to answer all the questions.' ☐
- 'It's hard to think well on the spot.' ☐
- 'My memory goes under pressure.' ☐
- 'Doing well is all about luck.' ☐

If any of these are part of the way you think and feel at this point, work on changing it. Here are some ideas that might help you to reframe your ideas, to set yourself up for much more enjoyable and effective study, and a considerably smoother ride through your exams.

'Exams are there to catch you out'

The exams you face have been set within your own academic community, by people with a clear interest in you doing well. Their content is based firmly on what you do in your course, and the questions are designed to show how much you've learned from all the different study activities you've done.

They're meant to be challenging, otherwise the work you've done wouldn't be worth much, and you wouldn't *gain* much by going through the exam process. But they're not just testing what you can do on the day. They're exploring the rich knowledge and real understanding you've built up over a considerable amount of time; so, if you've done the work, you'll have plenty to show off.

'Revision is boring'

Reading and rereading information can be *extremely* boring – but that's not what good revision is all about.

Revision, 'looking again', actually suggests a bit more than just repeating the same thing over and over, and you do need to be re-examining your work to check that you still understand it, as well as exploring a few new bits of research to add interest and energy.

But there's so much more to exam preparation than that. At its best, it involves a very active approach to learning – doing, talking, experimenting, making – and the thinking involved is practical and intense.

It's playful, too, because there's imagery to create, stories to write, mental journeys to invent, and any number of personal tricks to use to keep the memories strong and interest levels high.

Studying for exams has to be anything but boring if it's going to work.

'It's impossible to remember everything'

That's true – and it's also unnecessary. It could even be damaging to try.

Exams at this level demand that you respond to the exact questions set, finding the necessary information in your memory and then forming it into an answer that shows many different aspects of your ability. These aren't just tests of your recall, and training to repeat information would take your study way off track.

You need to use your memory well to *access, arrange* and *apply* things that you *know* and *understand.*

'There's never enough time to answer all the questions'

Exams add a level of urgency and intensity to your work to sharpen your focus and push you to be precise – to get to the most valuable things you know.

They're also testing how well you can organize yourself and manage the time available, because that reveals more about your confidence with the subject-matter, as well as how well practised you are at some important process skills.

'It's hard to think well on the spot'

Most of your thinking needs to be done beforehand. If your memory is good enough, you'll be able to find the information you want to use without too much strain. The question will guide you about how to communicate your understanding, and you'll have some well-rehearsed strategies for putting together your response. So, there should still be enough mental energy left to address the precise needs of the question and solve the exact problem it asks – which is very much what you're being tested on.

'My memory goes under pressure'

It can definitely be more difficult to use your memory when you're stressed. Humans are built like that: to prioritize threats and immediate needs over long-term learning. So, you need to be selective about what to remember, then make sure that it's all particularly well stored, with a number of different mental routes to retrieving it.

It's important to reduce stress as much as possible – which happens mostly by studying well and knowing you've done what it takes to succeed.

And you have to be a confident learner, with some very conscious memory techniques and plenty of practice under your belt.

'Doing well is all about luck'

These exams aren't add-on extras: they're part of your course, and your success in them will reflect how well you've done every other aspect of your studies. A strategic approach will be important to make the most of your time and match your effort to the exact requirements of each exam you face.

There's certainly some unpredictability in the subjects that come up, and in how well everything falls into place on the day. But part of learning to be a student is coping with the uncertainties, looking ahead, putting contingency plans in place, thinking on your feet ... and using your abilities well, whatever's thrown at you.

If your study's threatened by luck, or relies on it, something's definitely not right.

2 Make everything help

All the study strategies explored in this book have exams in mind. When exam time comes near, it's important to realize that you've already done huge amounts of work to prepare.

Notes. Good study involves making notes that help you to select useful information, organize it in a way that's meaningful, connect it to other learning to make it memorable, and also remember it *as* notes, recorded logically, spatially, creatively, with your own reactions added.

> **Go to: Chapter 12** *for a guide to making your notes as memorable as possible.*

Maps. At this level you explore what's known in a particular subject, but also *how*: how knowledge, understanding and skills have been developed over time. You become familiar with the key figures in its history, the schools of thought that have shaped it, the publications, speeches, experiments and events that have moved it on. Your course itself is structured to reflect what's important to know, and all the work you do trains you to get involved in the way new knowledge and understanding will be constructed from here.

And the work you do forms a valuable subject map – of what you've learned, and how you've learned it. Each new research document, page of notes and written assignment enriches the knowledge, but it also helps you to navigate it all, to see how it all fits together – and that's exactly what you'll be tested on in the exam.

> *Go to: Chapter 12* *for guidance on mapping your learning from the very start of your course.*

Cycles. If you're studying actively, the knowledge you gain isn't taken in and locked away somewhere until exams come around. It's constantly being put to use, helping you to work well in your chosen field and to seize all the new opportunities to learn.

If you start returning to work you've done earlier in the course and refreshing your memory about it, it soon becomes a habit – especially when you see how much it helps. But this cycle of learning relies on more than just rereading. You need to *do* something with it: maybe test yourself, write some quiz questions about it or enrich it with some extra research.

When exams are near, all the learning you've done is still familiar and fresh, and you can use your time polishing it ready to be examined (and you even had some ready-made resources to help).

> *Go to: Chapter 12* *to see how to build this cycle of learning into your study.*

> *Go to: Chapter 2* *to assess your ability to engage actively in study throughout your course.*

3 Be strategic

As well as high-quality, active learning all the time, it's important to leave room for some specific preparation in the build-up to an exam. This is where you work on detailed understanding and precise recall, getting ready to show off what you know and what you can do under pressure. The exam is a specialist challenge; you need a very clear overall strategy for success (including one for when you're in the exam room itself).

Academic Advice

'I try to show students that calling it 'revision' isn't very helpful. It needs to involve so much more than looking at the work repeatedly. You're not just reminding yourself what you learned at some point in the past. This should be some of the best learning you do on the whole course.' **Gill, university tutor**

Time

It starts with good time-planning.

- Don't leave the focused work until the last minute. You can't do anything well if you're stressed and tired, and there won't be any time to fill in gaps or solve problems.
- Decide how long it's going to take to do this kind of revision properly, depending on what's in the exam, how important it is, and how confident you are already.
- Start with a list of everything you could possibly be tested on in each exam you're taking – either an official document provided through your course, or one you make yourself. Make notes on it to show how much time you think you'll need to study each bit of it between now and the exam.

- Use your list to help you create a specific timetable (bearing in mind what else you'll have to fit in during this time). You'll be able to refer to this when you're compiling your weekly and daily plans.
- Make a note on the list whenever you've done enough on a particular topic. You'll be able to do more if there's time, but this will help you to see the areas that still need work when you're allocating time day by day. It should also boost your motivation to see each element being ticked off.

Balance

Keep doing everything you can to balance your work, rest and play. The extra pressure around exams, longer working hours and higher level of focus required can all take their toll if you're not careful.

- Plan in opportunities to relax and have fun.
- Let other people know how and why you're guarding more time than usual for study, but also make sure you stay connected to the people that boost your wellbeing (and especially the ones that might be able to help with things like shopping, cleaning and childcare).
- Use your learning journal to keep a check on your feelings, and access support if you're not coping – as early as you can.
- *Some* extra stress is probably inevitable, and the urgency of exams can energize you. But your study will quickly suffer if you're really not feeling well, so take your feelings seriously, and stay close to the people who can help if they notice something's not right.

> **Go to: Chapter 3** *for ideas about looking after your physical, mental and emotional health while you're studying, and to consider all the resources you have to support your wellbeing.*

Plans

Write down what you're aiming to cover each day, and the sort of learning strategies you're likely to use. You'll need to be flexible in practice and adapt to the way it's all going, but it's important to have a clear overall plan of attack. You may have time for just a short session each day among all your other work, or a clear timetable to focus solely on exams. In *both* cases, careful planning is essential.

Day	Exam preparation
Monday	*Macbeth*: recap main themes, using original notes; memorize the key points in the two coursework essays
Tuesday	Shakespeare's comedies: learn the material covered in the three coursework essays; use flashcards to memorize quotations
Wednesday	*King Lear* and *Richard III*: compare/contrast; notes/extended essay
Thursday	The Globe Theatre: recap its influence on the plays; use lecture notes and watch online theatre tour; predict and plan exam essay questions

Day	Exam preparation
Friday	*The Tempest*: revise detailed work on imagery; use presentation notes/ slides; practise writing answers to relevant past paper questions
Saturday	The history plays: revise all notes about historical accuracy; use last year's paper to practise planning and writing at speed
Sunday	Shakespeare's sources: recap the essay; memorize key points, particularly relevant dates; create and answer possible exam questions

Resources

Lots of your strategies will come directly from the resources provided by your course itself. Make the most of everything on offer. Many providers put a range of useful materials online:

Past papers. You can get a general sense of the way they tend to look, but the papers you end up sitting might be quite different – so use these examples to practise reading instructions, checking how many questions there are, and looking for clues about which parts of your course they refer to. Think about which questions you'd choose to tackle, and write plans for them. Think carefully about how you'd have to pace yourself to get through everything these papers ask you to do – but find out as much as you can about the *exact* papers you're going to be facing.

Model answers. Read these alongside the marking criteria (see below). Try to spot every element that was rewarded in some way. Look carefully at language and style (because this is what the examiners in your subject are expecting to see). Focus on the depth of the information included and the amount of analysis on display. Look at the similarities and differences between this kind of writing and the essays you've done during your course. What are the techniques used to write the correct amount of information, quickly and clearly enough to get the marks? What do these answers reveal about the knowledge, understanding and academic skills of the student who wrote them?

Marking criteria. Think like an examiner: how would you know if a student could do these things? What could make it easier for you to be sure they'd met the standards? Try to see which aspects of your work are going to be most valuable in terms of marks.

Even if you can't get hold of the exact assessment guidelines for the exam you're doing, you can still take a strategic approach based on some common principles.

Use the following themes to focus your preparations, helping you to decide what sort of information to focus on, what level of learning to do, and which skills to practise.

At this stage of education, your exam answers need to demonstrate:

- **relevant content** – you know what information to draw on to answer the questions
- **the necessary depth of understanding** – your writing reflects a solid grasp of specific ideas and their wider context
- **appropriate detail** – you're precise about *what* you focus on, and clear about how *much* is necessary to show what you know

- **a clear basis in research** – you refer to enough sources to show that you've read widely
- **suitable examples** – your evidence suits the questions and backs up your answers
- **effective style** – you can use academic writing techniques to explain what you think and why
- **the required level of analysis** – you can examine material in the way a question asks, to give opinions about it that are subtle and convincing
- **sufficient originality** – you can think well in the exam and, whenever possible, present information from a persuasive personal viewpoint
- **adequate presentation** – you write quickly but neatly enough to be accurate and clear.

You're likely to be marked *down* for:

- not addressing the exact question you've been asked
- approaching the question in the wrong way; for example, describing rather than analysing, or focusing on facts instead of the underlying themes
- only giving one perspective on the subject when you were asked for several
- being inaccurate or objectively incorrect
- failing to demonstrate the thinking and working involved in arriving at your answer.

Academic Advice

'Don't forget to use any feedback you got on your last assessment to help you improve your performance this time.' **Gill, university tutor**

Find out everything you can about how success is measured in this specific exam. If there are multiple choice or short answer questions, do they all earn marks equally? If you don't know an answer, is it worth guessing – or are marks deducted as penalties for getting anything wrong?

Understanding the assessment criteria and marking system will help you to design your strategy for tackling the exam itself. Make sure you've got a past paper in front of you as you work out the best use of time and effort and think of the most effective way to take on the challenge. Look carefully at the way marks are awarded throughout the paper, but also think about how long it's likely to take to get each section done. What would be the ideal way to allocate your time?

The best order

Think about the best order to do things in.

Would it help to plan all the essay answers at the same time?

- One topic might give you ideas about another.
- The deeper thinking involved in planning is probably better done when you're still feeling fresh.
- While you're writing the first answer, your subconscious mind can still be working on ideas to add to the other plans.
- You could even hand in the plan for the essay if you completely ran out of time at the end.

Could the questions in one section help to prepare you for what you're asked to do in another?

- Some people like to start with the one they're most comfortable with, to get into their flow.
- Others do the hardest one first, when there's a bit less time pressure and their energy levels are still high.
- With practice you'll find out which approach tends to get you the highest marks. Some things only really come through experience: for example, what sort of questions you can do fine even when time's ticking away at the very end, or which ones help you to stay energized in the middle.

4 Bring it all together

The study you do in the focused preparation period building up to an exam needs to draw on everything you know about learning.

- Check that the key conditions are in place.
> *Go to: Chapter 2.*

- Monitor how you're feeling about the challenge.
> *Go to: Chapter 4.*

- Pay particular attention to your environment.
> *Go to: Chapter 7.*

All of that should provide a strong context for the work you do now – which is driven by three key questions:

Have you got everything you need?

Get out all the materials and resources you've collected that have any connection with the exam. Work out the best way to keep them together during this phase. You should have plenty of documents – by other people, and ones you've created yourself – but you might still need to do some extra research or get hold of additional information, from fellow students or members of staff.

> ### Student Tip:
>
> 'I've got a book where I write down important details that are hard to remember – but really useful if you do. Things like definitions, scientific laws, dates, even some important quotations that keep being referred to. I just list them to start with, so I know I've got them safe. And then I look for ways to practise with them. I've made some of them into flashcards to test myself with. I made up a set of quiz questions and got people to test me. Nearer the exams I think I'll write some up on posters around my room. I've struggled in exams before, and it's details like these that have caught me out – so it gives me a lot more confidence to be on top of them. They often come up in lectures and classes too, and I use that for extra practice.' **Lin, Geography undergraduate**

Do you understand it all?

Can you explain the main ideas from memory? Saying it out loud is a good way to test how strong your understanding *really* is. Give yourself a little time for it to come back into focus – then quickly fill in any gaps by researching it yourself or asking friends or staff members for help. The *exam* isn't the moment to do thinking like this; you need to be completely clear in your understanding well ahead of time.

Will you remember it on the day?

However confident you think you are, it's a good idea to test yourself to find out how much you really know. Be honest about what you find, and adapt your schedule accordingly.

You'll *keep* testing your memory throughout this period, to guide what you work on – and, just as importantly, to strengthen the learning itself – but there's also plenty of very active memorizing to do. This is the time to make sure you're going to remember everything you need to excel.

Condense your material. From a full source document, detailed page of notes or complete essay, create a summarized version, structured around the main points. Then, can you make a more condensed version of *that*?

You're trying to boil it all down to a set of key points that will act as a framework for the rest of the information, but be simple enough to remember. As always, think about what's right for your subject and for this specific exam. How deeply do you need to know this information to be able to work well? Use single words or short phrases and abbreviations whenever possible. You'll be able to add details back in if you need to, using some of the techniques explained below; but for now you've got a summary version that holds the most important ideas.

Doing this forces you to think really carefully about what it all means. It tests your comprehension, sharpens your analyses and pushes you to draw out the essential elements.

It's up to you how you present your condensed version. You could do it as a page of notes, put key words and phrases on file cards, or design something clear and memorable on your computer. See whether adding colours, images or even feelings about the information helps to make it stick in your mind.

These summaries become valuable study resources to your collection, and it's a good idea to keep a record of them within the maps you make of your learning.

❯ *Go to: Chapter 12.*

Get used to thinking about them when you're remembering or writing about the information. Try to picture them in your mind's eye.

The really important ones can even be taken a step further and turned into memory journeys, using the ancient system for memorizing spatially.

> *Go to: Chapter 14 to see how you invent images to represent your ideas, then fix them in place around familiar buildings or real-world routes – entirely in your imagination.*

If you'd condensed an essay about *Macbeth*, for example, you might have ended up with a summary list of key themes:

- ambition
- the supernatural
- reality and appearance
- loyalty and guilt.

Any familiar location could be used to store them in your mind – your local supermarket, for example. The stranger the events going on there, the better. So, imagine the following scenarios:

- Someone's set up an incredibly long ladder in the middle of the car park and is trying to see just how high they can climb. (AMBITION)
- A ghost is sitting in one of the shopping trolleys lined up at the entrance. (THE SUPERNATURAL)
- The fruit inside the door looks lovely at a distance – but close up, it's all mouldy and rotten. (REALITY AND APPEARANCE)
- At the fish counter, someone's dropped their loyalty card into all the fresh food – and they're looking extremely guilty as they run away. (LOYALTY AND GUILT)

Maybe you'd change the name of the supermarket to Macbeth's … and then, in the exam, you'd know exactly where to go in your mind to find reminders of all the key ideas on your list.

Sometimes a stand-alone story is the easiest way to memorize a set of words.

In 2018 the seven richest countries by median wealth (so the ones with the highest proportion of rich people) were:

- Australia
- Switzerland
- Belgium
- Netherlands
- France
- Canada
- Japan.

It would make sense to start the story in a way that reminds you what the real information is about.

> *So, maybe there are bags of money stacked on Sydney Harbour Bridge. And what if they all turned out to be made of chocolate? The great detective Hercule Poirot might have to be called in to investigate. Imagine him taking a canal ride through Amsterdam while he gathered his thoughts, eating a croissant covered with maple syrup – when suddenly a samurai warrior leapt on board.*

Try it now. Read that story again – aloud if you can. Really try to imagine watching it happen. Make it as clear and colourful as you can. Emphasize senses, such as the taste of the croissant, and feelings, such as the shock at seeing a samurai. Then, see whether you can say the list of countries aloud, purely from memory, using seven clues woven into the story to help.

Experiment with the memory techniques that work best for you. Some people like to turn important lists into sentences based on the initial letters:

> *The order of biological taxonomy – domain, kingdom, phylum, class, order, family, genus, species – could become: **Do kangaroos prefer chips or fresh green salad?***

For centuries people have learned famous dates in rhyme.

> *Columbus sailed the ocean blue / In fourteen hundred and ninety-two.*

Sometimes you can find clues within words themselves:

> *Stalactites have to hold on **tight** because they hang from the cave roof.*

> *Always be SURE of your meaSUREments.*

> *If you imagine the initials of **Bactrian** and **dromedary** on their side, you'll remember that Bactrian camels have two humps, and dromedaries only one.*

Techniques like these can help you get the details right, enriching the larger structures you build to hold onto the main ideas … which helps keep *all* your learning in place, ready to be explored and extracted during an exam.

 # Ask yourself

→ **How well are you concentrating and how much of the learning is actually going in?**

Keep checking in with yourself, and be honest: if you're drifting, stop. Take a short break, maybe have something to eat or drink, do something different for a few minutes … then come back and see whether you're able to start studying well again.

And if you *still* can't, make a clear plan for how you're going to make up the time – then go and have a rest. That will benefit you more than tiring yourself out while you're learning nothing.

Creative planning

Practise using these condensed, creative memory stories to write answers to exam-style questions. They're particularly useful when you're planning essays, giving you quick access to key points – perhaps dipping into several mental journeys or memorable stories to find ideas to include. There's logic within the stories and routes you've used to fix the details into position, but this is also a highly creative way of thinking, and the images can help you spot patterns and highlight connections and themes. Your brain's being used well: you're in a good place to produce energetic, clear, confident work.

Practical skills

You can also use your memory like this to help you learn any practical skills you're going to be tested on.

If your assessments include lab or studio work, always look out for ways to deconstruct complex physical techniques into their component parts – which can be given visual reminders, linked into stories or arranged around routes, and memorized like any other kind of information. Thinking about the memory triggers as you practise can be a powerful way to boost your confidence and help you keep repeating the actions until you're fluent. At this level it's also an excellent way of analysing the component parts of practical processes, helping you to deepen your understanding of what you're doing and why.

Strength tests

Keep testing yourself: to assess your abilities at the start of a session, to guide your effort; and later when you've learned something new.

But make sure you re-test when your memory's had a chance to fade a little – maybe the next day, and again later that week – because that bit of extra struggle in the memory process can make a huge difference to the strength and durability of the learning.

Make every session a very conscious collection of study activities: testing current knowledge, adding extra information, creating new reminders, practising, using, doing, testing again ...

> *Go to: Chapter 12 to see how you can plan for this level of active learning in every preparation session you do.*

 # Ask yourself

→ Does it help to share your exam prep with others?

This is another of those questions that you need to be really honest about.

It's a very good idea to *try* doing joint learning sessions with friends. Put each other's memory to the test. Check your understanding by telling them everything you know about a topic. Spend five minutes learning new things individually, then teach and test each other. Share advice about learning, new perspectives on the work, motivational ideas.

You may well find it much more enjoyable to be working with a friend, and feeling good about learning is always important.

But is it working? Reflect very carefully on the impact of working together. Maybe it works well for some things but not others. What's the right balance for you – between working with a partner and just getting on with it alone?

❯ *Go to: Chapter 6 to check/update the **exam preparation** section in your Core Development Plan.*

5 Turn it on

After investing so much to get ready – in everything you've done in the build-up – you owe it to yourself to finish the job well and put in your best possible performance in the exam itself.

You're always in charge of your own learning, but it matters more than ever when the pressure's on. It's up to you to make sure nothing gets in the way of you showing off all the abilities you've worked so hard to achieve.

A week before

Double-check all the details of the exam. Exactly where is it: certainly what room in what building – but maybe even the desk you'll be sitting at. What time does it start? How long before that do you have to arrive? Make your travel plans and leave plenty of time for delays.

Think carefully about everything you'll need to take with you: equipment, identification, glasses …? It's also well worth checking what you're not allowed to take in, and what arrangements there are for storing your possessions while you work.

> ### Student Tip:
>
> 'Try a few different pens beforehand, to see which works best for fast, clear writing. Check it's allowed for the paper you're sitting. Get used to it before the exam – and take a few spares on the day.' **David, final-year Physics undergraduate**

It might help to do some mental rehearsal for the experience that awaits.

Now that you've done the bulk of the work, picture yourself settling down at your seat in the exam hall.

Imagine yourself confident, organized and sharp. Visualize yourself following your strategy to read through the paper, draw up your plans, complete each section at the right pace, and leave enough time to check your work at the end.

See whether this feels like a useful exercise. If it doesn't, and maybe makes you feel anxious or demotivated, stop (but ask yourself why you're feeling like that, and what you'll need to do in the coming week to change things).

But if it does seem to help you feel ready, make it a habit to rehearse for success like this, almost creating a memory of it going well, one that you can keep drawing on for motivation.

It can help you to develop strong task-management skills – so that you remember to check everything at the end, for example – and also push you to spot any details you still need to sort out (like if you realized from your virtual run-through that you needed to buy a watch to help you keep track of time on the day).

The night before

Get a good night's sleep. A little work won't hurt, reading through notes, recapping the key ideas, thinking about memory techniques. But don't do anything new. Just give what you've already got a quick final polish, pack your things ready for the morning ... then rest.

On the day

Try to keep everything as normal as possible. Do all the things you usually do to feel your best. Pay particular attention to your feelings. Steer clear of anything (or anyone) likely to lower your mood.

As you go through your morning routine, gradually start tuning in to the thinking you'll need to do in the exam, rehearsing some of the key things you've learned and looking ahead to how you'll soon be putting it all to use.

In the exam hall

Find your place in good time, get out your equipment, settle in. Check you can see a clock.

Get a sense of who's going to be moving around the room, and where people might be coming in and out, so that any movements and noise are less likely to surprise you when you're concentrating.

If you've spent any time visualizing this moment, give yourself a few seconds to engage with your memories of that: the positive feelings you strengthened, and the practical strategies you rehearsed – ready to do them now for real.

During the exam

Read the instructions carefully, even if this looks exactly like a past paper you're familiar with.

Check you've read through the *whole* paper, every side of every page, before you do anything else.

If you have choices to make, analyse them quickly, be clear in your rationale – and then commit (unless your planning reveals you got it wrong; in which case, change, *quickly*). Remember to choose topics that you've learned well recently – which may not necessarily be your favourites, or even the ones you've worked on most throughout your course. Be strategic about the questions that will get you the best marks.

Stick to the time-management strategy you agreed with yourself – unless something clearly forces you to change your plans. It might help to jot down timings on the front cover or next to particular sections or questions to help you keep to the pacing you worked out.

Go through the paper in the order you decided beforehand, confident you know what's coming up – but also alert to any changes from previous exams.

Answer the exact questions you're set. Read them a couple of times, especially essay questions. Underline key words and keep checking you know what you've been asked to do – when you're planning, before you start writing, and several times after that. These key words are useful for getting your plans started. Quickly map out the points you want to make, in a structure that matches the sort of thinking the question is asking you to demonstrate. Plan energetically, using the process to help you address *this* question rather than trying to reproduce a related answer from memory.

Academic Advice

'I always tell students to try to work with the question – to use it to fire up their thinking. It's tempting to feel like you can remember the answer, and just reel it off; but it's much better to imagine it's a completely original question, examine it really carefully, and then think of the things you know that answer it. It's somewhere between believing it's easy, and deciding it's impossible. Have faith that the question will guide you to the answer.' **Mike, university course leader**

You can stick to the typical writing structures for your subject – but now everything needs to be more succinct and direct than ever.

Introduce your approach to answering the question but don't waste time repeating anything that's printed on the page: get into *responding* to it as soon as you can.

There's a lot to show in your answer, even if there's not much time to do it: how well you can apply your knowledge to the question you've been set; analyse material that's valuable in your subject; synthesize elements from different areas of your work; and evaluate information and ideas. So, make it as easy as possible for the examiner to see all of that and give you the marks you deserve.

Your signposting techniques can be less subtle than usual: *clearly* spell out how many points you're making, what's the same, what's different, how ideas connect and combine. Outline your argument with precision and confidence.

You don't need references, there's much less expectation for detail, so the clarity of your reasoning and the strength of your tone are particularly important. Crisply presenting several well-made points can reflect extensive background knowledge (just as talking *around* a subject without actually offering anything specific suggests very little that's worth any marks).

The trick is to show how well you can *select* from everything you know, to address the specific question you've been set; and that you can communicate your understanding from memory and at speed. There are necessary differences from the work you do when you've got all your research around you and as much time as you need, but you can still demonstrate the core higher-level abilities you've developed.

If you have a complete mental block about a specific answer, give yourself a little time to think it through – but if that doesn't work, make a note to come back later, and move on. Other questions may nudge your brain in the meantime.

Leave yourself enough time at the end to check your answers are correctly numbered and that everything you've written is as clear for the examiner as possible. Make sure anything you changed your mind about is very obviously crossed out.

Look for any obvious errors in spelling, punctuation and grammar. If your work involves any calculations, you'll need to leave extra time to check those – and, if you can, to use a different method as corroboration. But don't change any answers at the last minute until you're absolutely sure you made a mistake earlier (when you were less rushed and more *likely* to have been right).

Check any loose pages are correctly labelled and collated, and that everything you want to be submitted *is*.

Academic Advice

'Although an increasing number of higher-level exams are being done electronically, many students still find themselves having to write by hand, so it's important not to lose the ability to write quickly and legibly.' **Alejandro, university tutor**

Afterwards

Have something to eat and drink and give yourself a chance to rest. Once again, make sensible decisions about what to do and who to talk to, bearing in mind how you usually feel as a result – especially if there's another exam on the horizon.

The day after

Reflect on your experiences. Make some notes in your learning journal about how well you coped with the emotional, intellectual and academic challenges involved. Did anything have a particular effect on your emotion? How did your memory work under pressure? Which strategies worked best for tackling this paper, and what would you do differently next time? What have you learned from the whole exam process that will help you in any tests you take from now on?

Be careful not to over-analyse. Remind yourself there's nothing you can do now about that particular exam. People tend to remember more of the bits they found difficult anyway (and talking to others about exams seems to make that happen even more). Worrying about it could stop you preparing properly for other exams coming up. Use your journal to record any useful ideas for next time – but also try to leave any worries behind when you finish the entry and close the book.

Student Tip:

'If you're offered a chance to receive feedback after an exam, take it. I know lots of students who pass up these opportunities, but I've always found them to be extremely useful for improving my exam technique and stopping me repeating mistakes.' **James, final-year Law undergraduate**

 > *Go to: Chapter 6 to check/update the* **exam performance** *section in your Core Development Plan.*

⑩ Ten-point summary

1. You may have to confront some exam experiences from the past in order to set yourself up for success now.

2. Done well, every aspect of higher-level study is part of your preparation for exams.

3. Good time-management is vital, to do the extra learning and practising required, and to maintain healthy balance in your life.

4. Take every chance to see previous papers, model answers, and official guidance about exactly what success involves.

5. Gather together everything you'll be tested on and check that you understand it well.

6. Condense complex material to make it manageable and memorable.

7. Use memory techniques to fix particularly important information in your mind.

8. Combine learning, practising and testing in a carefully planned period of focused preparation.

9. Check all the practical arrangements in advance, but also work on feeling your best when you get there.

10. Be strategic in the way you plan and write your answers, to show clear evidence of your knowledge and understanding of the subject, and high levels of confidence in the way you think and work.

▷ Where to next?

Part 6 will make sure that you now put everything you've learned in this book into practice.

Part 6

The journey on

Analysing your experiences and continually updating your development plans

Development plans

All the abilities and attitudes explored in this book will only really mean anything when you put them into *action*. They have to be developed over time, in the specific context of the subject you've chosen, within a community of other learners. It's important to prepare and practise beforehand, but it's the things that happen when you're studying that will allow you to make these skills your own.

The plans in this part of the book are designed to help you carry forward all the work you've started here – and to see what happens when you do. Being committed to an active and ambitious approach, reflecting on your experiences, and responding accordingly, is how you'll keep on developing, in the places where it matters. You'll find out what good study really means for you.

We learn by doing something new, and then *thinking* about what we've done.

Use these plans to continue the self-reflection you've begun in this book, coming back here whenever you want to focus on a particular aspect of your development, to regain your momentum, to add new ideas, or to record what's taking you forward: the things you're learning about studying, and about yourself.

In each plan, use the **Areas to focus on** column to make notes about the elements you know need more work. It could be because you're finding them difficult, or you haven't had enough experience of them – or they're particularly important, and need to be priorities.

In the space for **Ideas to try**, jot down any strategies you see, read, hear, or have your own insights about, that could be worth a go.

And under **Things that have worked**, record specific examples of success whenever they happen, so that you'll know what to keep doing in future.

Use these plans dynamically. Keep looking for ideas, trying new things, thinking about what happened, celebrating your wins – and staying ambitious for more.

Look inside yourself continually, but also reach out and take everything you need to succeed. See the benefits of strengthening yourself through the struggles of study – and have fun finding out what happens in all the challenges, all the *opportunities* ahead.

Studying well by … FEELING POSITIVE ABOUT LEARNING		
Areas to focus on	*Ideas to try*	*Things that have worked*

Studying well by … STAYING WELL		
Areas to focus on	*Ideas to try*	*Things that have worked*

Studying well by ... ACCESSING SUPPORT		
Areas to focus on	Ideas to try	Things that have worked

Studying well by ... BEING ORGANIZED		
Areas to focus on	Ideas to try	Things that have worked

Studying well by … USING TIME WELL		
Areas to focus on	*Ideas to try*	*Things that have worked*

Studying well by … IMPROVING LEARNING ENVIRONMENTS		
Areas to focus on	*Ideas to try*	*Things that have worked*

Studying well by ... LEARNING ACTIVELY		
Areas to focus on	Ideas to try	Things that have worked

Studying well by ... RESEARCHING EXISTING INFORMATION		
Areas to focus on	Ideas to try	Things that have worked

Studying well by … CONDUCTING ORIGINAL RESEARCH		
Areas to focus on	*Ideas to try*	*Things that have worked*

Studying well by … READING		
Areas to focus on	*Ideas to try*	*Things that have worked*

Studying well by ... THINKING ANALYTICALLY		
Areas to focus on	Ideas to try	Things that have worked

Studying well by ... THINKING LOGICALLY		
Areas to focus on	Ideas to try	Things that have worked

Studying well by ... THINKING CREATIVELY		
Areas to focus on	*Ideas to try*	*Things that have worked*

Studying well by ... USING MEMORY TECHNIQUES		
Areas to focus on	*Ideas to try*	*Things that have worked*

328

Studying well by ... WRITING		
Areas to focus on	Ideas to try	Things that have worked

Studying well by ... COMPLETING ACADEMIC TASKS		
Areas to focus on	Ideas to try	Things that have worked

Studying well by ... MANAGING RESEARCH PROJECTS		
Areas to focus on	*Ideas to try*	*Things that have worked*

Studying well by ... BENEFITING FROM TEACHING		
Areas to focus on	*Ideas to try*	*Things that have worked*

Studying well by ...
WORKING IN GROUPS

Areas to focus on	Ideas to try	Things that have worked

Studying well by ...
ENGAGING IN DIALOGUE

Areas to focus on	Ideas to try	Things that have worked

Studying well by … GIVING PRESENTATIONS		
Areas to focus on	*Ideas to try*	*Things that have worked*

Studying well by … PREPARING FOR ASSESSMENTS		
Areas to focus on	*Ideas to try*	*Things that have worked*

Studying well by ...
PERFORMING UNDER PRESSURE

Areas to focus on	Ideas to try	Things that have worked

Studying well by ...
WORKING TO STANDARDS AND PROTOCOLS

Areas to focus on	Ideas to try	Things that have worked

Studying well by ... DEVELOPING ACADEMIC CONFIDENCE		
Areas to focus on	*Ideas to try*	*Things that have worked*

Studying well by ... REFLECTING ON LEARNING		
Areas to focus on	*Ideas to try*	*Things that have worked*

Further resources

www.skillsyouneed.com

Resources to help you develop a wide range of key personal and academic skills, many of which are crucial for success in higher-level education.

https://help.open.ac.uk/topic/study-skills

Advice from the Open University on many different aspects of study, including core reading, writing and maths skills; computing; assignments; presentations; and preparing for tests and exams.

www.theguardian.com/education/advice-for-students

Regularly updated features, reports and support guides from the Guardian, relevant for students before, during and after university.

www.mind.org.uk

Down-to earth general information, and routes to getting specialist support, from the leading UK mental health charity.

www.nhs.uk/moodzone

Search for 'students' to get authoritative information and practical advice about staying well at university.

www.studentmindsorg.uk

The home of the UK's student mental health charity, which helps students to look after themselves, take care of their friends, and get involved in campaigns to improve wellbeing for all.

www.nus.org.uk

Trusted, realistic and empowering advice about studying well and living the student life to the full.

www.thecompleteuniversityguide.co.uk

An independent guide to higher-level courses and providers, offering information on all aspects of life as a student, and advice about planning for further studies, work experience and employment.

www.thestudentroom.co.uk

The UK's largest online student community, with links to events and opportunities; channels for communicating with other members; and tips for success at every stage of your studies.

www.ukcisa.org.uk

Resources for current and prospective international students, with advice on immigration issues, fees, support services, and all aspects of working and living in the UK.

www.moneyadviceservice.org.uk

Put 'students' in the search box to find out about the costs involved in higher-level education; the different forms of support on offer; and the best ways to manage your budget while you study.

www.mindtools.com

A vast collection of online learning resources with much to appeal to students, including help with learning skills, time-management, team-working, and planning for success in the world of work.

Index

Notes